O9-BTM-426

Modern Critical Interpretations

Adventures of Huckleberry Finn
All Quiet on the Western Front
Animal Farm
Beloved
Beowulf
Billy Budd, Benito Cereno, Bartleby the Scrivener, and Other Tales
The Bluest Eye
The Catcher in the Rye
Catch-22
The Color Purple
Crime and Punishment
The Crucible
Daisy Miller, The Turn of the Screw, and Other Tales
David Copperfield
Death of a Salesman
The Divine Comedy
Don Quixote
Dubliners
Emma
Fahrenheit 451
A Farewell to Arms
Frankenstein
The General Prologue to the Canterbury Tales
The Glass Menagerie
The Grapes of Wrath
Great Expectations
The Great Gatsby
Gulliver's Travels
Hamlet
The Handmaid's Tale
Heart of Darkness
I Know Why the Caged Bird Sings
The Iliad
The Interpretation of Dreams
Invisible Man
Jane Eyre
Julius Caesar
King Lear
Long Day's Journey into Night
Lord Jim
Lord of the Flies
The Lord of the Rings
Macbeth
The Merchant of Venice
The Metamorphosis
A Midsummer Night's Dream
Moby-Dick
My Ántonia
Native Son
Night
1984
The Odyssey
Oedipus Rex
The Old Man and the Sea
Othello
Paradise Lost
The Pardoner's Tale
A Portrait of the Artist as a Young Man
Pride and Prejudice
The Red Badge of Courage
The Rime of the Ancient Mariner
Romeo and Juliet
The Scarlet Letter
A Scholarly Look at the Diary of Anne Frank
A Separate Peace
Slaughterhouse Five
Song of Solomon
The Sonnets
The Sound and the Fury
The Stranger
A Streetcar Named Desire
Sula
The Sun Also Rises
A Tale of Two Cities
The Tales of Poe
The Tempest
Tess of the D'Urbervilles
Their Eyes Were Watching God
To Kill a Mockingbird
Ulysses
Waiting for Godot
Walden
The Waste Land
Wuthering Heights

Modern Critical Interpretations

Elie Wiesel's *Night*

Edited and with an introduction by
Harold Bloom
Sterling Professor of the Humanities
Yale University

CHELSEA HOUSE PUBLISHERS
Philadelphia

Printed and bound in the United States of America

10 9 8 7 6 5 4 3 2 1

∞ The paper used in this publication meets the minimum requirements of the American National Standard for Permanence of Paper for Printed Library Materials, Z39.48-1984

Library of Congress Cataloging-in-Publication Data

Elie Wiesel's Night / Harold Bloom, editor.
p.cm. — (Modern critical interpretations)
Includes bibliographical references and index.
ISBN 0-7910-5924-3 (alk. paper) 1. Wiesel, Elie, 1928–
Nuit. 2. Authors, french—Biography History and criticism.
3. Holocaust, Jewish (1939–1945), in literature.
I. Bloom, Harold. II. Series.
PQ2683.I32 N8534 2001
940.53'18'092—dc21 00-052357

Chelsea House Publishers
1974 Sproul Road, Suite 400
Broomall, PA 19008-0914

http://www.chelseahouse.com

Contributing Editor: Janyce Marson

Produced by: Robert Gerson Publisher's Services, Santa Barbara, CA

Contents

Editor's Note vii

Introduction 1
Harold Bloom

The Dominion of Death 3
Lawrence L. Langer

The Experience of the Void 17
Michael Berenbaum

In the Beginning 31
John K. Roth

Witness of the Night 47
Ellen S. Fine

Darkness That Eclipses Light 69
Robert McAfee Brown

The Conversion to Ambiguity 95
Colin Davis

Beyond Psychoanalysis: Elie Wiesel's *Night* in Historical Perspective 129
Ora Avni

Victims to Victors: The Trilogy 145
Simon P. Sibelman

Chronology 173

Contributors 177

Bibliography 179

Acknowledgments 183

Index 185

Editor's Note

My Introduction addresses Holocaust literature in general, rather than focusing specifically on Wiesel's memoir-novel, which originally was published in France as *Un di velt hot geshgivn* in 1956 and was followed by a shorter version, *La Nuit*, two years later and an English translation, *Night*, in 1960.

Introduction

Rather than comment directly upon Elie Wiesel's *Night*, which is the subject of all the essays in this volume, I will address myself to the larger question of Holocaust literature. My starting point will be Geoffrey Hartman's poignant and brilliant *The Longest Shadow: In the Aftermath of the Holocaust* (1996). Trauma, primary and secondary, respectively that of survivor or of audience, is at the center of Hartman's insights:

I am hardly the first to worry about the increasing prevalence of psychic numbing accompanied by fascination, and which is usually the consequence of *primary* trauma. It would be ironic and sad if all that education could achieve were to transmit a trauma to later generations in secondary form. In this fifth decade after the collapse of the National Socialist regime, the disaster still has not run its course. No closure is in sight: the contradictory imperatives of remembering and forgetting are no less strong than before.

But that leads to the question of artistic representation: can you, should you try to transmute the Holocaust into literature? Hartman defends the possibility of this transmutation against the Frankfurt Jewish philosopher, Theodor Adorno:

> After the Holocaust there is a spiritual hunt to de-aestheticize everything—politics and culture as well as art. As Adorno phrased in his harshest and most famous statement, it is a sign of the barbaric (that is, of lack of culture) to write poetry after Auschwitz. He refused the arts a role even in mourning the destruction, because they might stylize it too much, or "make unthinkable fate appear to have some meaning." Yet art creates an unreality effect in a way that is *not* alienating or desensitizing. At best, it also provides something of a safe-house for emotion and empathy. The tears we shed, like those of Aeneas when he sees the destruction of Troy

> depicted on the walls of Carthage, are an acknowledgment and not an exploitation of the past.

To acknowledge without exploiting is a difficult burden: are any of us strong enough for that? Hartman crucially goes on to consider a great poet, Paul Celan, Romanian-Jewish by birth, who wrote in a purified German. Celan's parents were murdered in the Holocaust; the poet himself survived a labor camp, but killed himself in Paris, at the age of fifty. His art was one of reticence, stripping words of their images. Hartman again is precise and eloquent upon the effect:

> Trauma is given a form and disappears into the stammer we call poetry, into a fissure between speech on the page, seemingly so absolute, and an invisible writing that may not be retrievable. This is, in truth, a disaster notation.

Paul Celan was a great (and very difficult) literary artist. Elie Wiesel is an eminent Witness, but hardly a canonical writer of narrative. Yet only a moral idiot would react to Wiesel's *Night* by refusing the burden of secondary trauma. A purely aesthetic reaction to *Night* is impossible, and not to be urged upon anyone. There remains what I find most problematical for Wiesel's reader: how to find the strength to acknowledge *Night* without exploiting it?

LAWRENCE L. LANGER

The Dominion of Death

The most frightening aspect of our present world is not the horrors in themselves, the atrocities, the technological exterminations, but the one fact at the very root of it all: the fading away of any human criterion. . . .
—Erich Kahler

. . . a man can cross the threshold of death before his body is lifeless.
—Alexander Solzhenitsyn

Death too can be a way of life.
—Jakov Lind

True art, says Erich Kahler, expanding Erich Auerbach's idea of "mimesis" or imitation, is and has to be

> an act of conquest, the discovery of a new sphere of human consciousness, and thereby of new reality. It lifts into the light of our consciousness a state of affairs, a layer of existence, that was dormant in the depth of our unconscious, that was buried under obsolete forms, conventions, habits of thought and experience. And by showing this latent reality, by making it visible to us,

> open to our grasp, the work of art actually *creates* this new reality as a new sphere of our conscious life. There is no true art without this exploratory quality, without this frontier venture to make conscious the preconscious, to express what has never been expressed before and what heretofore had seemed inexpressible.

Once we recognize that critical dogmas of this sort are not to be measured for their "truth"—if this were the case, most critical principles would cancel each other out—but for their relevance, their appropriateness, their consistency with a given body of material—once we recognize this, then Kahler's definition of art proves singularly applicable to the literature of atrocity. All serious art undoubtedly aspires toward the revelation of a new sense of reality, but the literature we are concerned with possessed the curious advantage of having such a "new" reality already available, pressing with equal force on the conscious and (as we have just seen) the preconscious life of the artist, and seeking only a way of being convincingly presented to an audience of contemporary readers. Normally, nonfiction is excluded from such definitions of art, since by its very nature it seeks to reflect a historical reality without manipulating or distorting details, drawing on the very conventions and habits of thought and experience that Kahler excludes. Most autobiographies, for example, orient us toward the past rather than shaping fresh visions of the future. Yet Kahler's terms are broad enough, and the nature of the Holocaust experience sufficiently unique, to permit autobiography to be included in his definition of art—if one could be found.

Most of the autobiographies concerned with *l'univers concentrationnaire* numb the consciousness without enlarging it and providing it with a fresh or unique perception of the nature of reality, chiefly because the enormity of the atrocities they recount finally forces the reader to lose his orientation altogether and to feel as though he were wandering in a wilderness of evil totally divorced from any time and place he has ever known—a reality not latent in, but external to, his own experience. The most impressive exception to this general rule is a work that has already become a classic in our time, an autobiography which, in its compressed imaginative power and artful presentation of the circumstances of the author's internment in Auschwitz, yields the effect of an authentic *Bildungsroman*—except that the youthful protagonist becomes an initiate into death rather than life—Elie Wiesel's *Night.*

A reader confronted with this slim volume himself becomes an initiate into death, into the dark world of human suffering and moral chaos we call the Holocaust; and by the end he is persuaded that he inhabits the kind of negative universe which Lear invokes when he enters with Cordelia dead in his arms: "Thou'lt come no more;/Never, never, never, never, never," and is prompted to intone together with Lear: "No, no, no life"—a final rejection of love, of family, of the past, of order, of "normality"—that lies dead on the stage at his feet. Wiesel's *Night* is the terminus a quo for any investigation of the implications of the Holocaust, no matter what the terminus ad quem; on its final page a world lies dead at our feet, a world we have come to know as our own as well as Wiesel's, and whatever civilization may be rebuilt from its ruins, the silhouette of its visage will never look the same.

Night conveys in gradual detail the principle that Hermann Kasack had evoked in his dream: death has replaced life as the measure of our existence, and the vision of human potentiality nurtured by centuries of Christian and humanistic optimism has been so completely effaced by the events of the Holocaust that the future stretches gloomily down an endless vista into futility. The bleakness of the prospect sounds melodramatic but actually testifies to the reluctance of the human spirit to release the moorings that have lashed it to hope and to accept the consequences of total abandonment. Disappointed in a second coming, man has suffered a second going, a second fall and expulsion, not from grace this time but from humanity itself; and indeed, as we shall see in one of the most moving episodes in his harrowing book, Wiesel introduces a kind of second crucifixion, consecrating man not to immortality but to fruitless torture and ignominious death. Yet one is never permitted to forget what is being sacrificed, what price, unwillingly, the human creature has had to pay for *l'univers concentrationnaire*, what heritage it has bequeathed to a humanity not yet fully aware of the terms of the will.

Works like *Night* furnish illumination for this inheritance, an illumination all the more necessary (especially if one is to go on to explore the literature succeeding it) when we consider how unprepared the human mind is to confront the visions it reveals. A book like *Anne Frank: The Diary of a Young Girl*, incontestably more popular and influential than Wiesel's *Night*, by its very widespread acceptance confirms our unpreparedness to respond to the grimmer realities and the imaginative re-creations of the literature of atrocity. In many respects *Anne Frank* is the reverse of *Night*—in its premises, in the nature of the experiences it narrates, and in its conclusions; in fact, it draws on the very "obsolete forms, conventions, habits of thought and experience" which, in Erich Kahler's formulation, the writer must burrow through if he is to create for his reader the new reality we dignify by the name of art.

Of course, the comparison is meant to be objective rather than invidious; Anne Frank was indeed a young girl, and her eventual fate was more terrifyingly final, if no more fearful, than Wiesel's. But her *Diary*, cherished since its appearance as a celebration of human courage in the face of impending disaster, is in actuality a conservative and even old-fashioned book which appeals to nostalgia and does not pretend to concern itself with the uniqueness of the reality transforming life outside the attic walls that insulated her vision. Bruno Bettelheim long ago provoked angry criticism for suggesting the limitations in the tactics of the Frank family; whether or not it was justified is irrelevant here, but it further confirms the sentimentality of an audience that pursues Anne's reality—like Anne herself—only to the arrival of the "green police," that is unable or unwilling to peer beyond the end of her tale to the "new" reality symbolized by her wretched death in the barracks of Bergen-Belsen.

Anne Frank's *Diary* was written in the innocence (and the "ignorance") of youth, but its conclusions form the point of departure for Wiesel's *Night* and most authors in the tradition of atrocity; indeed, their work constitutes a sequel to hers and ultimately challenges the principle that for her was both premise and epitaph—"In spite of everything, I still think people are good at heart"—a conception of character which dies hard, but dies pitilessly, in *Night* and in literature of atrocity in general. The optimism which nurtured her faith in humanity is symbolized by her family's quarantine from reality during their years of hiding; their real story, and the story of the transformed world that determined their destiny, began after Anne's diary ended. The values it preserves—love, devotion, courage, family unity, charity—are mocked by the fate she suffered (mocked too, one is inclined to add, by the fate of Lear and Cordelia), and to the informed reader only dramatize the inadequacy of heart-warming terms to describe the soul-chilling universe that destroyed her.

Yet Elie Wiesel recognized, as Anne Frank could not, that the values she celebrated might form an indispensable core for creating a magnetic field to attract fragments of atrocity, so that a permanent tension could be established between the two "forces"—a similar tension exists in some of the dreams we examined—a kind of polarity between memory and truth, nostalgia and a landscape of horror eerily highlighted by the pale reflection from vacant moral spaces. The literary effect is that memory ceases to offer consolation but itself becomes an affliction, intensifying the torment of the sufferer. Or rather, the usual content of memory is replaced by the harsh events of life in the concentration camp, until the past loses the hard edge of reality and the victim finds that both past and future, memory and hope—the "luxuries" of normal existence—are abruptly absorbed by an eternal and terrifying present, a present whose abnormality suddenly becomes routine. At this moment, life becomes too much for man and death assumes the throne in the human imagination.

A prospect like this must have led Camus to begin *The Myth of Sisyphus* with the statement that the only truly serious philosophical problem is suicide. In fact, Camus offers a lucid description of the consequences for man of his familiar world disappearing (consequences which Elie Wiesel presents in greater detail in *Night*):

> in a universe suddenly divested of illusions and lights, man feels an alien, a stranger. His exile is without remedy since he is deprived of the memory of a lost home or the hope of a promised land. This divorce between man and his life, the actor and his setting, is properly the feeling of absurdity.

Too lucid, perhaps: Camus built intellectual defenses against a universe ruled by atrocity and the irrational in an attempt to prevent man's total defeat at its hands; Wiesel's relationship to *l'univers concentrationnaire* was far more tentative, and he was concerned no less with its effect than with its essence. The unreal reality of *Night* and most literature of atrocity exists in a world halfway between Camus's alternatives of suicide or recovery.

Perhaps even *essence* is an inexact word for Wiesel's appeal to the imagination as well as to the intelligence of the reader: asked some years after the liberation if he himself believed what had happened in Auschwitz, he replied, "I do not believe it. The event seems unreal, as if it occurred on a different planet." Even more paradoxically, he commented on the difficulty of coming to terms, not with the Holocaust—"one never comes to terms with it"—but with its tale:

> The full story of the Holocaust has not yet been told [1967!] All that we know is fragmentary, perhaps even untrue. Perhaps what we tell about what happened and what really happened has nothing to do one with the other. We want to remember. But remember what? And what for? Does anyone know the answer to this?

What this ambiguity conceals we may never know, but it emphasizes the difficult struggle between language and truth that every author must engage in when he turns to this theme; and the important distinctions it draws between the Holocaust itself and its tale, "what really happened" and "what we tell about what happened," explains why Wiesel's autobiographical narrative reads more like fiction than "truth," since the power of the imagination to evoke an atmosphere does far more than the historian's fidelity to fact to involve the uninitiated reader in the atmosphere of the Holocaust.

Night is an account of a young boy's divorce from life, a drama of recognition whose scenes record the impotence of the familiar in the face of modern atrocity; at its heart lies the profoundest symbolic confrontation of our century, the meeting of man and Auschwitz (a meeting reenacted by Rolf Hochhuth in the culminating episode of *The Deputy*)—and this confrontation in turn confirms (as in Anthony Hecht's "More Light! More Light!") the defeat of man's tragic potentiality in our time, and the triumph of death in its most nihilistic guise. The book begins with the familiar, a devout Jewish family whose faith supports their human aspirations and who find their greatest solace—and assurance—in the opportunity of approaching, through diligent study, the divine intentions implicit in reality. The premises behind these aspirations are clarified for the boy narrator by Moché the Beadle, a humble, sagelike man-of-all-work in the Hasidic synagogue in the Transylvanian town where the boy grows up:

> "Man raises himself toward God by the questions he asks Him. . . . That is the true dialogue. Man questions God and God answers. But we don't understand his answers. We can't understand them. Because they come from the depths of the soul, and they stay there until death. You will find the true answers . . . only within yourself."

With this counsel, says the narrator, "my initiation began"; but the kind of questions one asks in his dialogue with God are determined by tradition and education and assumptions that have withstood the assault of adversity. Moché's wisdom is tested when he is deported, together with other foreign Jews, from the small Hungarian town. One day (having escaped, miraculously, from his captors), he reappears with tales of Jews digging their own graves and being slaughtered, "without passion, without haste," and of babies who were thrown into the air while "the machine gunners used them as targets." The joy was extinguished from his eyes as he told these tales, but no one believed him—including the young narrator.

The inability of humanity to accept the version of reality proclaimed by Moché the Beadle brings us once again to the world of despair transcending tragedy inhabited by King Lear. For just as Lear attributes to the symbols of royalty more power than they possess, and stubbornly refuses to believe that his daughters are capable of the monstrous behavior and attitudes which his situation confirms, so the citizens of Sighet, the narrator's town, depend on the material "items" of their civilization, almost as if they were sacred talismans, for security. Their abandoned possessions, after their deportation, become symbols of a vanished people, a forgotten and now useless culture.

Throughout *Night*, Wiesel displays a remarkable talent for investing the "items" of reality, and of the fantastic "irreality" that replaces it, with an animistic quality, and then setting both on a pathway leading to an identical destination: death. For example, in this description of a landscape without figures, crowded with things but devoid of life—less macabre than Borchert's bomb-ruined Hamburg but equally devastating to the imagination—in this passage, presided over by an indifferent nature, symbols of an exhausted past turn into harbingers of a ghastly future:

> The street was like a market place that had suddenly been abandoned. Everything could be found there: suitcases, portfolios, briefcases, knives, plates, banknotes, papers, faded portraits. All those things that people had thought of taking with them, and which in the end they had left behind. They had lost all value.
>
> Everywhere rooms lay open. Doors and windows gaped onto the emptiness. Everything was free for anyone, belonging to nobody. It was simply a matter of helping oneself. An open tomb.
>
> A hot summer sun.

Just as Lear undergoes a physical disrobing and a spiritual denudation before he gains a measure of self-knowledge and a more valid conception of reality, so the fifteen-year-old narrator of *Night* is gradually deprived of the props which have sustained him in his youth; but his experience is such that self-knowledge (as ultimately for Lear) becomes more of a burden than a consolation, and "a more valid conception of reality" sounds like a piece of impious rhetoric.

The displacement of life by death as a measure of existence is metaphorically reinforced in *Night*—as it is in some of Nelly Sachs's poems—by imagery that has become standard fare for much literature of atrocity, imagery facilitating the transition from one world to the other—the boxcars, for example, in which victims were transported:

> The doors were closed. We were caught in a trap, right up to our necks. The doors were nailed up; the way back was finally cut off. The world was a cattle wagon hermetically sealed.

"Liberation" from this hermetic world upon arrival in the camp, however, changes nothing; the "way back" ceases to have meaning, and man must turn his attention to absorbing the nature of the fearful "way ahead," and of finding methods to survive in spite of it, though the price he must pay for his survival is not calculable in figures inherited from the familiar past. He must somehow accommodate himself to an environment dominated by the macabre images of furnace and chimney, of flames in the night and smoke and reeking human flesh; and he must further acknowledge, against all his human impulses and religious training, the authenticity of this harsh, incredible fate:

> "Do you see that chimney over there? See it? Do you see those flames? (Yes, we did see the flames.) Over there—that's where you're going to be taken. That's your grave, over there. Haven't you realized it yet? You dumb bastards, don't you understand anything? You're going to be burned. Frizzled away. Turned into ashes."
>
> Those absent no longer touched even the surface of our memories. We still spoke of them—"Who knows what may have become of them?"—but we had little concern for their fate. We were incapable of thinking of anything at all. Our senses were blunted; everything was blurred as in a fog. It was no longer possible to grasp anything. The instincts of self-preservation, of self-defense, of pride, had all deserted us. In one ultimate moment of lucidity it seemed to me that we were damned souls wandering in the half-world, souls condemned to wander through space till the generations of man came to an end, seeking their redemption, seeking oblivion—without hope of finding it.

The narrator's response introduces a tension that permeates the literature of atrocity: "Surely it was all a nightmare? An unimaginable nightmare?" With a desperate insistence he clings to a kind of emotional nostalgia, as if the stability of his being depends on an affirmative answer; but a subsequent experience shatters that stability permanently, and his efforts henceforth are devoted to making the reader relive the nightmare that continues to haunt him.

His world crumbles—as did Ivan Karamazov's—over the suffering of little children: his first night in the camp he sees babies hurled into a huge ditch from which gigantic flames are leaping:

> I pinched my face. Was I still alive? Was I awake? I could not believe it. How could it be possible for them to burn people, children, and for the world to keep silent? No, none of this could

> be true. It was a nightmare. . . . Soon I should wake with a start, my heart pounding, and find myself back in the bedroom of my childhood, among my books. . . .

The waking dream, haunted by the omnipresence of death, filled with "truths" unacceptable to reason but vivid, nevertheless, in their unquestionable actuality, leads first to disorientation—the new inmates of the camp begin reciting the Jewish prayer for the dead *for themselves*—then to an attempt, at least by the young narrator, to discover mental attitudes commensurate with what the mind initially finds incomprehensible. The ritual incantation which marks his inauguration into *l'univers concentrationnaire* inverts the traditional pattern of autobiography and *Bildungsroman* by beginning with a repudiation that depletes the possibilities of life scarcely after it has begun; it signifies not only a boy's despair, but the exhaustion of meaning in a world henceforth unlike anything men have ever encountered:

> Never shall I forget that night, the first night in camp, which has turned my life into one long night, seven times cursed and seven times sealed. Never shall I forget that smoke. Never shall I forget the little faces of the children, whose bodies I saw turned into wreaths of smoke beneath a silent blue sky.
>
> Never shall I forget those flames which consumed my faith forever.
>
> Never shall I forget that nocturnal silence which deprived me, for all eternity, of the desire to live. Never shall I forget those moments which murdered my God and my soul and turned my dreams to dust. Never shall I forget these things, even if I am condemned to live as long as God Himself. Never.

When the author of these words said a decade later that the events seemed unreal, that he did not believe they had happened to him, he emphasized not only their uniqueness, but also the paradoxical situation that life goes on even after it has "stopped," that Wiesel the man survives and talks about what happened—or remains silent—while Wiesel the writer, certainly in *Night*, has transcended history and autobiography and used the imagery of atrocity and his own experience to involve the nonparticipant in the essence of its world. With due respect to the suffering of the victims, one may repeat what has often been reported by students of the Holocaust—after a particular point, catalogues of brutalities and lists of statistics cease to affect the mind or the imagination, *not* because what they seek to convey lacks significance, but because the mind and imagination lack a suitable context for the information. Hence Wiesel's gradual shift in focus to the *implications* of the events, and his dramatic juxtaposition of carefully selected—though always genuine—scenes and feelings, create an indispensable vestibule for anyone wishing to venture farther into the mansion of Holocaust fiction.

When the first night ends, the narrator presumably has left normality behind, and death has infected his future: "The student of the Talmud, the child that I was, had been consumed in the flames. There remained only a shape that looked like me. A dark flame had entered into my soul and devoured it." The flame illuminates a vision of the self which under ordinary circumstances might be called self-knowledge, but here leads to a futility that negates tragedy and prefigures an exile more complete than anything Camus ever conjured up, a human condition that will have to create new terms for its existence, since Auschwitz has irrevocably breached any meaningful alliance between it and the past.

Even *oblivion* and *redemption*, once the sacred and universally recognizable alternatives in Dante's *Inferno* and *Paradiso*, are goals consigned to the limbo of language, words drawn from memory because reality affords no exact vocabulary for what Wiesel wishes to describe; Wiesel's "half-world," in many of its features remarkably like Hermann Kasack's purely imaginary *Totentraum* or Dream of Death, responds to evocation through vague images rather than specific ideas. Language is not reduced to silence, but it must be used more sparingly, and its range of allusion is governed by concrete experiences rather than by abstract conceptions: for example, the word *furnace*, which was not, says Wiesel, "a word empty of meaning: it floated on the air, mingling with the smoke. It was perhaps the only word which did have any real meaning here."

For Stephen Dedalus, words—"A day of dappled seaborne clouds," for instance—unlocked the mysteries of reality and disclosed vistas of beauty that inspired him to affirm his spirit before a hostile or indifferent world and trust his powers of creation to shape the future. In *l'univers concentrationnaire* of Wiesel's narrator, a diametrically opposite principle of negation prevails, whereby events silence the creative spirit, destroy the longings of youth, and cast over reality an all-embracing shadow of death.

One of the dramatic pinnacles of *Night* illustrates with unmitigated horror this reversal of the *Bildungsroman* formula: three prisoners, two men and a young boy, have been "convicted" of sabotage within the camp and are sentenced to be hanged before thousands of inmates. One imagines the boy, a "sad-eyed angel" on the gallows in the middle, the older victims on either side of him, a grotesque and painful parody—though literally true—of the original redemptive sufferer; the sentence is executed, and the prisoners are forced to march by the dangling bodies, face to face with their own potential fate;

> The two adults were no longer alive. Their tongues hung swollen, blue-tinged. But the third rope was still moving; being so light, the child was still alive. . . .
>
> For more than half an hour he stayed there, struggling between life and death, dying in slow agony under our eyes. And we had to look him full in the face. He was still alive when I passed in front of him. His tongue was still red, his eyes were not yet glazed.
>
> Behind me, I heard [a] man asking:
>
> "Where is God now?"
>
> And I heard a voice within me answer him:
>
> "Where is He? Here He is—He is hanging here on this gallows. . . ."
>
> That night the soup tasted of corpses.

More than one boy's life and another boy's faith is extinguished here, and more than soup loses its familiar taste—a rationale for being, a sense of identification with the human species (as well as a divine inheritance), all the feelings which somehow define our world as a "civilized" place of habitation, are sacrificed on this gallows crucifix, until it is no longer possible to establish a connection between one's intelligence and its apprehension of surrounding reality. The ritual of death, the agonizing struggle between living and dying which always has one inevitable outcome, even if some fortunate few should literally survive—for a time—the ritual of death ungraced by the possibility of resurrection, becomes the focus of existence and shrouds reality in an atmosphere of irrational, impenetrable gloom—"Our senses were blunted," as Wiesel wrote earlier; "everything was blurred as in a fog."

Under such circumstances men learn to adopt toward totally irrational events attitudes that one would expect only from insane or otherwise bewildered human beings: the result is that the incredible assumes some of the vestments of ordinary reality, while normality appears slightly off-center, recognizable, one might say, "north-north-west." Neither total confusion nor absolute comprehension, neither a mad world in which men behave sanely, nor a reasonable one in which human conduct seems deranged—this is the schizophrenic effect Wiesel achieves in his autobiographical narrative. It is scarcely necessary to arrange literal episodes or invent new ones to create the nightmare atmosphere which imaginative works in the tradition will strive for—such is the unique nature of reality in *l'univers concentrationnaire*. For example, shortly after the episode of the hanging of the boy, the Jewish New Year arrives, and Wiesel establishes a counterpoint between the traditional celebration of the inmates, who offer the familiar prayers of praise—"All creation bears witness to the Greatness of God!"—and his own religious disillusionment, which makes him resemble a solitary shrub on a desolate island of faith, which itself appears diminutive and even slightly ludicrous in an endless sea of atrocity:

> My eyes were open and I was alone—terribly alone in a world without God and without man. Without love or mercy. I had ceased to be anything but ashes, yet I felt myself to be stronger than the Almighty, to whom my life had been tied for so long. I stood amid that praying congregation, observing it like a stranger.

Nevertheless, a short time later the apostate narrator seriously debates with fellow inmates living in the shadow of the crematorium whether or not they should fast on Yom Kippur, the Day of Atonement. No participant in this discussion could appreciate more intensively than the innocent, horrified spectator–reader the scathing irony, not to say the insane logic, of this situation: starving men choosing not to eat. The narrator ultimately nibbles his bread and feels a void in his heart, a void intensified by the futility of religious values in a universe that not only refuses to acknowledge them, but is built on premises so cynical that such values mock the men who espouse them.

For the victims who seek sustenance in their faith are reduced to a more degrading role by the subsequent episode, a "selection"—which in plain language meant that some men, usually those physically weaker, were periodically designated for death in a ritual that resembled the weeding-out of defective parts in a machine-assembly plant. Men who know in advance that their life depends on the opinion of an SS "doctor" run past this official, hoping that their numbers will not be written down; most pass the "test," but a few are aware that they "fail," that in two or three days they will be taken to the "hospital" and never be seen again. After such knowledge, what humanity? What logic or reason or connection between what men do and what they suffer, can prevail in one's conception of the universe? In one's conception of one's self? For the narrator, existence is reduced to an elemental struggle between acquiescence to death—"Death wrapped itself around me till I was stifled. It stuck to me. I felt that I could touch it. The idea of dying, of no longer being, began to fascinate me."—and the need to live, in order to support his weakening father, broken in health and spirit by the rigorous discipline of the camp.

Ultimately, the contest between Death and the Father, the one representing *l'univers concentrationnaire* with its insidious and macabre dissolution of reasonable longings, the other all those familiar inheritances which constitute the basis of civilized existence—ultimately, this contest assumes symbolic dimensions, as if normalcy in its dying gasp makes one final effort to assert its authority over the gruesome power seeking to dispossess it. But when death intrudes on the imagination to the point where memory and hope are excluded—as happens in *Night*—then this rivalry, with the accompanying gesture of resistance, proves futile; a kind of inner momentum has already determined the necessary triumph of death in a world disrupted beyond the capacity of man to alter it. The extent of the disruption, and the transformation in humanity wrought by it, is painfully illustrated by the cry of SS guards to the prisoners being transported westward in open cattle-cars from Auschwitz (because of the approaching Russian troops) to Buchenwald: "Throw out all the dead! All corpses outside!"—and by the response of those still surviving: "The living rejoiced. There would be more room."

Thus disinherited, bereft of any value that might permit him to confront the inevitable death of his father with at least the dignity of an illusion, and compelled in the depths of his heart to accept the desolate rule of *l'univers concentrationnaire*—"Here there are no fathers, no brothers, no friends. Everyone lives and dies for himself alone."—the narrator helplessly watches his last living link with the familiar world of the past expire and learns that grief has expired with him. Not only have normal feelings lapsed—plunging us into a shadowy realm where men cease to respond to reality by following any predictable pattern—but they have been replaced by attitudes which a "normally" disposed reader, still bound by the moral premises of pre-Holocaust experience, would characterize as verging on the inhuman. But to the reader who has himself submitted imaginatively to the hallucination-become-fact of this experience, the narrator's reaction to his father's death can more accurately be described as one illustration of what happens when human character is pressed beyond the limits of the human: "in the recesses of my weakened conscience, could I have searched it, I might perhaps have found something like—free at last!"

At this moment, to follow Camus's language, man is divorced from his life, the actor from his setting, and the son (in a manner quite different from the conventional *Bildungsroman*) severed from his patrimony and thrust forth onto a stage which requires the drama of existence to continue, though without a script, *sans* director, the plot consisting of a single unanswerable question: How shall I enact my survival in a world I know to be darkened by the shadow of irrational death, before an audience anticipating a performance that will be illuminated by the light of reason and the glow of the future? Out of some such query as this, representing a paradox of private existence, is born a principle of schizophrenic art, the art of atrocity.

The final, haunting moment of *Night* occurs when the narrator, Wiesel himself, following his liberation, gazes at his own visage after lingering between life and death (a result of food poisoning):

> One day I was able to get up, after gathering all my strength.I wanted to see myself in the mirror hanging on the opposite wall. I had not seen myself since the ghetto.
>
> From the depths of the mirror, a corpse gazed back at me.
>
> The look in his eyes, as they stared into mine, has never left me.

An unrecognizable face from the past and a living death-mask—variations on this confrontation, spanning two worlds with a current linking regret to despair, characterizes the literature that grew out of the nightmare of history which transformed a fifteen-year-old boy into a breathing corpse.

Wiesel's account is ballasted with the freight of fiction: scenic organization, characterization through dialogue, periodic climaxes, elimination of superfluous or repetitive episodes, and especially an ability to arouse the empathy of his readers, which is an elusive ideal of the writer bound by fidelity to fact. His narrative approaches fiction in its ability to evoke rather than describe the two worlds that eventually create a Karamazov-like "double" in the narrator on the final page. It demonstrates more clearly than any other literal account of the Holocaust how powerfully the paradoxes of this historical horror will challenge and exasperate the imagination of the artist—the painter as well as the writer, one might add—who tries to create a form appropriate to its jagged revelations. The young boy who stared at the inarticulate knowledge and suffering in the eyes of his reflection at that crucial moment in his life was destined to become a novelist himself, though his fictional concern with the implications of his ordeal—understandably enough, perhaps—would be more philosophical than dramatic; but the *sensibilité concentrationnaire*, roused by similar knowledge, if not always similar suffering, drew this portion of history into the unlimited aspirations of literary art, and gave it a resonance and universality which only imaginative literature could achieve.

MICHAEL BERENBAUM

The Experience of the Void

All of Wiesel's writings are concerned with the ramifications of the Holocaust for man, God and Israel. Peter Berger has argued that death is the marginal experience *par excellence* which threatens to reveal the innate precariousness of all socially constructed universes. If death is the marginal experience *par excellence*, then the death of six million Jews in the Holocaust is the marginal experience *extraordinaire* which has undermined the socially constructed universe of normative Judaism. Wiesel's writings are an attempt to come to terms with that marginal experience and to construct a new universe to replace the one that was shattered.

The progression in Wiesel's first three novels, *Night*, *Dawn*, and *Le Jour* (*The Accident*), from night to dawn to day, is not merely a positive progression from a world of darkness to a world of light, but also a progression from a world in which God is present (at the beginning of *Night*), to a world in which God is killed so that man can live (in *Dawn*), and finally to a world in which God is absent (in *Le Jour*). In *Le Jour* God's presence is no longer felt, and the individual lives without meaning and without God. It is ironic that Wiesel's titles become brighter as the presence of God becomes dimmer, but this irony reflects Wiesel's reliance upon man in a world devoid of God. Nonetheless, the transition from a God-filled world to a Godless world is not easy for Wiesel. He continually emphasizes

---

From *The Vision of the Void: Theological Reflections on the Works of Elie Wiesel.*

not only the initial suffering that brought him to his view of a Godless world, but also the internal pain that accompanies this new consciousness. He yearns to return to the God-filled world and to the shtetl in the Carpathian Mountains from which he was prematurely snatched and taken into the kingdom of night.

Theodicy in *Night*

There are few better illustrations of Hegel's famous statement that "history is the slaughter bench at which the happiness of peoples, the wisdom of states and the virtue of individuals have been sacrificed" than Wiesel's 1958 memoir *Night*. In *Night* Wiesel vividly describes the transition from belief to disillusionment. At the beginning of *Night* Wiesel's world is dominated by his involvement with God. The author describes himself as a young boy who is fascinated by the mystery of God's transcendence and yearns to bring about the awaited redemption. The young boy studies the Talmud by day and the mysteries of the Kabbalah by night. He rises at midnight to keep the *Shekinah* company, for she is in exile, and he weeps bitterly over the destruction of the Temple and the exile of both Israel and God. The boy's life and faith were one. When asked why he prays, the boy was puzzled by the question. "Why did I pray? A strange question. Why did I live? Why did I breathe?" He was aware of the contradictions and the questions of historical existence, but like Rabbi Nachman of Bratzlav, he withstood the questions with a staunch faith that looked toward the dimension of eternity, the level at which question and answer were one.

Wiesel begins to reveal an erosion of faith when he describes its deceptive power. He explains that in Sighet, the Transylvanian town of his youth, the signs of the imminent slaughter were apparent, but that only the discerning eyes of a few—a madman, a visionary, and a prophet, or those who had seen the end and returned to tell the tale—could really face the truth. For the rest of the community, and for the author himself, an illusion of safety prevailed and life continued normally. The illusion of a merciful universe sustained some people, faith in humanity nourished the hopes of others, while for Wiesel the lure of eternity clouded his sense of reality. Tragically, it was faith and not wickedness that misled the people of Sighet.

As the story of *Night* unfolds, Wiesel describes how his faith was slowly and painfully consumed by the flames that sent the souls of the young and the innocent skyward. Wiesel's faith and the faith of many of the characters he describes had been fortified against the encroachment of anomic forces by the teachings of Jewish tradition. In other words, Wiesel was not psychically unarmed to confront the problem of evil that the concentration camp experience raised. He knew both the history of the problem within Jewish tradition and the many possible defenses against the incursion of *anomie*. However, none of these defenses ultimately worked for Wiesel on an existential level, and it is on the existential level that the religious problem of evil must be faced. (The theoretical problem can easily be resolved by either challenging God's goodness, diminishing His power, or denying His existence.) Through the incidents and reflections presented in *Night*, Wiesel undermines the traditional strategies for explaining and handling the presence of evil.

One traditional strategy of the Rabbis for preserving the belief in God's justice is expressed in the prayer book for the Holidays. This strategy is a moral one which seeks to understand the historical situation of Israel in light of its wrongdoings and its evil ways. According to this strategy, Israel has sinned and consequently must be punished: "Because of our sins we were exiled from our land." However, Wiesel is unable to accept this strategy. He never even entertains the possibility that the iniquities of the people led to their annihilation. In fact, Wiesel angrily rejects this strategy. Speaking of his teachers, he said:

> I had another teacher who taught me to sing. . . . He taught me a song *U'mipnai Chata'enu*, it is because of our sins that we had been exiled. I sang it then. I sing it now, and now I resent it. No, it is not because of our sins. There were no sins, not that many. I refuse to believe that there could have been so many sins to provoke such a punishment. If there was such a punishment, it is because someone else had sinned, not we, not the people of Israel.

By rejecting this explanation, Wiesel refuses to relieve God of His responsibility. Both Wiesel's love of Israel and his respect for the God that Israel revered precluded that possibility.

Another traditional strategy for explaining the existence of evil seeks to defer ultimate justice to the time of the Messiah or the world to come. One such strategy is put most succinctly by Raba, the Babylonian *amora* (sage) of the fourth generation, who said that Job's sin was his lack of belief in the resurrection of the dead. Job's complaint could only arise in a situation where historical existence is considered the sole form of existence and where life itself is expected to be rewarding. The Jewish view that the Messiah will restore Israel serves as a powerful force for defending the plausibility structure of Judaism by deferring justice and reward to a future time. In the words of Gershom Scholem, the Jewish view of the Messiah is a "theory of catastrophe." It would seem that this theory is most applicable in the presence of catastrophes. Wiesel realizes the healing potential of the belief in a messianic solution, but he seems to reject the ultimate reality of such a solution or its ability to 'explain' or 'dismiss' the present. Wiesel's style of writing itself emphasizes the reality of present experiences as opposed to explanation or abstract analysis. Wiesel primarily chooses to describe rather than to explain. He thereby lets his incidents tell their own tale. Experience speaks louder than explanations and cannot be silenced by answers. Furthermore, Wiesel's treatment of the theological explanations themselves reveals their lack of connection with the experiences they seek to explain.

This discontinuity is illustrated by Wiesel's description of a conversation among the inmates shortly after their arrival at Auschwitz.

> In the evening, lying on our beds, we would try to sing some of the Hasidic melodies, and Akiba Drumer would break our hearts with his deep, solemn voice.
>
> Some talked of God, of his mysterious ways, of the sins of the Jewish people, and of their future deliverance. But I had ceased to pray. How I sympathized with Job! I did not deny God's existence, but I doubted His absolute justice.
>
> Akiba Drumer said: "God is testing us. He wants to find out whether we can dominate our base instincts and kill the Satan within us. We have no right to despair. And if he punishes us relentlessly, it's a sign that He loves us all the more."
>
> Hersh Genud, well versed in the cabbala, spoke of the end of the world and the coming of the Messiah.
>
> Only occasionally during these conversations did the thought occur to me: "Where is my mother at this moment? And Tzipora . . . ?

Although this discussion may have distracted the young Wiesel from his terrible plight, it hardly spoke to his reality. The author's juxtaposition of the discussion of theology and his recollection of his infrequent thoughts of his family emphasizes the lack of connection between the two. The distinction between the historical present and the messianic future did help to sustain individual communities through their misery and thus helped to preserve not only the individual but the belief in Judaism as well. However, Wiesel cannot accept messianism as an alternative to facing the Holocaust nor can he accept a Messiah who refused to appear at the time when he was so crucially needed. After the experience of Auschwitz, Wiesel was forced to take history with the utmost seriousness. It became for him the principal level of existence. The Rabbinic strategies, which deferred the explanation of evil until the messianic future or the world to come, did not work for Wiesel. Wiesel had once been prepared for eternity; his life was shattered by history.

The Zohar, the central Kabbalistic text in Jewish mysticism, presents a third strategy for defending the traditional theodicy in the face of evil. The Zohar relates the following parable:

> It is the will of the Holy One that men should worship Him and walk in the way of truth that they may be rewarded with many benefits. How, then, can an evil servant come and counteract the will of his Master by tempting man to walk in an evil way, seducing him from the good way and causing him to disobey the will of his Lord? But, indeed, the "evil inclination" also does this through the will of its Lord. It is as if a king had an only son whom he dearly loved, and just for that cause he warned him not to be enticed by bad women, saying that anyone defiled might not enter his palace. The son promised his father to do his will in love. Outside the palace, however, there lived a beautiful harlot. After a while the King thought: "I will see how far my son is devoted to me." So he sent to the woman and commanded her, saying: "Entice my son, for I wish to test his obedience to my will." So she used every blandishment to lure him into her embraces.

According to this parable, evil is God's test of Israel's love and obedience. Evil tempts people to renounce or abandon God's moral commandments. Thus, evil is viewed as a part of God's greater plan, and the nature of the evil itself is denied ultimate significance. Evil becomes a creation of God in service of a greater good. Wiesel rejects this explanation of the Holocaust for many of the same reasons he rejected the first two explanations. In addition to the negative characterization that would have to be ascribed to a God who would devise such a 'test' as the Holocaust, the text explanation, like the messianic explanation, does not really relate to the actual experience of suffering. Like the other theological explanations, the concept of the test leads the mind away from the reality that raised the question of evil rather than speaking to that reality. Thus, Wiesel's existential situation could not be explained by traditional theology, and he therefore lost his faith in the traditional solutions. These solutions were ultimately ineffective in lessening his suffering or in protecting him from the encroachment of anomie.

Wiesel describes in *Night* how he first expressed his rejection of traditional theology in terms of religious rebellion. He was shocked by the incongruity of a liturgy that praised God and a reality that indicted Him. Wiesel refused to repress this incongruity and therefore defiantly refused to praise God. Wiesel describes how the new arrivals at Auschwitz began to recite Kaddish when they came to recognize the true nature of their situation. The Kaddish, a prayer in praise of God that is recited by the mourner following the death of a close relative, symbolically serves as a proclamation of God's justice in the face of death. Wiesel was revolted at this recitation. He writes:

> For the first time, I felt revolt rise up in me. Why should I bless His name? The Eternal, Lord of the Universe, the All-Powerful and Terrible, was silent. What had I to thank Him for?

Yet moments later, in spite of himself, Wiesel began to pray. He could not dismiss God so he confronted and condemned Him. In one prayer, for example, he thanked God for the magnificence of the universe in which mud could hide the shine of even a new pair of shoes. Wiesel continued to express this feeling of revolt against God throughout the book.

As Wiesel's anger intensified, his rebellion became defiance. The author describes the New Year services in the camps, services in which God is proclaimed King and is praised for recalling His covenant with Israel and in which Israel is praised as the Chosen of God. Wiesel became angered at his fellow inmates for having surrendered to the drama of the liturgy and for still being troubled (as indeed he himself still was) by the question of God or, perhaps more accurately, by the burden of God. The juxtaposition of the New Year liturgy and the reality of Auschwitz proved an outrage to Wiesel. In rebellion, he refused to bless God's name and to praise a universe in which there were factories of death and in which Israel was the chosen victim. Wiesel describes the service and his rejection of it.

> "All creation bears witness to the Greatness of God!"
>
> Once, New Year's Day had dominated my life. I knew that my sins grieved the Eternal; I implored his forgiveness. Once, I had believed profoundly that upon one solitary deed of mine, one solitary prayer, depended the salvation of the world.
>
> This day I had ceased to plead. I was no longer capable of lamentation. On the contrary, I felt very strong. I was the accuser, God the accused. My eyes were open and I was alone—terribly alone in a world without God and without man. Without

> love or mercy . . . I stood amid that praying congregation, observing it like a stranger.

In this passage Wiesel reveals how he had moved beyond rebellion and defiance to alienation and radical loneliness. This sense of estrangement is not confined to Wiesel's immediate experience in the camps nor to his descriptions of that experience in *Night.* He returns to the feeling of alienation time and again in his novels and short stories. The alienation that Wiesel describes involves not only a severance from eternity but an integral involvement in history. Thus, the drama of the New Year in the camps which he describes in *Night* was not played out in the domain of the divine but in the human arena.

Wiesel further undercuts the divine-human encounter of Yom Kippur, the encounter in which the individual stands naked before God and asks that his deeds be examined and that he be judged for life, by choosing to describe Yom Kippur as the day for a selection by the earthly masters, the S.S. The penitents who had besieged the Lord with prayer the evening before were forced to test their skills on far more attentive masters as they tried to pass an inspection by the S.S. doctor who had within *his* power the decision of life and death. Wiesel describes how the S.S. made Yom Kippur into a Day of Judgment where the fate of men was decided by their masters. The drama of the Day of Judgment came true in a manner never envisioned by the tradition.

Wiesel's rebellion in *Night* is not limited to diatribes alone. Wiesel describes the arrival of the Day of Atonement, the sacred day of judgment, when he was forced to express his rebellion and alienation in deed as well as in thought. He was forced to question whether he should eat on Yom Kippur, whether one should fast in the camps. He wrestled painfully with the place of tradition and obedience in the world of night. Wiesel resolved the question by eating. He describes the occasion:

> . . . there was no longer any reason why I should fast. I no longer accepted God's silence. As I swallowed my bowl of soup, I saw in the gesture an act of rebellion and protest against Him.
>
> And I nibbled my crust of bread.
>
> In the depths of my heart, I felt a great void.

The void of personal separation from God, the void of meaninglessness in life, and the void of God's absence in history are all acutely expressed by the author. In a sense, the entire corpus of Wiesel's writings is an attempt to confront absence, to describe the beauty that preceded it, the pain of separation, the yearning for return, and the failure of all efforts to return.

The void that Wiesel experienced was precipitated by the gap between his religion and his reality, between the realm of eternity and the realm of history. Throughout *Night* he underscores his rejection of faith by contrasting the reality of pain with the language of liturgy and with the hopes generated by faith. Each of the characters Wiesel develops feels the acute anxiety of disappointment. None survive with their faith intact. Old Rabbis declare their heretical feelings. Akiba Drumer, a formerly pious man, abandons his belief in both God and life. Mercifully, others die before they can fully lose their faith. The author survives, having witnessed the "other side" of man and God, feeling the abyss of a Godless world and the guilt of knowing that he has both betrayed others and been the victim himself of betrayal. He alone must look in the mirror and begin again, if only to tell his tale.

Theodicy in *Dawn*

Wiesel's second novel, *Dawn*, was first published in France in 1960. The novel is set in Palestine just prior to the foundation of the state of Israel. Elisha, the protagonist of the novel, is the chosen executioner of a British soldier, Captain Dawson, whose life is to be taken in retaliation for the execution of a young Jewish terrorist.

Elisha is a former concentration camp inmate who later became a student of philosophy in order to understand the perennial questions of eternity and to ascribe blame to man and God for the events that so marred his adolescence. Elisha's course of studies in Paris was interrupted by a Sabra, a native-born Palestinian Jew, who wished to solicit him for a terrorist organization and train him in the art of force. Elisha's solicitor took him to Palestine where he met his new master who instructed him in the art of combat, an art that did not allow him to discern cosmic patterns but that provided him with a new sense of power and control over his fate. During his period of training, Elisha was forced to undergo a radical change in both his character and aspirations. He finally qualified as a terrorist.

The central theme explored by Wiesel in *Dawn* is the relationship between God's dominion and man's obedience. In *Night* God does not intervene to save His people and enforce His laws. In *Dawn* Wiesel describes how man obliterated God's dominion when he tried to enforce justice himself and how he destroyed his trust in God in order to save himself.

The story Wiesel tells in *Dawn* details how the establishment of the state of Israel and the new reliance of the Jewish people on their own power involves a rejection of the God of Israel who was expected to reveal himself through history. Although Elisha does not fully understand his confrontation with God, it is primarily this conquest of God through complete self-reliance that is taught him by his terrorist master. During his instruction Elisha recalls an earlier master who had taught him Kabbalah before the war. Elisha recounts some of his teachings and presents his reaction to it.

> I remembered how the grizzled master had explained the sixth commandment to me. Why has a man no right to commit murder? Because in so doing he takes upon himself the function of God. And this must not be done too easily. Well, I said to myself, *if in order to change the course of our history we have to become God, we shall become Him. How easy that is we shall see. No, it was not easy.* (italics mine)

People must act in order to affect history. People must create in a world functionally devoid of God, a world that does not turn to God for salvation. Wiesel restates this point even more explicitly in a later work with reference to the state of Israel during a situation of war. "Whoever kills, becomes God. Whoever kills, kills God. Each murder is a suicide, with the Eternal eternally the victim." In order to live and shape history, in order to be independent and self-reliant, humanity must kill its sense of reliance upon God and affect its own salvation.

The climax of *Dawn* comes near the end of the novel when Elisha must finally confirm the course of his training and the degree of his transformation by executing a British hostage. Elisha is convinced that this execution is necessary to insure the foundation of an independent Jewish state in Palestine. In the final scene of the novel, after Elisha has executed his victim, he comes to the realization that he himself was the victim. Elisha considers the situation: "That's it, I said to myself. It's done. I've killed. I've killed Elisha."

The interpretation of this passage beyond the literal level hinges on the meaning of the name Elisha. It is obvious that in killing another person Elisha has also killed a part of himself, but I am convinced that Wiesel implies far more by this passage than is immediately apparent. To elucidate the meaning of Elisha's critical statement, it is important to consider the significance of names themselves within the Jewish tradition for this tradition is so much a part of Wiesel's idiom. The importance of names for Wiesel can be verified by reference to his use of them in his other works. In connection with this work, the specific meaning of the name Elisha, in addition to the implied reference to the two famous Elishas in Jewish tradition, exposes deeper levels of meaning in Elisha's climactic statement.

A glance at some of Wiesel's other novels reveals that Wiesel chooses his names very carefully for their historical overtones and for their exact meaning in Hebrew. In *The Town Beyond the Wall*, for example, the central character's name is Michael, and the name Michael, *Mi ca el*, in Hebrew literally means "who is like god." Throughout the novel, Michael in fact struggles to achieve the strength and omnipotence of God. In addition, when considered in the interrogative "who is like God?" Michael's name expresses the central question that remains unresolved throughout the novel. Similarly, in *A Beggar in Jerusalem* the narrator's name, David, is particularly significant. The name David reinforces many of the historical and messianic overtones present throughout the novel for the name connotes not merely the legendary king of Israel who captured Jerusalem and made it his capital, but also the Messiah who, according to tradition, will be a descendant of David. Wiesel's emphasis on the significance of names themselves is an extension of the importance of names within Jewish tradition for, according to Jewish lore, names are thought to reveal the essence of one's being.

Within Jewish literature the specific name Elisha is held by two important figures, the prophet Elisha who was the successor of Elijah, and Elisha ben Abuyah, the heretic who was the teacher of Rabbi Meir and an important man in his own right. Elisha the prophet was not only the principal successor of Elijah but his faithful companion as well. According to Rabbinic lore, Elisha was both a disciple and a colleague who surpassed his master as a miracle worker by performing sixteen miracles (twice the number performed by Elijah). These miracles ranged from crossing the river and healing the leper to reviving the dead. Elisha the heretic was a contemporary of Rabbi Akivah and one of the four rabbis to enter the sacred realm of mystery. Of the four rabbis, only Akivah emerged unscathed. Ben Zoma went mad, Ben Azzai died, and Elisha lost his faith. According to some Rabbinic traditions, Elisha is depicted as a dualist. According to others, his apostasy was a total denial of the theodicy of Israel. Elisha once declared: the world is "let din v'let dayan," without justice and without a judge. Ironically, the name Elisha itself has the literal Hebrew meaning "God will save."

Theodicy in *Le Jour*

The struggle between life and death continues to dominate Wiesel's third novel of the trilogy, *Le Jour*. However, in this novel alone God is not implicated either in life or in death. In *Night* God was implicated in the anguish of the living as He was in the extermination of the dead. In *Dawn* God was implicated in the death of Captain Dawson. The execution was in fact the execution of God. In *Le Jour*, however, the struggle is no longer between man and God or even between man and man. The struggle is within Eliezer, now a newspaper correspondent for an Israeli paper. The battle rages between Eliezer's desire to live and create and his yearning for death and peace.

The battle between life and death is constant in *Le Jour.* The accident that brought Eliezer to the brink of death was in fact not an accident but rather the occasion chosen subconsciously by the correspondent to dramatize the battle waging within him. After the accident, a lover, a friend, the sky, and the light help retain the correspondent's thin hold on life, while his mother and grandmother, the sea, and the rivers tempt him to yield to death. Fever and physical pain combine with his emotional suffering and with his sense of fragmentation to battle for death while a pragmatic American doctor struggles to preserve his life. The doctor tells the correspondent:

> "Every man is like the river . . . Rivers flow toward the sea, which is never full. Men are swallowed up by death which is never satiated."

Yet, in spite of himself, Eliezer repeats Dylan Thomas' famous line, ". . . rage, rage, against the dying of the light."

Both the historical references and the literal meaning of the name Elisha are relevant to the character Elisha in *Dawn.* The image of a pupil who comes to equal if not surpass his master (particularly if his master is The Master) and who has learned to work his own miracles, as well as the image of a heretic who has lost his faith and expresses that loss either in dualism or denial are both images that relate to Wiesel's Elisha. (In addition, the miracles performed by the prophet Elisha are symbolically relevant to the story in *Dawn.* The crossing of the river recalls both the Exodus and the entrance into the promised land and can thus be applied to the foundation of the state of Israel as the return to the promised land. The healing of the leper can represent the leprous isolation of the Jewish people throughout the Holocaust by the other nations of the world and the end to the isolation that the foundation of the state of Israel seemed to provide. Most powerfully, the revival of the dead can represent the revival of the Jewish people after the catastrophic destruction of the Holocaust.) Furthermore, the literal Hebrew meaning of the name Elisha, which refers to a saving God, is most relevant to Wiesel's Elisha. If we apply these historical and literal references to Elisha's crucial statement "I've killed Elisha," additional levels of meaning appear in the statement. When Elisha and his Jewish compatriots consent to war and killing in order to form a state, we must ask ourselves whom they really have killed. Which Elisha has been killed? Does the foundation of the state of Israel by violence entail the death of Elisha the prophet who revives the dead? Does the assumption of power by the Jewish people and their own enforcement of justice by violence entail the end of Elisha the heretic who proclaimed there was no justice? Does the foundation of the state of Israel signify an act of deicide, the murder of Elisha, the saving God? It is my belief that the execution that Elisha commits primarily signifies an act of deicide. The price for the historical survival of the Jewish people involves the functional death (if not the deliberate murder) of a saving God.

As Elisha learns, deicide is never an easy act to commit. Although he recognizes the necessity of doing without God in order to affect history, this recognition is not without its inner turmoil. Elisha knows that there can be no return to the sacred cosmos of the past, yet in the very depths of his being he never ceases to yearn for a return to such a cosmos.

What is God's role in such a universe? The narrator of *Le Jour* relates the difference between his first and second experience in surgery. During his first experience, when the narrator was still a child, he dreamed of approaching the heavenly throne and of asking the questions that have always been sacred mysteries to Israel. "When will the exile end?" "When will the anointed one, the Messiah, come?" The narrator distinctly remembers the fact that God did respond, although when he awoke he could not recall the content of the response. There were answers to his questions, and even if he did not remember the answers later, he knew that there was a realm where question and answer were one. By the time the narrator undergoes his second experience in surgery, he has become an adult. After this surgery the narrator relates to the doctor, "I didn't see God in my dream. He was no longer there." God's absence during the second experience was as pronounced as His presence had formerly been.

If there is a God in *Le Jour*, He is not the God of Israel, a just and saving God, but rather a compassionless sadist. The correspondent explains:

> Man prefers to blame himself for all possible sins and crimes rather than come to the conclusion that God is capable of the most flagrant injustice. I still blush every time I think of the way God makes fun of human beings, his favorite toys.

Wiesel continues to elaborate his negative image of God by citing a concept from Lurrianic Kabbalism and then twisting it into a demonic form. In Lurrianic Kabbalism, God was considered dependent upon humanity in order to become one again. Human salvation and God's liberation were integrally related. In a bitter passage the correspondent reaffirms God's dependence upon man and God's radical loneliness. However, God is now depicted as dependent upon humanity solely for entertainment and diversion:

> Yes, God needs man. Condemned to eternal solitude, he made man only to use him as a toy, to amuse himself. That's what philosophers and poets have refused to admit: in the beginning there was neither the Word, nor Love, but laughter, the roaring, eternal laughter whose echoes are more deceitful than the mirages of the desert.

The correspondent's deliberate denunciation of God establishes the distance between him and the theodicy of traditional Judaism, and the ontological structure that he chooses in place of the tradition does not insulate him against death. The victory of life at the end of the novel is in no way assured. Wiesel wishes to illustrate that the outcome of any individual battle is uncertain, that it is in fact 'accidental.' Even if life wins the immediate battle, death cannot be overcome. Death ultimately triumphs. Though the correspondent does rage against death and though he does outwit death a second time, the external forces of death and his own desire for death do remain. The ashes of the past will inevitably return to haunt him as they have haunted him before. All being is being unto death. In *Le Jour* Wiesel exposes a world in which God is at best absent in the struggle between life and death. At worst, God may even be an ally of the forces of death.

Conclusions

The questions that preoccupied Wiesel in *Night* concerning the suffering of the innocent and the absence of redemption are harshly answered in *Le Jour*. Wiesel explains that there is no reason why the innocent suffer and that the hour of redemption is death. This is the sad truth that humanity avoids and tries to repress at all costs.

> Men cast aside the one who has known pure suffering, if they cannot make a god out of him; the one who tells them: I suffered not because I was God, nor because I was a saint trying to imitate Him, but only because I am a man, a man like you, with your weaknesses, your cowardice, your sins, your rebellions, and your ridiculous ambitions; such a man frightens men, because he makes them feel ashamed. They pull away from him as if he were

> guilty. As if he were usurping God's place to illuminate the great vacuum that we find at the end of all adventures.

In the beginning as night descended there was hope and faith. In the end when the day arrived there is a vacuum, death. The trilogy of *Night*, *Dawn*, and *Le Jour* marks the transition from a God-infused world to a Godless world, the transition from a world in which redemption can be expected to one in which all that is left is to rage against the dying of the light. Surely no critic who has carefully read these three volumes can see in them a vision of hope and a restoration of the sacred cosmos of normative Judaism. At this stage in his writing, Wiesel affirms human finitude in a world unconducive to the ultimate realization of human desires.

JOHN K. ROTH

In the Beginning

> And God said, "Let there be light"; and there was light. And God saw that the light was good; and God separated the light from the darkness. God called the light Day, and the darkness he called Night. And there was evening and there was morning, one day.
>
> (Gen. 1:3–5)

> This is the message we have heard from him and proclaim to you, that God is light and in him is no darkness at all.
>
> (1 John 1:5)

> "Man raises himself toward God by the questions he asks Him. . . . I pray to the God within me that He will give me the strength to ask Him the right questions."
>
> (*Night*)

Haven't You Heard About It?

A transport arrives at Birkenau, reception center for Auschwitz. Bewildered Jews from Sighet and other Rumanian towns emerge from train-car prisons into midnight air fouled by burning flesh. Elie Wiesel, his father, mother, and little sister are among them. Separated by the Nazi guards, the boy loses sight of his mother and sister, not fully aware that parting is forever.

Father and son stick together. In the commotion, a guard provokes someone within their hearing: "'What have you come here for, you sons of bitches? What are you doing here? . . . You'd have done better to have hanged yourselves where you were than to come here. Didn't you know what was in store for you at Auschwitz? Haven't you heard about it? In 1944?'"

To the guard's amazement, the Jews of Sighet did not know what awaited them. So near and yet so far away, the final solution had reached them late. Forewarning would have made a difference? At least some persons could have fled for their lives. But forewarning might have counted for nothing, too. The Holocaust, after all, was—and still is—received repeatedly as news too bad to be believed. Soon enough, however, Wiesel and his father learned what to expect. They were sent "left" by Dr. Mengele, the SS medical official whose baton directed life and death. Normally left was death's way, and for a time their line marched directly toward a pit of flaming bodies. Steps from the edge, a guard's order turned them toward the barracks. But the fire left its mark: "Never shall I forget those flames which consumed my faith forever."

Elie Wiesel survived that first night and the days that followed. For ten years after his release, he wrote nothing, sifting and wrestling with the questions that must be asked . . . in the right way. *Night* came first. Originally a manuscript of some eight hundred pages, the English version available since 1960 is a memoir, lean and spare, describing Wiesel's death camp experiences in 1944–45. It begins with a boy who "believed profoundly." It ends with this reflection: "From the depths of the mirror, a corpse gazed back at me. The look in his eyes, as they stared into mine, has never left me."

Some readers find *Night* telling of an anti-Exodus, an anti-Covenant, a triumph for death. The account *is* a reversal of the release of Egyptian slaves into a land flowing with milk and honey. True, Wiesel's story concludes with liberation, but the fundamental action is a journey always deeper into captivity that strips good away. Life-affirming covenants with God disappear, replaced by their opposite: promises of death kept all too faithfully by Hitler. In its images of time and space, in its portrayal of ruined life, the book is a record of death and dying. All of these readings fit, and yet neither singly nor collectively do they exhaust it. *Night* eludes fixed interpretations because of the questions it raises.

Beginnings make all the difference in the world. No less so what we make of them. Our aim is to inquire how things stand between God and humankind after Auschwitz, and especially to explore what Christian testimony is possible in that setting. At first glance, *Night* appears to provide anything but an auspicious beginning, at least if hope is premised on the conviction that Christianity provides trustworthy clues about relations between God and the world. For *Night* probes a void that kills not only Elie Wiesel's parental father, but his faith in God the Father, too.

There would be simpler ways to proceed. The Holocaust could have been ignored. We could try even now to forget it, and then faith might be easier. Still, notes of rebellion are real. In gut-level honesty, people with religious faith usually want a stance that, if not simply corroborated by experience, is at least able to face its tests without fleeing from them. Faith is strong just to the extent that it can stand aware of, in spite of, even because of facts that count against it. A tall order. It brings a host of complications. For example, the very honesty that propels a person to keep open eyes trained on the dark undersides of existence may also lead one to conclude that religious paths followed once can be taken no more.

Not by his own choosing, Elie Wiesel learned that life can kill trust and hope. Indeed he learned that there are times when it *should* do so, because the alternative is a self-deception that betrays. At this point the line draws finely. Wiesel's objective is never to shatter faith as an end in itself. If his death camp experience forced a form of religious rejection upon him, it also revealed that hopes, dreams, even illusions—religious or otherwise—can be life-giving. To threaten them needlessly is to become a killer. Thus, one of the greatest sins located in the Holocaust is that men and women created conditions in which faith in God's justice, mercy, and love became all but impossible.

What makes the difference, then, between ways in which people—writers especially—put faith to the test? Everything depends on whether the motive is that of tearing down or building up. "One can say anything," writes Wiesel, "as long as it is for man, not against him." That norm and test, however, lead to a second complication.

No individual can work out another's relationship with God. But by what we say and do, we are responsible for shaping options that a person perceives in that area. Religiously speaking, one profound aspect of Holocaust encounters is that they open the options so far, always in the direction of complexity and mystery. That is, the Holocaust forecloses quick spiritual resolutions. Leaving nothing unchanged, it makes faith less "the *assurance of* things hoped for, the *conviction of* things not seen," (Heb. 11:1, my emphasis) and more *a search and quest for them.* It also interrogates other dispositions—atheism and agnosticism, humanism and cynicism—because its range of experience renders everything uncertain except uncertainty itself.

Uncertainty often takes the form of questions. Questions push us back toward beginnings, whether the universe or *Night* is concerned. Can we encounter God in the questions we ask? Can we uplift ourselves through the inquiries we put to God and each other? If we can do so with the Holocaust at the heart of the matter, then Paul may be right: "For I am sure that neither death, nor life, nor angels, nor principalities, nor things present, nor things to come, nor powers, nor height, nor depth, nor anything else in all creation, will be able to separate us from the love of God in Christ Jesus our Lord." (Rom 8:38–39) And if we cannot, then one search will lead to another. In either case, we shall find that we are in the beginning.

Genesis says that "in the beginning God created the heavens and the earth." At first "the earth was without form and void, and darkness was upon the face of the deep." (Gen. 1:1–2) Then God separated light from the darkness. Day and Night were born; order emerged out of chaos. Other beginnings, recorded in *Night* millennia later, quiz the Creator about darkness and the void. Why were those qualities not erased by God's formative power? Why were they only refashioned, and even then so as to build the possibility of Auschwitz into the world's foundations? Genesis makes a point of calling good that first day's light. About darkness it is silent. At the end of the mythical sixth day, all creation is called good. Even darkness may be included. But the original silence is heavy, at least in retrospect from 1944. Destruction without justification. Waste without reason. Suffering without merit. In a word, *radical evil* stalks what God found good. To speak of the powers of darkness, as we do, should leave us searching: why are they here?

"In the beginning was the Word, and the Word was with God, and the Word was God" (John 1:1)—that is the message that Christians receive. Referring to Jesus the Messiah, it is taken to imply that "God is light and in him is no darkness at all." (1 John 1:5) Jewish questions test those prologues and every Christian touched by them. Elie Wiesel puts to God the question he heard upon entering Auschwitz: "Haven't you heard about it?" And in *Night* his questioning is not meek and beholden. Things are too far out of hand for subservient piety. "I was the accuser," writes Wiesel, "God the accused." And the questions come as steadily as the silence that returns: "Why should I bless His name? . . . What had I to thank Him for?" . . . "'What are You, my God, compared to this afflicted crowd, proclaiming to You their faith, their anger, their revolt? What does Your greatness mean, Lord of the Universe, in the face of all this weakness, this decomposition, and this decay?'" "'Where is the divine Mercy? . . .'"

Once Wiesel felt an answer. It formed as he witnessed the execution of three fellow-prisoners. One of them, the center of his concern, was a child:

> Behind me, I heard the same man asking:
> "Where is God now?"
> And I heard a voice within me answer him:

> "Where is He? Here He is—He is hanging here on this gallows. . . ."
>
> That night the soup tasted of corpses.

If the scene parallels the crucifixion, remember that no resurrection followed. There was only agonized death, prolonged because the boy's starved body was too light to make the noose work efficiently. The words and scene form a microcosm of the darkness created by the Holocaust. Nevertheless, the image is an enigma. Its meaning is neither single nor announced directly.

Who, what, is dying on that gallows? One child, all children, and Elie Wiesel among them. A world of faith and possibly all worlds of faith, whether they are oriented toward optimism about humanity or toward trust in God. Meanings such as those can be seen, but there is more. For instance, what about the God who is dying in the body of a tortured child?

The child was beautiful, gentle, weak. He may also have been involved in plans for violent resistance, and certainly he showed himself to be tough and courageous in maintaining silence during interrogation torture. Still, he does not quite fit the idea of "The Eternal, Lord of the Universe, the All-Powerful and Terrible" that Wiesel had learned as a boy to associate with God. The additional fact that Wiesel never gives up a relation to God—"I did not deny God's existence, but I doubted His absolute justice"—also denies that this death of God is an acceptance of atheism. At most the child could represent a fragment, an aspect of God. And what might that be? The part that transforms the universe. Wiesel writes that the executed boy was "loved by all." The aspect of God that is dying is that which can be loved, at least that which can be loved easily.

A Holocaust Universe can be the outcome of no God at all. It can also be the result of a God who creates, and it can even be linked to a God who watches over and intervenes in history. But it is extremely difficult to relate such a universe to a God providential and moral, to One who organizes and moves history so as to reveal a care "that means life to you." (Deut. 30:20) In witnessing the death of a child, Wiesel suggests that to be with God is to encounter a silent presence—perhaps beyond good and evil, beyond love—who gives life only to leave us alone. That relationship makes the world unsafe: "'Today anything is allowed. Anything is possible, even these crematories. . . .'"

The answer heard within while Wiesel watched a child die ("Here He is—He is hanging here on this gallows") quizzes more than it resolves. *Night* brings that process to no resolution. Reasons? *Night* is truth that must be told to honor the dead, to bear witness for them, to convey the message that darkness can extinguish light. But what are those reasons if not affirmations that life can be good, that we must not forsake it, even if it is so maimed for us that looking in mirrors we see corpses that make us want to drop.

Speaking in God's name, Moses told his people to choose life. (Deut. 30:19–20) With *Night* as back and foreground, all of Wiesel's books explore, refine, and underwrite that command. Always that effort encounters darkness, often so thick that nothing but despondency seems possible. And yet there is always something more. Heavily shadowed, especially in his early works, Wiesel's appeal remains: choose life.

As Wiesel has learned from Moses and his legacy, that conclusion is forever a beginning because it decides nothing specific for anyone. Instead we are moved into troubling questions about ourselves and God. Elie Wiesel thinks that a Jew "defines himself more by what troubles him than by what reassures him. . . . To me, the Jew and his questioning are one." Christianity tries to be more reassuring: the Messiah has come to reveal an unshakable kingdom—so the story goes. But when such claims enter Auschwitz they turn into dilemmas that should lead Christians to opt for a more Jewish identity. As *Night* moves toward *Dawn* a step is taken in that direction.

What Do You Want of Me?

Elisha, 18, finds himself in Paris. Liberated from Buchenwald by Americans, his plan is to study philosophy at the Sorbonne "because I wanted to understand the meaning of the events of which I had been the victim." Gad interrupts. This man is a stranger, but Gad knows why he is in Elisha's room. His answer to Elisha's question—"'What do you want of me?'"—is simple: "'I want you to give me your future.'"

Gad needs Elisha's future for the sake of a people. His aim is to make Elisha choose life by engaging in the battle to free Palestine from British rule and thus to achieve the rebirth of a nation, a new Israel. Elisha is moved by Gad's vision. At the same time his religious upbringing, not consumed entirely by the Holocaust, warns him that men and women do not seize holy land with impunity. A Jewish return to Israel, to Zion, still feels like a messianic hope. It is God's prerogative, not his people's. But the experience of Auschwitz is also irrepressible: apparently God will not act, at least not in any way that guarantees Jewish well-being. If there is a God who chooses life, he does so in ways that put it always under threat. Men and women must become their own providence and security. They must become what God never was or what he now refuses to be.

The vision of Gad prevails. It *is* more important to change the world than to interpret it, and the works of the freedom fighter replace those of philosophers. But once called by Gad to play political roles refused by God, Elisha learns how ambiguous it is to choose life: "Well, I said to myself, if in order to change the course of our history we have to become God, we shall become Him. How easy that is we shall see. No, it was not easy." The ambiguous twist is that choosing life in this particular situation requires choosing death as well.

Elisha, once the possible victim, is now cast as executioner. His order: retribution for the British slaying of an Israeli soldier. His target: Captain John Dawson, a man he does not hate and has, in fact, come to like. Of course, there are circumstances that warrant this Englishman's death. The cause of liberty is just and good; the means necessary to achieve that end are not blameworthy. Israel is worlds away from Treblinka. To equate Elisha's act with that of a *Kapo* or an SS would be blasphemy. But the invalidity of such comparisons is incomplete: "The shot had left me deaf and dumb. That's it, I said to myself. It's done. I've killed. I've killed Elisha."

Killed Elisha? . . . How? . . . In what sense? Elisha's aim is God's eclipse: by taking the prerogative to determine who shall die and who shall live; by deciding that human deeds alone can create and inhabit promised lands, and then only if they show enough strength to shatter resistance and defend against encroachments. So if *Dawn* is the willed continuation of a death of God experienced unwillingly in *Night*, then some of the Jew in Elisha dies as well: that portion which trusts the Lord too much.

Scruples against violence, murder, and execution? Folly in a world where people must be their own providence. To choose life in this Holocaust Universe no one—least of all a Jew—must refuse to kill when survival dictates. Besides, violence, even executions and terrorism, have their own cleansing effect, especially when carried out for a good cause. And they are not only cathartic. They also can be politically effective by showing others that you mean business and that tampering with one's life, liberty, and happiness carries a high price.

And yet . . . it is not, must not be so simple. Elisha's killing brings little release and even less clarity. Oh, he knows that he has executed John Dawson and that he has changed his life and heritage in the process. But to what end and at what cost? History and perhaps God himself had forced Elisha's hand, and there was no better choice than to take history into his own hands. But the result of that action is an ambiguity deepened by the clarity that he had to act in place of God's missing providence. "Ambiguity," says Wiesel, "is the name of our sickness, of everybody's sickness." He could add that it is a sickness that can lead to despair and death as we experience disillusionment at our own hands. He could also add that there is one sickness worse: namely, the sickness of a false clarity that feels no anguish when life is taken away. No, it is not easy to become God . . . unless one becomes a God who lacks sensitivity and decency. That incarnation occurs more than we care to admit.

What do you want of me? Should we be silent? Not ask that question of each other, ourselves, God, or life itself? Or, unable to resist the asking, should we train ourselves to resist expecting answers? The problem is that neither strategy works very well. Life is a series of what-do-you-want-of-me's. Sooner or later most of us thrust them to the sky if not to God. As for answers? Our expectations or the lack of them drag us, however unwillingly, back down to the one suggested by *Dawn*: existence fractures. It will not—cannot be—set right.

Life forces change. Nice if we could read that development as an always upward, progressive movement, but such an evaluation is a luxury all too rare. In most of us the impotence, and thus relative innocence, of youth is replaced by power, and then by tendencies to use it that require massive efforts to keep them from inflicting more suffering than they relieve. Initial anticipations are more optimistic. A Gad or a God or even self-interrogations are first-glanced as more benign. But push does come to shove, and then enough ambiguity recedes to make us aware of the labyrinth we inhabit. We learn with Elisha that life is not easy just because part of the answer to "What do you want of me?" is our own undoing.

What do you want of me? Given that men and women have some capacity to figure out what is going on, that question prods us to seek reasons, explanations, solutions. That prodding, however, is as much burden as it is blessing. Nowhere does Paul speak more truth than when he says that now we see in a mirror dimly and know only in part. But that realization does nothing to calm human restlessness. For we do understand a great deal, and we are convinced that we may understand more, and so we are impelled to keep asking questions and to keep on trying to answer them until we find something that satisfies. The difficulty is that events like the Holocaust defy satisfactions. This ultimate critique of pure reason yields reasons in abundance, but they all raise issues of their own. Consider, for example, some attempts to "explain" the death camps.

At least since the time of Job, human consciousness has been tempted to assume that devastation falls on those who earn it. Likewise with prosperity and peace. At least since the time of Job, human consciousness has also known better, but not well enough to put the former assumptions to rest. Still linked with strands of Judaism and Christianity, themes of retribution and punishment infiltrate efforts to comprehend Auschwitz. Such infiltration kills.

Holocaust-as-judgment? For Jewish failure to obey God's will—a failure understood as collective more than individual—punishment is meted out. By implication the SS becomes God's instrument, not for the annihilation of a people but for their chastisement and correction. The instrument itself, of course, is not without flaw. It also gets justice. Nazi ruins testify that God's judgment is a two-edged sword.

Questions agitate immediately. Does the punishment fit the crime? What kind of God are we dealing with in this scenario? At the heart of the matter, one answer proclaims, is the sovereignty, the holiness, of God. Human life—the existence of the world—is a gift. Nothing forced God to create, and nothing but his own will commits himself ultimately to anything or to anybody. The human story may have started in Eden, and God may have chosen special identity with a particular people. But a permanent rose garden on this earth was not his promise. Divine will and human obedience to it: on those factors everything depends. And what a will it was and is. At times its decisions support our perceptions of rationality, justice, and goodness. At times they confound human standards, and we learn in laughter and tears alike that these words are sound: "'For my thoughts are not your thoughts, neither are your ways my ways, says the LORD.'" (Isa. 55:8)

The will of God is not capricious might alone. At least the tradition that runs from Moses to the prophets and then on to Jesus and Paul emphasizes the *holiness* of God, and that holiness is not merely naked power. God's holiness-as-power is awesome indeed. Even more so as it includes goodness and righteousness. Those ingredients fill—and frequently dominate—the biblical narratives from start to finish. They are present when great expectations take dust and breathe into it God's image. They are found as God calls Abraham and promises to make him the father of a great people. They project through the exodus of Egyptian slaves, to the covenant between God and his people mediated by Moses and the Law, to the prophecy of Jeremiah and Amos, and for Christians to the conviction that "God so loved the world that he gave his only Son, that whoever believes in him should not perish but have eternal life." (John 3:16)

So the pieces of this Holocaust puzzle are put together as follows: devastation there has been, is, and shall be, but it is not the result of divine wrath alone. There is a corrective purpose, a call to repent and obey. If the correction seems overly harsh, we should remember that life is a gift and that God's holiness is not confined by human desire. God owes us nothing. We are the debtors. What do you want of me? Jews are called to sanctify God's name through adherence to the Law. Christians are taught not only to trust but also to help make real the promise "that in everything God works for good with those who love him, who are called according to his purpose." (Rom. 8:28)

Two additional pieces try to squeeze into this resolution. Although officially disavowed, vestiges remain that make Christians prone to see the

Holocaust as God's punishment against Jews for their refusal to accept Jesus as the Messiah. Second, whether related to the first idea or quite independent of it, the emergence of the modern state of Israel is looked on as verification that God brings good out of evil. God's wrath mellowed, and Phoenix-like Israel was reborn out of ashes.

Harsh though they are, these explanations have their comforts. Covenant. Commandment. Disobedience. Punishment. Redemption. One leads to another with simplicity. Those ingredients take an event that seems to explode the moral structure of the universe, and they work it back into a framework that accentuates purpose within early history and even redemption beyond it. For reasons of that kind, a reading of the Holocaust that sees providence as judgment and vice versa always exerts appeal. But the simplicity of such logic is dangerous. To see how, think again about Elisha's dawn.

In theory and practice Elisha's circumstances give him ample justification for killing John Dawson without qualm. More than that, the circumstances seem to make it necessary for Elisha to kill. But the drama in the dawn revolves around some counterpointing questions. Is the execution of John Dawson really unavoidable? Do Elisha's circumstances—or any circumstances—completely justify suffering that may not have to be? Elisha feels the pull of questions like those . . . and then he pulls the trigger. To what end? So that a greater good can emerge? As judgment, as punishment—retributive or corrective—brought to bear against forces that oppose good causes? Or just because an order was given, and orders must be obeyed?

Moments before Elisha kills him, John Dawson is smiling. He tells Elisha that he is smiling "'because all of a sudden it has occurred to me that I don't know why I am dying.' And after a moment of silence he added: 'Do you?'" Yes and no . . . and the shot tries to kill twice, taking Dawson and the no at once. The success and failure mix together, and *Dawn*, like *Night*, ends with a mirror-image: "The night lited, leaving behind it a grayish light the color of stagnant water. Soon there was only a tattered fragment of darkness, hanging in midair, the other side of the window. Fear caught my throat. The tattered fragment of darkness had a face. Looking at it, I understood the reason for my fear. The face was my own."

Not remorse or grief. Not even guilt. Fear is what Elisha feels. That quality puts the emphasis on what may yet occur as well as on what has already happened. Is Elisha afraid that one killing will lead to another? Does he fear that killing will be easier and easier until it becomes the most natural thing in the world? So it seems, and with those possibilities Elisha ties us back to tempting "explanations" of the Holocaust. *Like him, we should fear any tendency that makes killing easier and suffering merely understandable.*

Reasons? One appropriate response is that none should be offered. If the reasons are not obvious, no statement or analysis can make them so. On the other hand, we have a great propensity for missing the obvious, and attention to it may help. Rightly, then, we could argue that with every justification of suffering and killing we open ourselves to indifference, and with indifference comes the likelihood that suffering and killing will go unchecked. We could emphasize that such attitudes violate every ethical and religious norm that humanizes life by directing us to love our neighbors as ourselves. Although it would be harder, we might even try to show that we should fear any outlook that justifies suffering and killing because it can undercut self-interest. But all those lines of thought pale in comparison to the best reason of all: the Holocaust itself.

Anything is possible. But hardly anyone alive—let alone the victims—would argue that the Holocaust in-and-of-itself was good. Instead it should not have been permitted. But happen it did, and one crucial ingredient was that people developed, believed, and enforced reasons for killing and justifications for suffering. Any view that allows us to see killing and suffering as natural, expected, as a means to a better end, *without protesting against that same set of perceptions*, plays into the hands of destruction that reached Holocaust proportions once and can do so again. Religious thought is not immune. Unintentional though the result might be, the Holocaust "explanations" that we have examined play into the hands of suffering and killing, just as versions of them contributed to the Holocaust in the first place. They did and do so by taking attention away from the actual plight of human victims, by arguing that the horrible has a justifying logic and that in the long- if not the short-run evil is not as bad as it seems.

To what, then, did Elisha give his future? The answer depends on how he confronts explanations for John Dawson's death. To accept them without recognizing that there are no satisfactory explanations is to invite death to take strides forward. To hear explanations, to follow their logic, and then to refuse to accept them as sufficient—even as one admits that killing deeds have occurred and at times may be unavoidable—that approach is one that could keep us from succumbing altogether.

Relations to God fit a similar pattern. With the Holocaust as measure to help us judge what is for humanity and what against it, we must put to the test what we say or refuse to say about God and to God. *To justify God may be to speak against human life. To protest against God may be to defend what is good. Not simply to accept God's will but to question it long and hard can be essential for sensitizing us to each other.*

One of the best stories about a biblical Elisha tells how that man of God restored life to a dead child (2 Kings 4:8-37). His namesake in *Dawn* appears to stand in stark contrast. And yet no final comparisons can be made so long as the Elishas in us all keep asking "What do you want of me?" and decline to give the future away to explanations that make misery intelligible. The biblical writers remembered a Shunammite woman and Elisha's saving of her son because that man and woman refused to let despondency and grief have the final words. Wiesel's Elisha is memorable not because of his firm convictions in that regard, but because he helps us to see how difficult, and therefore how important, it is to resist temptation to accept too much. That temptation and resistance to it put God and humanity on trial together as we move toward broad daylight and an accident.

Why Should He Want to Kill a Man Who Succeeds in Seeing Him?

On first meeting Gad, Elisha told him that "'the future is of limited interest to me.'" Did his experiences with Gad and his post-execution struggles make the future urgent for Elisha? Uncertain. We do know that Elie Wiesel rounds off his beginning trilogy with the French-titled *Le Jour* (*Day*). But even that work is not the emergence of light out of darkness, not without ambiguity. Both *Night* and *Dawn* reveal that the swords of politics and history cut many ways; once one has experienced this kind of destruction *Day* asks: "Is life worth living at all?"

His present and future overwhelmed by what he has witnessed in the past, another in a long line of young people—all the same, all different—doubts that he can endure his Holocaust survival. The world will not be changed; the dead cannot be brought back to life, even though they haunt the living too much, creating feelings of guilt, frustration, anger, and rebellion that make joy and happiness all but impossible. In spite of the fact that he has friends, and even a woman who loves him, the young man's life is "the tragic fate of those who came back, left over, living-dead." And so, not only because he feels that "'I am my past,'" but also because he knows that his inability to move beyond makes others suffer, this person senses that life will demand him to lie in ways that he has neither the desire nor the strength to sustain.

Not feeling well, worn out by the heat and a reporting job that seems of no consequence, the young man still manages to keep his date with Kathleen. They decide on a film. Then, crossing a busy street, the young man is struck and dragged by a car: *Le Jour*, rendered in English, becomes *The Accident*. "On the fifth day I at last regained consciousness. . . . I felt alone, abandoned. Deep inside I discovered a regret: I would have preferred to die. An hour later, Dr. Russel came into the room and told me I was going to live. . . . That I was still alive had left me indifferent, or nearly so. But the knowledge that I could still speak filled me with an emotion that I couldn't hide." Nurtured by friends, continuing under the care of a doctor who takes death as a personal enemy, life returns to be chosen again.

As Wiesel weaves past and present together, it remains uncertain whether the accident was premeditated. It is clear, though, that the young man comes to interpret the accident as a choice of death. Thus, *The Accident* is no melodramatic account of bungled suicide. Instead it probes more deeply as Wiesel catches his character in between: In between recognizing how much he wanted to die and how much others want him to live; in between sensing that he will live on and yet not seeing how to do so well. "The problem," Wiesel proposes, "is not: to be or not to be. But rather: to be and not to be." At least for survivors, life conspires to make people choose it; suicides are exceptions that prove the rule. And therefore the issue for most persons, most of the time, is not whether to be but what to be, and we face the latter always in the midst of tragedy. Such nothingness threatens to consume us. Not so much by leading people to take their own lives, but by making us living-dead who pass those qualities to others.

Why does life come to so much grief? If not through wrongdoing, judgment, and punishment alone, then because suffering itself is instructive and redemptive? It teaches us our limits and possibilities alike, and should it be prolonged unto death, accompanying heroism and even martyrdom can lift the spirits of men and women everywhere. The suffering servant . . . the dying Christ . . . a God pained by his own love of earth . . . images like those come down through the ages to suggest that suffering means more than meets the eye. No doubt such outlooks contain some truth. What man or woman has not learned some constructive lesson via pain, or communicated a helpful strength to others by enduring or dying well? Yes . . . and then *but*.

The Accident was caused by a "yes, but." It occurred because too much suffering had been witnessed to balance out instructive or redemptive scales. Martyrs, saints, . . . maybe even Saviors . . . "'are those who die before the end of the story.'" Such is the response when Kathleen asks her friend—long before the accident—whether suffering leads to saintliness. He thinks instead that there is "'a phase of suffering you reach beyond which you become a brute: beyond it you sell your soul—and worse, the souls of your friends—for a piece of bread, for some warmth, for a moment of oblivion, of sleep.'" To be sure, it is possible to say that a person broken by suffering is simply one who cannot "take it." And no judgments hit harder than the self-doubts that intrude when survival or well-being seem to follow from a "giving in" that a better use of will would not have tolerated.

Paul promises that "you can trust God not to let you be tried beyond your strength, and with any trial he will give you a way out of it and the strength to bear it." (1 Cor. 10:13) Who has the burden of proof? Is it only to those whose faith is sufficiently strong that the promise is made good? Either that, or we have to see death itself as the Messiah. Both views have problems. On the one hand, faith is neither necessary nor sufficient for earthly survival. On the other, it is neither necessary nor sufficient for losing one's life in Auschwitz or anywhere else. Beyond that, death-as-Messiah so often comes too late, and thus can be no Messiah at all. To die after one's life is in pieces may well be a release. But even if there is life beyond the grave, such a way of finding Paul's promise fulfilled is ironic, if not callous and cynical.

The Accident signals that every person has a breaking point. Individually no one knows where it is, not until too late. Maybe things are better that way, because then we are really left responsible. But like God's promises, responsibility is a mixed blessing because it brings so much guilt in its wake. To be sure, all adults have good reasons to feel guilty. But just as we overestimate the value of suffering, so we may assess guilt unfairly and therefore in ways that harm. And not only with respect to each other. God figures in as well, in spite and because of the fact that "man prefers to blame himself for all possible sins and crimes rather than come to the conclusion that God is capable of the most flagrant injustice."

Do we honor God and ourselves by holding him blameless? Or is it just a fearful hope that leads people to absolve God of sin? The victim of the accident has seen too much to pursue either course any longer. He understands that to hold God blameless only intensifies despair that is already more than many human hearts can bear. His desire to live is not unequivocal, but it is sufficient to rule out any piety that legitimates the ways of God at humanity's expense. And thus the abuse endured by Sarah, namesake of a people's mother, indicts God harshly.

"Whoever listens to Sarah and doesn't change, whoever enters Sarah's world and doesn't invent new gods and new religions," writes Wiesel, "deserves death and destruction." Sarah's world? In *The Accident* it is that of a Paris prostitute, but as the accident victim relives his encounter with her, he and Sarah are taken back to an earlier time and place. That Sarah's world is built on a question: "'Did you ever sleep with a twelve-year-old woman?'" And the place where it was asked and answered with a vengeance was in the special barracks of Nazi concentration camps, erected for the camp officers' diversion.

A biblical tale says that God once told Moses that "'man shall not see me and live.'" (Exod. 33.20) God's word to Moses is usually interpreted to mean that a human person cannot see God and live because of the disproportion between the might and righteousness of God on the one hand and the weakness and sin of men and women on the other (see Isaiah 6:5). Indeed the fact that God is hidden, obscure, revealed to us indirectly, is often seen as a form of grace that enables human life to have its chance. *The Accident* is premised on ideas of that kind, but Sarah's world turns them and makes God's warning say something more:

> Why should He want to kill a man who succeeded in seeing Him? Now, everything became clear. God was ashamed. God likes to sleep with twelve-year-old girls. And He doesn't want us to know. Whoever sees it or guesses it must die so as not to divulge the secret. Death is only the guard who protects God, the doorkeeper of the immense brothel that we call the universe.

That estimate cuts even more deeply when Sarah discloses that her purity as a victim is forever compromised: she recalls that she sometimes felt pleasure in those barracks, and probably survived because of it.

What about this round of question-and-answer? Doesn't it just sour already bitter experience? Wouldn't it be better to reject the implication that God is a cosmic sadist and keep on affirming, in spite of the world, that "God is light and in him is no darkness at all"? Or would it be better to refuse both options? The first because it is morally intolerable; the second because concentration camp brothels disconfirm the claim except for Gods too weak to make their goodness matter. Wouldn't it be better to embrace no personal, purposive God at all? Or would it be better still just to stop pursuing such lines of thought completely?

The Accident does not answer straight out. Its victim is alive in a hospital at the end, or he is even released and telling his story from an unidentified time and place. The truth is that we don't know whether this man's questions raised himself toward God, or if they did what he discovered in the process. We do know that Elie Wiesel survived *The Accident* to write another day, which is to say that he persists in tracing the issues raised in the beginning of his authorship and indeed of the world itself. But why? What is to be achieved by such effort?

> "Stories."
> *"But there must be more to it than that."*
> "Yes, there is more to it than that."
> *"What, then?"*
> "I am afraid of what will happen if the effort ends."

"What will happen?"

"Nothing."

"And that makes you afraid?"

"Exactly."

"But what if we make the effort?"

"I am still afraid."

"Why?"

"Because even in making it we may stop and rest with a conclusion."

"But isn't that the point, to draw a conclusion?"

"No, that's not the point."

"Then what is?"

"There isn't any . . . except to keep asking 'What's the next step?' . . . except to keep wondering 'And yet? . . . and yet' . . . except to keep willing 'In spite of . . . because of . . .'"

"So how does God figure into this equation?"

"He doesn't, at least not clearly enough, and that's what makes our lives hang in the balance of our asking."

"Are you suggesting that encounters with God—whether and how we have them—make the future?"

Night . . . Dawn . . . Le Jour/The Accident . . . their questions set an agenda for encounters between Creator and creature after Auschwitz. Specifically for those who claim to encounter God through Jesus of Nazareth. Desolation in the Kingdom of Night. Despair produced by dawn's ambiguity. An evening accident and a tortured spirit who will leave a hospital only half healed in the light of day. These are beginnings that the Holocaust beckons us to share. They show that nothing about the first day in the beginning was quite as good as God pronounced it—or that devastating differences of opinion were destined to follow from the original separation of light and darkness. But the message of those differences is not to shirk responsibility by blaming God. It is rather to explore how crucial is human responsibility in a world which not only lacks enough insurance for the good but even permits our doing—as well as thinking—the unthinkable. That message is enough to make one give up. And yet . . . ?

ELLEN S. FINE

Witness of the Night

> Dans *La Nuit*, on trouve la mort, on atteint l'oubli. Mais cette autre nuit est la mort qu'on ne trouve pas, est l'oubli qui s'oublie, qui est au sein de l'oubli, le souvenir sans repos.
>
> —Maurice Blanchot

> Je fuis la nuit et je la porte sur mes épaules.
>
> —Elie Wiesel

Elie Wiesel's first book, *Night*, published originally in Yiddish in 1956, translated into French in 1958, and into English in 1960, depicts the long journey into Holocaust darkness. The work defies all categories. It has been described as personal memoir, autobiographical narrative, fictionalized autobiography, nonfictional novel, and human document. Essentially, it is a *témoignage*, a first-hand account of the concentration camp experience, succinctly related by the fifteen-year-old narrator, Eliezer. With Kafka-like lucidity, the narrator initiates us, the readers, into the grotesque world of the Holocaust and compels us to observe the event taking place before our eyes. Before all else, Eliezer is a witness, who tells the tale in a direct and linear mode. He does not interpret or explain the facts but allows them to speak for themselves. The young boy lacks the self-consciousness of later Wieselean protagonists who are more aware of their mission to testify.

However, *Night* is more than a *témoignage*, and the narrator is more than a witness. While he effaces himself before the events, we also hear his own voice—a voice that recounts more than mere circumstances. "The child in *Night* is too old to write about children," Wiesel has remarked. Indeed, the words of the author-narrator depict the metamorphosis of a child into an old man, his abrupt passage into the blackness and silence of nonbeing in one never-ending night. The voice of the child-witness reveals the effect of the landscape of violence upon the psyche of one individual. It communicates the vision of a nightmare: the voyage from a familiar to an unknown world, a son's perception of the slow death of his father and the spiritual death of himself. As François Mauriac, who wrote the foreword to *Night*, points out: "In truth, it is much less a deposition dealing with historical facts than the inner adventure of a soul who believed for a time that God, too, had been massacred—God, the eternally innocent."

Ten years after the actual experience, Elie Wiesel brought forth this "inner" testimony and was thus able to reconstitute his fragmented memories in such a way as to form a structured and coherent narrative. The result is a text of literary quality, rich in themes that lay the foundation for the author's subsequent works. A close examination of two of the book's principal motifs—*night* and *father-son*—help to shed light on the central theme of the witness, the generating principle of Wiesel's literary universe. For, to live through the forces of darkness and to care for another shows the persistence of self in a system principally designed to annihilate the self. To survive and to testify affirms the will to remain human in the aftermath of the inhuman. The event is unthinkable, the story impossible to transmit. Yet from another level of consciousness, the voice of the witness transcends Night's sovereignty and takes on a life of its own.

THE KINGDOM OF NIGHT

The theme of night pervades Elie Wiesel's memoir as suggested by the title itself, which encompasses the overall Holocaust landscape—*l'univers concentrationnaire*—a world synonymous with methodical brutality and radical evil. The dark country presented to us is self-contained and self-structured, governed by its own criminal gods who have created laws based upon a death-dominated ideology. Wiesel uses the word *Night* throughout his writing to denote this strange sphere, unreal and unimaginable in its otherworldliness. He speaks of that "kingdom of the night where one breathed only hate, contempt and self-disgust" in "A Plea for the Dead"; and in one of his speeches, refers to "the dark kingdom which . . . represented the other side of Sinai, the dark face of Sinai." "We were the children of Night," he proclaims, "and we knew more about truth and the paths leading to it than the wisest philosophers on earth."

Eliezer, the narrator of the book, is, in effect, a child of the Night, who relates the journey from the friendly Jewish community tucked away in the mountains of Transylvania to Auschwitz—the frightening and foreign capital of the kingdom of Night. During the course of the trip certain events take place which stand out in the narrator's memory and often occur during the nocturnal hours. The theme of night is linked to the passage of time in the account itself. Within the larger framework, more specific phases, characterized by the motifs of the *first* and *last* night, structure the descent into terror and madness, and point to the demarcations between the known and unknown.

Once Eliezer enters Auschwitz, he loses his sense of time and reality. Darkness envelops him and penetrates within: his spirit is shrouded, his God eclipsed, the blackness eternal. Pushed to his limits, the narrator experiences the *other* haunted and interminable night defined by Maurice Blanchot as "the death that one does not find"; "the borders of which must not be crossed." The intermingling of particular nights with Night, the measuring of time alongside timelessness, corresponds to a style that interweaves a direct narration of events with subtle reflections upon the experience.

In 1941, when the narrative begins, Eliezer is a deeply Orthodox boy of twelve, living in the town of Sighet, situated on the Hungarian-Rumanian border. The word *night* is first mentioned with regard to his evening visits to the synagogue: "During the day I studied the Talmud, and at night I ran to the synagogue to weep over the destruction of the Temple." While this nocturnal lamentation is part of a religious tradition, its prominent position in the text can be interpreted as a prediction of the bleak shadow cast upon Jewish communities throughout twentieth-century Europe.

Eliezer spends many of his evenings in the semidarkness of the synagogue where half-burned candles flicker as he converses with Moché, his chosen master of the Kabbala; they exchange ideas about the nature of God, man, mysticism, and faith. Night, here, exudes a poetic and pious atmosphere as the time for prayer, interrogation and dialogue within the context of the secure and the traditional. Indeed, the narrator's experience of benevolent night begins to change with Moché's expulsion from Sighet. Deported because he is a foreign Jew, Moché is sent to Poland, driven to a forest along with hundreds of other Jews, and shot in front of freshly dug pits. Wounded in the leg only, he rises from the mass grave and miraculously makes his way back to Sighet to recount what he calls "the story of my own death." "Jews, listen to me," he cries out. "It's all I ask of you, I don't want money or pity. Only listen to me." No one in the *shtetl*, including Eliezer, believes his tale, and Moché is forced into silence, Wiesel's first example of the unheeded witness whose futile warnings predict the fate of the entire Jewish community. This occurs towards the end of 1942.

Without being explicit, Wiesel's narrative closely follows the historical events that led to the expulsion of the Hungarian Jews. The years 1942 and 1943 as rapidly described in the text were fairly normal for the Jews of Sighet. While anti-Jewish legislation was enacted and periods of calm alternated with those of turbulence, day still predominated over night. From 1938 to 1944, Hungarian prime ministers ranged from eager collaborators to those who collaborated reluctantly, resulting in cycles of despair and hope for the Jews who were unable to assess their situation realistically. In 1944 the Jewish community of Hungary was the only large group still intact. The circumstances changed drastically, however, in March, with the German takeover of the country and the installation of the pro-German Sztójay government. Adolph Eichmann, commander of the Special Action Unit (*Sondereinsatzkommando*) came to Hungary to personally carry out one of the most concentrated and systematic destruction operations in Europe. In the spring of 1944, with the end of the war in sight, the Nazis deported and eventually wiped out 450,000 Jews, 70 percent of the Jews of Greater Hungary. The Jews from the Carpathian region and Transylvania were among the first to be ghettoized and then rounded up. Of the fifteen thousand Jews in Sighet's community alone, about fifty families survived.

The Germans were notorious for their methods of deceiving their victims by dispelling notions of fear and creating the illusion of normality as they went about setting the machinery of extermination in motion. Eliezer speaks of life's returning to normal, even after the Nazis forced the Jews of Sighet into two ghettos fenced off from the rest of the population by barbed wire. At least, he remarks, Jews were living among their brothers and the atmosphere was somewhat peaceful. This deceptively secure setting was soon to be shattered.

"Night fell," says the narrator, describing an evening gathering of friends in the courtyard of his family's house in the large ghetto. A group of about twenty was listening attentively to tales told by his father, when suddenly a Jewish policeman entered and interrupted his father's story, summoning him to an emergency session of the Jewish council. "The good story he had been in the middle of telling us was to remain unfinished," Eliezer notes.

The theme of *the unfinished story* becomes a key to the entire text and to Wiesel's work in general, linking day and night, father and son, voice and silence. Suspended in the midst of its natural flow, the father's story is a metaphor for Jewish life and lives abruptly brought to a standstill in the middle of the *night*. When the father returns at midnight from the council meeting, he announces news of the deportation to be held the following day.

From this point on, time is defined by the first and last night. Eliezer refers to "our last night at home," spent in the large ghetto after watching the first transport of victims parade through the streets under the blazing sun, the infernal counterpart to Night. Then, there is the last evening in the small ghetto, where Eliezer, his parents, and three sisters observe the traditional Sabbath meal: "We were, we felt, gathered for the last time round the family table. I spent the night turning over thoughts and memories in my mind, unable to find sleep."

Expelled from the small ghetto, Eliezer and his family, along with other members of the community, are thrown into cattle cars where they endure three long nights. Day is left far behind. The theme of night corresponds here to the reduction of space. Whereas the gentle gloom of the synagogue provided the framework for a boundless exploration of sacred doctrines, the ghetto period—in its progression from larger to smaller—serves as a transitional space, leading to the nailed-up doors of the cattle wagons, which plunge the prisoners into the confinement and extreme darkness of a night without limits.

The night of the cattle wagons is hallucinatory. Madame Schäcter, a woman of fifty, who along with her ten-year-old son had been deported separately from her husband and two elder sons, starts to go mad. On the third and last night in the train, she screams out as if possessed by an evil spirit, conjuring up vivid images of fire and a furnace. Some of the men peer through the barred train window to see what Madame Schäcter is pointing to, but all they can glimpse is blackness. Night is both within and without, surrounding the mad prophet who continuously cries out, as if to predict the end of the world, but who is forcefully silenced by those around her who do not want to believe in the foreboding signs. At the terminus, Birkenau–Auschwitz, Madame Schäcter gives one last howl: "Jews, look! Look through the window! Flames! Look!" As the train stops, the victims, in disbelief, observe red flames gushing out of the chimney into the black sky.

The theme of fire is present, indeed, throughout the text, from the half-burned candles of the synagogue, where Eliezer and Moché attempt to illuminate the mysteries of the universe, to the relentless sun of the ghetto liquidation, culminating in the savage blaze of the death pits and crematoria. "Here the word 'furnace' was not a word empty of meaning," the narrator notes, "it floated on the air, mingling with the smoke. It was perhaps the only word which did have any real meaning here." Fire is, indeed, an integral part of Night, as suggested by the term *Holocaust* itself, which signifies widespread destruction by fire or a sacrificial burnt offering.

When Eliezer sees the vivid flames leaping out of a ditch where little children are being burned alive, he pinches his face in order to know if he is awake or dreaming in this nightmarish atmosphere of "Hell *made immanent.*" The young boy watches babies thrown into the smouldering pits and people all around murmuring *Kaddish* (the Jewish prayer for the dead) for themselves—the living dead—as they slowly move in a kind of *danse macabre*. They give the eerie impression that they are participating in their own funeral. For a moment, the narrator contemplates throwing himself on the barbed wire, but the instinct for survival prevails. As he enters the Holocaust kingdom on that first night he recites a ritualistic incantation, which marks his initiation into one long and never-ending night and commits him to remember it always:

> Never shall I forget that night, the first night in camp, which has turned my life into one long night, seven times cursed and seven times sealed. Never shall I forget that smoke. Never shall I forget the little faces of the children, whose bodies I saw turned into wreaths of smoke beneath a silent blue sky.
>
> Never shall I forget those flames which consumed my faith forever.
>
> Never shall I forget that nocturnal silence which deprived me, for all eternity, to the desire to live. Never shall I forget those moments which murdered my God and my soul and turned my dreams to dust. Never shall I forget these things, even if I am condemned to live as long as God Himself. Never.

This invocation summarizes the principal themes of Wiesel's first book, joining the theme of night to those of fire, silence, and the death of children, of God, and of the self. The moment of arrival designates the end of the reality-oriented structure of "outer" night, and the shift to "inner" night, in which time is suspended. As dawn breaks Eliezer observes: "So much had happened within such a few hours that I had lost all sense of time. When had we left our houses? And the ghetto? And the train? Was it only a week? One night—*one single night*? . . . Surely it was a dream."

Indeed, like a dream sequence, the events of the camp journey have been accelerated and condensed into a short interval. "One of the most astonishing things," says Wiesel, "was that we lost all sense not only of time in the

French meaning of the word, of *durée*, but even in the concept of years. . . . The ten-year-old boy and the sixty-year-old man not only looked alike, felt alike and lived alike, but walked alike. There was a certain 'levelling.'" This levelling process seems to occur in one night, a notion often repeated by the author:

> In a single night, a single hour, one acquires knowledge and grows up. The child finds himself an old man. From one day to the next, familiar structures and concepts vanish, only to reappear in different forms. One gets used to the new order in spite of everything.

The concept of time that governs life in normal conditions thus changes radically in the concentrationary universe. But even more important than time is the highly organized and methodological procedure that deprives an individual of his humanness and transforms him into a thing while still alive. The *défaite du moi*, the "dissolution of the self," is the worst kind of living death and is a recurring theme in Holocaust literature.

After one single night in Auschwitz, Eliezer is turned into a subhuman, identified only by an anonymous number. Yesterday an active member of a community imbued with religious teachings and traditions, the boy is now bereft of all faith. A black flame, the demonic union of fire and night, has permeated his psyche. At the center of his soul lies a void:

> I too had become a completely different person. The student of the Talmud, the child that I was, had been consumed in the flames. There remained only a shape that looked like me. A dark flame had entered into my soul and devoured it.

On the eve of Rosh Hashanah, the last night of the Jewish year, Eliezer experiences a deep sense of alienation as he stands among his praying and sobbing compatriots who are observing the holiday. The once fervent youth is now a spectator of himself, a stranger to his beliefs, and in revolt against an absent God who has betrayed his people by allowing them to be tortured, gassed, and burned. "I was the accuser, God the accused. My eyes were open and I was alone—terribly alone in a world without God and without man." With blunted senses and branded flesh, the child turns away from his God and his heritage. His spirit is arrested in the confines of Night: the empire of darkness has taken possession of his inner being. For the boy of fifteen history has stopped.

Although time is essentially abolished in the kingdom of death, the narrator nevertheless continues to structure outer reality in the account itself by noting the nights that mark the principal stages of the trip. After three weeks in Auschwitz, he and his father are sent in a work transport to Buna, where they spend several weeks. The Germans finally evacuate the camp as Russian troops approach. Before the long cold voyage to Buchenwald, Eliezer meditates on the motif of *the last night*:

> The last night in Buna. Yet another last night. The last night at home, the last night in the ghetto, the last night in the train, and, now, the last night in Buna. How much longer were our lives to be dragged out from one 'last night' to another?

The march from Buna to Buchenwald takes place in blackness, amid glacial winds and falling snow. The boy realizes that the night he is leaving will be replaced by one even more unfathomable on the other side; the *invisible darkness* of the tomb. As the procession winds its way through the thick snow, numerous corpses are strewn upon its trail. After several days without food or water, the remaining prisoners are thrown into open cattle cars and transported to Buchenwald. For the starved skeletons who speed through the frozen landscape, "days were like nights and the nights left the dregs of their darkness in our souls." Suddenly, on the last day of this seemingly endless journey, a fierce cry rises up from among the inert bodies of the entire convoy—a collective death rattle that seems to emanate from beyond the grave. This shared song of death when no hope is left is a protest to the world which has abandoned them. A brutal expression of the agony of those who have reached their limits, this massive convulsion *is* the primeval language of Night. Finally, late in the evening, twelve survivors out of the hundred who started out reach Buchenwald.

The last night—and the most significant—is January 28, 1945. Eliezer's father, sick with dysentery, his head bloody from the blows of an SS guard, lies curled up miserably on his bunk bed. When his son awakens the next day, he realizes that his father has been carted away before dawn—perhaps still alive. It is the finality of this moment that virtually ends the narrative, plunging Eliezer into a realm where no light penetrates and where, on some level, the *child of Night* remains for the rest of his life.

Father and Son: A Residue of Humanism

If the nocturnal forces of death envelop and endure, miraculously, from within the depths of the Holocaust universe surges the will to survive. Father and son struggle to remain human, acting as lifelines for each other. They fight to keep alive by mutual care and manage to create a strong bond between them in the most extreme of circumstances. Yet competition for survival causes a conflict between self-interest and concern for the other. Close ties break down in the kingdom of Night and even the solidarity built up between Eliezer and his father is undermined by feelings of anger and ambivalence brought about by Nazi techniques specifically designed to destroy human relationships.

"A residue of humanism persists illogically enough in our world, where there is a 'void' at the center of things," Wylie Sypher observes, in *Loss of the Self in Modern Literature and Art.* For a child of fifteen entering the perverse world of the concentration camp, the "residue of humanism" is the presence of his father. Separated from his mother and three sisters upon their arrival at Birkenau, Eliezer becomes obsessed with the need to hold on tightly to his father's hand, the only object of life in a universe where every moment holds the possibility of death. "My hand shifted on my father's arm. I had one thought—not to lose him. Not to be left alone." Warned by an anonymous prisoner to lie about their ages, the fifteen-year-old boy and the fifty-year-old man instantly become eighteen and forty, and are thus able to follow Dr. Mengele's wand to the left-hand column (life) instead of the right-hand one (crematoria).

The fear of being torn apart from his last family link haunts the narrator throughout the book. During the "levelling" process, as he is being stripped bare of all possessions, he is fixated on one thought—to be with his father. Later, when the boy is recovering from a foot operation in the Buna hospital and finds out that the camp is about to be evacuated, he runs outside into the deep snow, a shoe in his hand because his foot is still swollen, and frantically searches for his father: "As for me, I was not thinking about death, but I did not want to be separated from my father. We had already suffered so much together; this was not the time to be separated." Upon arrival in Buchenwald after the long torturous convoy in the open wagons, Eliezer is again haunted by the familiar fear and fiercely clutches his father's hand.

This obsession to hold on to the father has been interpreted by the French scholar André Neher as juvenile. He feels that "Elie remains a small, dependent child in spite of the overabundant maturity resulting from his experience." However, if the gesture of grasping the hand is somewhat childlike, and the son's vow never to be severed from his father has a desperate tone, the primary relationship between father and son appears to be more an interdependency based upon mutual support in the midst of surrounding evil. Father and son, joined together in front of the sacrificial altar, recall the Biblical story of Abraham and Isaac (the *Akeda*), described by

Wiesel in *Messengers of God* with the emphasis on commitment in a world threatened by destruction: "And the father and son remained united. Together they reached the top of the mountain; together they erected the altar; together they prepared the wood and the fire." Wiesel cites a text from the Midrash in which the Biblical pair are envisaged as "victims together," bound by their communal offering.

Until the last pages of *Night*, reciprocal devotion sustains both Eliezer and his father and is linked to the recurring Wieselean theme of rescue—saving the life of another human being and thereby saving one's own. The narrator reports several instances during which his father's presence stops him from dying. When Eliezer files past the fiery pits on the first hallucinatory night in Auschwitz, he has thoughts of suicide. He is deterred from killing himself by the voice of his father who tells him that humanity no longer cares about their fate, and that at this time in history everything is permitted. The father's voice, though sad and choked, represents a life force, which combats the all-encompassing blackness.

During the long march from Buna to Gleiwitz, the prisoners are forced to gallop through the snow, and Eliezer, pained by his throbbing foot, is again drawn to death as an escape from suffering. Once more the paternal presence helps him to resist the appeal of death. Because he feels that his father needs him, the son does not have the right to succumb. His will to survive is ultimately linked to the existence of his father:

> Death wrapped itself around me till I was stifled. It stuck to me. I felt that I could touch it. The idea of dying, of no longer being, began to fascinate me. Not to exist any longer. Not to feel the horrible pains in my foot. . . . My father's presence was the only thing that stopped me . . . I had no right to let myself die. What would he do without me? I was his only support.

After seventy kilometers of running, as morning approaches, the survivors are allowed to rest. The narrator sinks into the soft snow, but his father persuades him to go into the ruins of a nearby brick factory, since to sleep in the snow means to freeze to death. The open shed, too, is crusted with a thick cold carpet enticing its weary victims, and Eliezer awakes to the frozen hand of his father patting his cheeks. A voice "damp with tears and snow" advises the boy not to be overcome by sleep. Eliezer and his father decide to watch over each other: they exchange vows of protection, which bind them together in revolt against the death that is silently transforming their sleeping comrades into stiffened corpses.

Later on, when the men pile on top of each other in the barracks of

Gleiwitz, Eliezer struggles to rid himself of an unknown assassin slowly suffocating him with the massiveness of his weight. When he finally liberates himself and swallows a mouthful of air, the boy's first words are to his father whose presence is acknowledged by the sound of his voice, "a distant voice, which seemed to come from another world." The voice once again is a lifeline, a reassurance against death. Yet the otherworldliness of the father's speech suggests that he is beginning to lose hold of his vital forces; eternal night beckons to him.

The last time the father rescues the son is in the open cattle car shuttling the victims from Gleiwitz to Buchenwald. On the third night of the trip, the narrator suddenly wakes up: somebody is trying to strangle him. He musters enough strength to cry out the one word synonymous with survival—"Father!" Too weak to throw off the attacker, his father calls upon Meir Katz, an old friend from his home town, who frees Eliezer. The father thus saves his son's life through a surrogate, one of the most robust in the group, but one who dies before the men reach Buchenwald and whose abandoned corpse is left on the train.

During the various phases of the nocturnal journey the other side of the rescue motif is also apparent: the son carefully watches over his father and at times delivers the latter from death. These brief moments of solidarity disrupt the machinery of destruction and prove to be examples of human resistance in the face of the inhuman. When Eliezer's father is selected for the gas chamber in Gleiwitz, the youth runs after him, creating enough confusion to finally reunite father and son in the right-hand column, this time the column of life. Shortly after this episode, Eliezer saves his father's life in the convoy to Buchenwald. Lying inert in the train, his father is taken for dead by the men who are throwing out the corpses. Eliezer desperately slaps his father's nearly lifeless face in an attempt to revive him and succeeds in making him move his eyelids slightly, a vital sign that he is still alive. The men leave him alone.

Upon arrival at the camp, the father reaches the breaking point. He sinks to the ground, resigned to dying. Eliezer is filled with rage at his father's passivity, and realizes he must now take charge. "I found my father weeping like a child," he says when later he finds him stretched across his bunk, crying bitterly after being beaten by the other inmates for not properly taking care of his bodily needs. The boy feeds his helpless father and brings him water. We see here the reversal of roles: the transformation of the once-powerful paternal authority into a weak, fearful child and that of the dependent child into an adult. By assuming responsibility for the sick old man, the son becomes a kind of father figure, illustrating Wiesel's contention that in the inverted world of the concentration camp, old men metamorphosed into children and children into old men in one never-ending night.

The reversal of roles in *Night* has been viewed by André Neher as "an anti-*Akeda*: not a father leading his son to be sacrificed, but a son guiding, dragging, carrying to the altar an old man who no longer has the strength to continue." Wiesel's text, he observes, is "a re-writing of the *Akeda* under the opaque light of Auschwitz. It is no longer a narrative invented by the imagination of a poet or philosopher. It is the reality of Auschwitz." This reality offers a sharp contrast to the Biblical event. Whereas in the Bible God saves Isaac from being sacrificed by sending a ram to replace him, He does not intervene to save the father at the altar of Auschwitz. God allows the father to be consumed by Holocaust flames and the son is forced to recognize the inevitable—that he is impotent in the face of death's conquest and God's injustice. He must slowly watch his father acquiesce to death. Symbol of reason, strength, and humanity, the father finally collapses under the barbaric tactics of the Nazi oppressor to which Eliezer is a silent witness.

If the theme of father-son is characterized, in general, by the reciprocal support necessary for survival in extremity, the sanctity of the relationship is nevertheless violated by the camp conditions. In contrast to the son's need to protect and be protected by his father, there appears the opposing motif: the abandonment of the father. The Nazi technique of attempting to eradicate all family ties and creating a state of mind in which men view each other as enemies or strangers—what can be called the *concentration camp philosophy*—is demonstrated in *Night* through a series of incidents showing the competition for survival between fathers and sons.

Bela Katz, the son of a merchant from Eliezer's hometown and a member of the *Sonderkommando* in Birkenau, is forced to shove the body of his own father into the crematory oven. A *pipel* in Buna beats his father because his father does not make his bed properly. A third instance, and the one the narrator constantly uses as a measure of his own behavior, is the deterioration of relations between Rabbi Eliahou and his son. Shunted from camp to camp for three years, the boy and his father have always managed to stay together. But after the seventy-kilometer march from Buna to Gleiwitz they are separated. The Rabbi reaches the shed and looks for his son. He tells Eliezer that in the obscurity of the night his son did not notice him fall to the rear of the column. However, Eliezer remembers seeing the youth run past the staggering old man and is horrified by this clear example of abandonment:

> A terrible thought loomed up in my mind: he had wanted to get rid of his father! He had felt that his father was growing weak, he

> had believed that the end was near and had sought this separation in order to get rid of the burden, to free himself from an encumbrance which could lessen his own chances of survival.

Eliezer prays to God to give him the strength never to do what Rabbi Eliahou's son has done.

Perhaps the most devastating example of the breakdown of human bonds occurs in the cattle cars going to Buchenwald during the final phase of the journey. Some workers amuse themselves by throwing pieces of bread into the open wagons and watching the starved men kill each other for a crumb. Eliezer sees an old man about to eat a bit of bread he was lucky enough to snatch from the crowd. Just as he brings the bread to his mouth, someone throws himself on top of him and beats him up. The old man cries out: "Meir, Meir, my boy! Don't you recognize me? I'm your father . . . you're hurting me . . . you're killing your father! I've got some bread . . . for you too . . . for you too . . ." The son grabs the bread from his father's fist; the father collapses, murmurs something and then dies. As the son begins to devour the bread two men hurl themselves upon him and others join them. The young narrator is witness to the entire event: "When they withdrew, next to me were two corpses, side by side, the father and the son. I was fifteen years old."

Having witnessed fathers beaten, abandoned, and killed, the author, through his narrator, has chosen to represent the *son's betrayal of the father* and has omitted situations in which the father mistreats the son. As Terrence Des Pres has pointed out in *The Survivor*, the principle of jungle rule in the camps is frequently belied by examples of human solidarity. Wiesel elects to record the acts of care and decency performed by his father. By not being critical of the paternal figure in a world too often governed by viciousness, the author protects his father's image and honors his memory. This unconscious process of selection reveals the subjective aspect of the eyewitness account and of the survivor's perceptions. The focus upon the abuses of the sons is perhaps a projection of the author-narrator's own feeling of guilt; he identifies with them at the same time that he condemns them for having let their fathers perish. Despite Eliezer's efforts to save his father's life throughout the camp experience, the boy is critical of his own reprehensible behavior, and ultimately takes the blame for his father's death upon himself.

From the first day, the son helplessly witnesses the debasement of his father. When Eliezer's father is seized with colic and politely asks the *Kapo* where the lavatories are, he is dealt such a heavy blow that he crawls back to his place on all fours like an animal. Instead of defending his father's honor by striking the *Kapo*, Eliezer remains paralyzed, afraid to speak out. This fear makes him aware that his values are changing:

> I did not move. What had happened to me? My father had just been struck, before my very eyes, and I had not flickered an eyelid. I had looked on and said nothing. Yesterday, I should have sunk my nails into the criminal's flesh. Had I changed so much, then? So quickly? Now remorse began to gnaw at me. I thought only: I shall never forgive them for that.

This feeling of impotence is repeated in Buna when Idek, the *Kapo*, in a fit of madness beats Eliezer's father with an iron bar. The son's reaction is not simply that of a passive onlooker; he is furious at his father:

> I had watched the whole scene without moving. I kept quiet. In fact I was thinking of how to get farther away so that I would not be hit myself. What is more, any anger I felt at that moment was directed not against the *Kapo*, but against my father. I was angry with him, for not knowing how to avoid Idek's outbreak. That is what concentration camp life had made of me.

At the end of the narrative, when an SS guard strikes the sick father on the head with his bludgeon, Eliezer again looks on without moving, terrified of being beaten himself.

We see here the brutal effect of concentration camp life upon an individual psyche. Rage against the aggressor has been displaced onto the victim, and concern for the other has regressed into a preoccupation with self-survival, reduced to primitive and instinctual bodily needs. Eliezer is condemned to the role of the impotent witness, incapable of crying out, of seeking revenge, or, finally, of saving his father's life. Although he has fantasies of destroying his father's assassins, he can only behold his bloody face in despair. He is unable to respond to his father's last summons for help—an utterance of his name, "Eliezer."

Yet more than the sense of complicity, after the father dies the son feels ambivalent and even somewhat liberated. Earlier in the text, his mixed emotions surface during an alert in Buchenwald, when Eliezer, separated from his father, does not bother to look for him. The next day he sets out but with highly conflicting feelings:

> Don't let me find him! If only I could get rid of this dead weight, so that I could use all my strength to struggle for my own survival, and only worry about myself. Immediately I felt ashamed of myself, ashamed forever.

Eliezer's desire to rid himself of his oppressive burden, to lose his dependent father in the crowd, makes him recall with horror Rabbi Eliahou's son during the evacuation from Buna. When the narrator finally locates the feverish and trembling old man lying on a plank outside, he frantically claws his way through the crowd to get him some coffee. Later, he halfheartedly offers his dying father what is left of his own soup. While his deeds demonstrate care and devotion, his thoughts are of withdrawal and abandonment. Actions and intentionality, behavior and fantasies, do not correspond. The fifteen-year-old judges himself guilty: "No better than Rabbi Eliahou's son had I withstood the test."

The head of the block tells Eliezer that it is too late to save his old father and that instead he should be eating his father's ration. In his innermost recesses, Eliezer believes that the *Kapo* is right, but is torn by shame and runs to find more soup for his father. We see here the clashing principles for survival that dominated the death camp universe. On one hand, the rule of eat or be eaten, devour or be devoured prevailed. In the struggle of all against all, the *Kapo* teaches Eliezer, "every man has to fight for himself and not think of anyone else. Even of his father. Here, there are no fathers, no brothers, no friends. Everyone lives and dies for himself alone." And yet on the other hand, a *Kapo* tells the prisoners: "We are all brothers, and we are all suffering the same fate. The same smoke floats above all our heads. Help one another. It is the only way to survive."

In Wiesel's tale "An Old Acquaintance," a similar situation reveals human beings at odds with themselves. In this instance the father offers his half-full bowl of soup to the son, who refuses it. Seeing this occur several times, the *Kapo* finally orders the son to eat his father's soup. As the son gulps it down, he has contradictory feelings: "At first I wanted to vomit but soon I felt an immense well-being spread through my limbs. I ate slowly to make this pleasure, stronger than my shame, last longer." He hates the *Kapo* but is grateful for his intervention. These mixed sensations of nourishment and regurgitation, well-being and disgust, are indicative of the opposing emotions constantly created in the camp inmates as their dignity, loyalty, and honor are assaulted by the barbaric choices they are forced to make.

The ambivalent feelings of the fifteen-year-old with regard to his father and food are intensified after his father dies:

> I did not weep, and it pained me that I could not weep. But I had no more tears. And in the depths of my being, in the recesses of my weakened conscience, could I have searched it, I might perhaps have found something like—free at last.

The relief soon turns into a deep sense of guilt, for having failed to save his father, for having survived in his place, and for having thoughts of being liberated by his death. The protector has been transformed into a betrayer. Unconsciously, the youth may even feel that he has acted out a son's worst Oedipal fear: he has physically become "his father's murderer."

The survival guilt that Eliezer painfully endures culminates with the face in the mirror at the end of the narrative. Several days after the liberation of Buchenwald by American soldiers, and after a severe bout of food poisoning during which the boy almost dies, he looks at himself in the mirror for the first time since the ghetto. A stranger—a child of Night—peers at him, and the text concludes with the dark image of death itself: "From the depths of the mirror, a corpse gazed back at me. The look in his eyes, as they stared into mine, has never left me." The distinction made between *his* eyes and *mine*, conveying the notion of the fragmented self, is stressed in the original French: "Son regard dans mes yeux ne me quitte plus" ("His look in my eyes no longer leaves me"). The staring corpse is a permanent reminder of the "dead" self, that part of the narrator which was engulfed by the black smoke of Auschwitz and which will plague him for the rest of his life.

The cadaverous reflection in the mirror also suggests the son's identification with his dead father, to whom he remains attached. According to Robert Jay Lifton, survival guilt is related to "the process of identification—the survivor's tendency to incorporate within himself an image of the dead, and then to think, feel and act as he imagines they would." At the end of the night, Eliezer incorporates his father into his own psyche and projects this image onto the mirror as his double. The haunting specter with its penetrating glance serves to keep the paternal presence alive and is the son's means of defending himself against his loss. The mirror image epitomizes Eliezer's state of mourning and his desire to join his father, whose death is experienced as a death of the self. "When my father died, I died," Wiesel reveals. "That means that one "I" in me died. . . . At least, something in me died."

The Unfinished Story

If Eliezer is spiritually reunited with his father in the ghostly visage of the glass tomb, the guilt-ridden, numbed, and nearly lifeless son is nevertheless condemned to survive. The "surviving" self emerges as witness and counteracts the "dead" self, an important theme in Wiesel's works, linked to the theme of father-son. In order to continue the succession, the son must take his father's place. An imperative reaching far beyond himself compels him to complete the story his father was in the midst of telling the night in the ghetto before news of the deportation interrupted his words; The son himself must become a storyteller, for the story is a mode of transcendence, and the power of the word a protest against the nihilism of the Holocaust. As heir to the aborted tale, the son's task is to bring the destroyed Jewish communities and their inhabitants back to life. The need to remember transcends the particular to include an entire tradition that has vanished in the night. Before all else, the author-narrator seeks to resurrect his father and to prolong his voice: *the father's unfinished story becomes the story of the father.*

The struggle to recover one's words in a dissolving world, to fight against silent suffocation in a universe where daily events all but fatally constrict one's breath, is dramatized through the theme of the voice—a counterforce to Night. With the progressive decay of the body, the human voice alone remains a sign of life. The Hungarian Jew dying next to Eliezer in the hospital room is a faceless mass of skin and bones, and yet is able to speak out and warn the boy to leave the hospital before the next selection. The man's ability to articulate is synonymous with survival. "I could only hear his voice," the narrator says; "it was the sole indication that he was alive. Where did he get the strength to talk?"

In the dark shed of Gleiwitz where exhausted men pile on top of each other, Eliezer wrestles against death. As he gasps for air under the heap of dying bodies, a weak but familiar voice cries out for help beneath him. He realizes that it is Juliek, the boy from Warsaw who played the violin in Buna. The narrator struggles to move away from his friend—to breathe and to let him breathe. He calls out to the young musician: "'How do you feel, Juliek?' I asked, less to know the answer than to hear that he could speak, that he was alive." The act of speaking becomes an act of resistance, the disembodied voice a vestige of humanity in a thoroughly dehumanized universe. After a long while, the hallucinatory notes of Juliek's violin miraculously punctuate the oppressive silence of the pitch-black living tomb and, for a brief' moment, evil is eclipsed by tones of purity and innocence. "I shall never forget Juliek," Eliezer says. "How could I forget that concert, given to an audience of dying and dead men!" In the morning, the corpse of Juliek lies next to his shattered instrument.

Whereas the utterance of sounds signifies life, death is the collapse into silence. At the end of the text, when Eliezer's father lies across his bunk bed, aware that his life is drawing to a close, he puts his parched lips to his son's ear and feverishly races against the end. Fearful that he will not have time to tell him everything, he verbally passes on his meager heritage to his successor. Eliezer listens carefully to his father, who can barely pronounce his final words. When the doctor comes and does nothing as the old man slowly dies, Eliezer is furious: "I felt like leaping at his throat, strangling him. . . . Oh, to strangle the doctor and the others! To burn the whole word! My father's murderers! But the cry stayed in my throat." The soundless scream is a form of death-in-life. This inability to protest further alienates Eliezer and severs him from his last living tie to the past. Unable to avenge his father's death by choking the enemy, it is inevitably the son who is stifled by impotent rage.

The theme of the stifled voice permeates the fiery landscape of Night, where the inmates can barely whisper because of "the thick smoke which poisoned the air and took one by the throat." In this polluted atmosphere, the cutting off of breath is most tragically exposed in the scene describing the hanging of the young boy with the face of a sad angel. The youth, who took part in an attempt to blow up the electric power station at Buna, is discovered and tortured for several days. He refuses to give the names of his accomplices and is condemned to be hanged along with two other men. The entire camp is summoned to witness the execution. The two adults die quickly, but the child, because his body is so light, suffers a delayed agonizing death. As the camp prisoners march past the gallows in total silence and look the child in the face, Eliezer hears a man behind him ask: "'Where is God now?' And I heard a voice within me answer him: 'Where is He? Here He is—He is hanging here on this gallows. . . .'"

The death of an innocent child calls to mind religious sacrifices of other sons—Isaac bound to the altar, and the crucifixion of Jesus. However, in Buna, God does not intervene to substitute a ram, nor does he resuscitate the young boy slowly dying on what Lawrence Langer calls a "gallows-crucifix." The camp ceremony is, as Langer observes, "the ritual of death ungraced by the possibility of resurrection." God Himself died on the gallows of Auschwitz, Wiesel has declared:

> I had the impression in Buchenwald of being present at the death of God. I have remained haunted by it. God died in each one of these deported children. I survived, but not completely. My heroes seek a supplementary death.

Friedrich Nietzsche's prophecy of the "death of God" is literally enacted here upon the death camp altar. However, Nietzsche points to man's abdication of religious values while advocating the establishment of a human deity to replace the state of godlessness. Wiesel's statement is more than an accusation against the God who has betrayed his people, "the God who kills, and therefore can kill himself." For Wiesel, no new order of human divinity can replace God; the loss of faith extends to all of mankind: "At Auschwitz, not only man died but also the idea of man. . . . It was its own heart the world incinerated at Auschwitz."

The scene of the hanging child has been viewed by many as the central event in *Night* because the death of God as experienced by a fifteen-year-old is inscribed into the concentrationary landscape. In his foreword to the book, François Mauriac speaks of the horror produced by the "death of God in the soul of a child who suddenly discovers absolute evil." This French writer sees in the dark, penetrating eyes of Wiesel "the reflection of that angelic sadness which had appeared one day upon the face of the hanged child." Alfred Kazin describes the hanging as

> the one particular scene that has already made this book famous in Europe. . . . It is the literal death of God and absolute emptiness in the soul, the blackness that in his mind means that there is no longer any light from a divine source, that Wiesel experienced most in the endless night of Auschwitz.

The figure of the innocent, saintly boy whose breath is cut off and whose young voice is permanently stilled on the camp gallows mirrors for Eliezer the annihilation of his own self—the self that once believed in God and humanity. But at the same time that he identifies with the strangled child, he is destined to survive as his witness. For the rest of his life, the author-narrator is torn by these conflicting selves: the self that has died, choked into stillness by the thick fumes of the death camps, and the one fighting to preserve itself in a post-Holocaust era.

Ultimately, the voice of the witness fills Night's void. The deaths of the child, the father, and God compel Eliezer to search for something to believe in. This "something" is his own ability to answer the disembodied voice from behind asking where God is as the youth swings from the gallows: "*And I heard a voice within me*" (my emphasis). What the narrator beholds lies infinitely beyond speech and can only be acknowledged in awesome silence. Yet the very existence of an inner voice is a sign of life—a trace of human identity in the universe of darkness.

This *voice from within* is the generative principle of the will to bear witness, source of survival, and residue of life in the kingdom of death. The narrator of *Night* has been reduced to a disembodied voice: the narrator *is* his voice. Yet this struggle against suffocation is what transforms the passive spectator into the active witness who must tell future generations what he has seen and lived through in order to warn them that fathers and sons have been murdered, that God is dead. The power to articulate emanates from a deeper level of the self and reaches far beyond words. What the narrator ultimately recounts is not only the outer reality but also the inner reality of the experience, thereby creating a new reality that combats "the finality of the event," as Wiesel points out:

> In *Night* I wanted to show the end, the finality of the event. Everything came to an end—man, history, literature, religion, God. There was nothing left. And yet we begin again with Night.

The author reveals here a basic contradiction—that of Night as the end and the beginning. This apparent opposition can be interpreted in light of the writing process. The world of death and degradation gives birth to the narrative. Ten years have distanced the survivor from the pain of the immediate but have given him the perspective and the courage, on the one hand, to detach himself from the experience and, on the other, to reenter it through the eyes of a fifteen-year-old. He has been able to relate and to order the events so as to transmit a coherent literary work. Language and memory are mobilized as instruments of healing, and telling the story becomes an act of restitution, as well as a protest against forgetfulness. By bearing witness the author transforms his voice into a life-giving force, so that he may infuse his dead father, the hanging child, and other victims of the Holocaust with breath.

Night terminates in silent darkness. The tomblike glass image looms before Eliezer, a terrifying conclusion to the child's unfathomable journey into the realm of the dead. Nonetheless, it is this unrecognizable reflection of himself that inspires Elie Wiesel to become a writer:

> One day as I was looking in a mirror, I didn't recognize myself . . . I then decided that since everything changes—even the face in the mirror changes—someone must speak about that change. Someone must speak about the former and that someone is I. I shall not speak about all the other things but I should speak, at least, about *that* face and *that* mirror and *that* change. That's when I knew I was going to write.

The author rises from the grave to tell the tale, a tale which depicts the zero point of existence, but which is also the point of departure for his future works:

> *Night*, my first book, became the basis of my entire edifice. Afterwards, I tried to construct concentric circles around this

> testimony. For me, the war represents the year zero and Auschwitz is as important as Sinai.

Night testifies to the destruction of man. At the same time, this work provides the foundation upon which Elie Wiesel rebuilds a structure for his life, and sets forth his legacy as witness to the Holocaust.

ROBERT McAFEE BROWN

Darkness That Eclipses Light (a moral journey—1)

The Holocaust is a sacred realm. One cannot enter this realm without realizing that only those who were there can know. But the outsider can come close to the gates. One can never know and yet one must try.
—Elie Wiesel, in *Counterpoint*, Fall 1980

There is a darkness that eclipses light. It is the darkness of Auschwitz into which Elie Wiesel entered. The rest of us can never enter that realm, can never know that darkness: "Only those who were there can know." But those who were there feel morally constrained to share what was there, so that we, the outsiders, "can come close to the gates." We can never know, and yet we must try.

Ten years after his liberation from Buchenwald—ten years during which he lived out a vow of silence so that he would not falsify—Elie Wiesel broke his silence with an account of the kingdom of night. A Yiddish version, *And the World Has Remained Silent*, appeared in 1956, and a condensed version, *La Nuit*, the version the world knows, was published in French in 1958, appearing in English in 1960 as *Night.* Once the authorial floodgates had been opened, five novels appeared in quick succession: *Dawn* (1960), *The Accident* (1961), *The Town Beyond the Wall* (1962), *The Gates of the Forest*

(1964), *A Beggar in Jerusalem* (1968). They conduct the reader on a moral journey of awesome proportions.

The journey's starting point is *Night*. Every subsequent book is commentary on that spare and unsparing text. Wiesel describes it as "a kind of testimony of one witness speaking of his own life, his own death," and then continues:

> All kinds of options were available: suicide, madness, killing, political action, hate, friendship. I note all of these options: faith, rejection of faith, blasphemy, atheism, denial, rejection of man, despair, and in each book I explore one aspect. In *Dawn* I explore the political action; in *The Accident*, suicide; in *The Town Beyond the Wall*, madness; in *The Gates of the Forest*, faith and friendship; in *A Beggar in Jerusalem*, history, the return. All the stories are one story except that I build them in concentric circles. The center is the same and is in *Night*.

The reality of *Night* is the reality of the monstrous moral evil that was the Holocaust. Wiesel copes in each book with a possible answer to the question: *how do we respond to monstrous moral evil*? Most of the answers turn out to be destructive, as though monstrous moral evil retained final power over all attempts to challenge it, a darkness unremittingly eclipsing light.

Can light ever penetrate the darkness again? We are not entitled to anticipate an affirmative answer easily, as though we could eliminate the intervening steps on the journey, because they are so painful. Our guide did not have that privilege, and we must deny it to ourselves, walking one step at a time with him, remembering that we will always be "outsiders," and yet remembering also, with gratitude, that he will help us.

Victim

Of all of Wiesel's works, *Night* is the one that most cries out not to be touched, interpreted, synthesized. It must be encountered at first hand. The only justification for the following pages is to force that encounter.

How, then, do we respond to monstrous moral evil? Sometimes human beings are not even given the privilege of asking the question. The decision is already made for them by the practitioners of evil; they are designated in advance as *victims*. It was a designation involuntarily assumed six million times during the reign of the kingdom of night by Jews in central Europe.

Many things happen to victims, so *Night* reports. At the heart of them all is shattering, a shattering of world, faith, self, and future.

The victim's world is shattered. The opening pages of *Night* breathe the serenity of a secure world. Sighet, nestled in the Carpathian mountains, is a town where Jews can live between memory and anticipation, drawing on the treasures of the past to create a hopeful future. Within Sighet there was a small boy who "believed profoundly," studying the Talmud by day and weeping over the destruction of the Temple by night. Praying was as natural as breathing to the small boy, who could await each Shabbat tremulous with anticipation that *this* might be the occasion of Messiah's coming. A secure world.

No, not a secure world. Instead, a world that was shattered, beginning with tiny actions at the edges that slowly accelerated, penetrating closer and closer to the vital center, until the entire world that was Sighet came crashing down. First it was the deportation of foreign Jews (Moché the Beadle, for one), followed by unbelievable stories of horrors being exacted against Jews outside the secure world; then, direct occupation by German soldiers, followed by the confiscation of the private property of Jews, the introduction of the yellow star, travel curfews, the creation of two ghettos, and finally, deportation.

The now-familiar scenario unfolded inexorably, but back then it was not familiar and therefore not seen as inexorable. Secure worlds do not shatter easily. Even as the screws of the Nazi machine were progressively tightened, Wiesel records three times with devastating honesty that it appeared that "life had returned to normal."

It never did. It only got worse, even though right up to the time the cattlecars of deportees arrived at Auschwitz, the reluctance to believe the worst persisted. Only crazy people would believe the reports that were circulating, and only crazy people would circulate them. Moché, with tales of Jews digging mass graves, lining up in front of them and being efficiently machine-gunned into them? Moché must be mad. Madame Schächter, screaming about fires and chimneys in the darkened cattlecar when everybody in the darkened cattlecar knew it contained nothing but frightened, thirst-crazed Jews? Madame Schächter must be mad. The real world was still Sighet, where God still dwelt and there were clean linens on Shabbat.

But the real world was no longer Sighet. The real world, which shattered the old world, was a railway station in upper Silesia, with a name no one in the cattlecars had even heard before. Auschwitz.

The last illusions disappeared when the cattlecar doors opened and the victims emerged on the platform at Birkenau—another unfamiliar name—the death camp of Auschwitz.

Close by were gigantic flames. The pious, deeply-believing boy reports: "They were burning something. A lorry drew up at the pit and delivered its load—little children. Babies! Yes, I saw it—saw it with my own eyes . . . those children in the flames"

What did that do to the piety and deep belief of the boy? In the most widely-quoted passage in Holocaust literature, he tells us:

> Never shall I forget that night, the first night in camp, which has turned my life into one long night, seven times cursed and seven times sealed. Never shall I forget that smoke. Never shall I forget the little faces of children, whose bodies I saw turned into wreathes of smoke beneath a silent blue sky.
>
> Never shall I forget those flames which consumed my faith forever.
>
> Never shall I forget that nocturnal silence which deprived me for all eternity, of the desire to live. Never shall I forget those moments which murdered my God and my soul and turned my dreams to dust. Never shall I forget these things, even if I am condemned to live as long as God Himself. Never.

Every word Wiesel has written since is commentary on that passage. Every bitterness and disappointment confirms it. Every sliver of light and hope is threatened by it. It is the end of a journey—not arrival at a promised land, but final expulsion from one. The exodus story in reverse.

The victim's faith is shattered. There is a shattering even more devastating than the shattering of one's world. It is the shattering of one's faith—in Wiesel's case the shattering of his faith in God.

He does not become an atheist or assert "the death of God" as many commentators assume. Years later, responding to Richard Rubenstein's assertion that Auschwitz has destroyed God and made denial of God morally mandatory, Wiesel said, "How strange that the philosophy denying God came not from the survivors. Those who came out with the so-called God is dead theology, not one of them had been in Auschwitz." Even in the passage just cited, it is not God, but Wiesel's "faith" that is consumed by the flames. What has been "murdered" is "my God and my soul," the God conceived of by the pious Hasidic child of fourteen years. Indeed, the next sentence speaks of the anguish of being "condemned to live as long as God Himself." Do not assume, Wiesel reminds us in every book, that it is consolation to believe that God is still alive. Rather than solution, it simply states the problem. Ever since that first night, Wiesel has struggled with two irreconcilable realities—

the reality of God and the reality of Auschwitz. Either seems able to cancel out the other, and yet neither will disappear. Either in isolation could be managed—Auschwitz and no God, or God and no Auschwitz. But Auschwitz *and* God, God *and* Auschwitz? That is the unbearable reality that haunts sleep and destroys wakefulness.

Auschwitz is not going to surrender its demonic power. Must God therefore be forced to surrender the divine power? Why should one say the *Kaddish*, the prayer for the dead, in a death camp? What is there to thank God for, in the land of burning children? He ceases to pray, and sympathizes with Job: "I did not deny God's existence, but I doubted His absolute justice."

The challenge comes to fever pitch at Rosh Hashanah, the Jewish new year. In a biting passage, the young boy records his reaction when ten thousand inmates repeat the ancient refrain, "Blessed be the Name of the Eternal."

> Why, but why should I bless Him? In every fiber I rebelled. Because He had had thousands of children burned in His pits? Because He kept six crematories working night and day, on Sundays and feast days? Because in His great might He had created Auschwitz, Birkenau, Buna, and so many factories of death? How could I say to Him: "Blessed art Thou, Eternal, Master of the Universe, Who chose us from among the races to be tortured day and night, to see our fathers, our mothers, our brothers, end in the crematory? Praised be Thy Holy Name, Thou Who hast chosen us to be butchered on Thine altar?"

He even begins to feel strong in his quarrel with God: "I was the accuser, God the accused. . . . I had ceased to be anything but ashes, yet I felt myself to be stronger than the Almighty." On Yom Kippur, the day of atonement, he decides not to fast (grotesque world, in which starving men debate whether to eat or not), and his eating bread and swallowing soup when fasting is prescribed, is a bitter rebellion against God.

And likewise a bitter acknowledgement of God.

Devastating discovery: the comment of a faceless neighbor in the barracks, who had once believed in the promises of God: "I've got more faith in Hitler than in anyone else. He's the only one who's kept his promises, all his promises, to the Jewish people."

Almost at the end, during the long march through the snow, in the face of the betrayal of a father by a son, Wiesel writes, "And, in spite of myself, a prayer rose in my heart, to that God in whom I no longer believed."

Two incidents at Buna, a camp near Auschwitz, encapsulate the shattering of faith.

The first involves the hanging of a prisoner caught stealing during an alert. The others are ordered to stand at attention and witness the execution, after which they are marched past the dead face at close range before being dismissed for supper. A routine incident. Wiesel comments, "I remember that I found the soup excellent that evening."

The second hanging—one of the most devastating scenes in all holocaust literature—involves three inmates, one of them a child, who were suspected of blowing up the power station at Buna. As they approach the gallows, someone behind Wiesel asks, "Where is God? Where is He?" And then the chairs are toppled and the three victims are supported only by the ropes around their necks. Once again the prisoners are marched by the victims at close range so that all may see the dead faces and be deterred.

> The two adults were no longer alive. Their tongues hung swollen, blue-tinged. But the third rope was still moving; being so light, the child was still alive . . .
>
> For more than half an hour he stayed there, struggling between life and death, dying in slow agony under our eyes. And we had to look him full in the face. He was still alive when I passed in front of him. His tongue was still red, his eyes not yet glazed.
>
> Behind me, I heard the same man asking:
>
> "Where is God now?"
>
> And I heard a voice within me answer him:
>
> "Where is He? Here He is—He is hanging here on this gallows . . ."
>
> That night the soup tasted of corpses.

Commenting on this passage verges on blasphemy, and yet we must. Some Christians see God's "hanging here on this gallows" as a replication of Christ's hanging on the cross for the redemption of the world, God's presence in the midst of evil. But this is no replication of the crucifixion story. At best it is parody of that event, and its message is despair, not hope: God on the gallows, God subjected to human demonry, God at the mercy of evil, God embodying death and impotence rather than life and power, God whose "real presence" is such that soup is transubstantiated into corpses.

The victim's self is shattered. When a world is shattered and a faith is shattered, the self who lives in the world and shares the faith is likewise shattered.

The first night in camp has passed. It has been long enough to complete the shattering of the self. The evening and the morning are the first day. Only the first day.

> The night was gone. The morning star was shining in the sky. I too had become a completely different person. The student of the Talmud, the child that I was, had been consumed in the flames. There remained only a shape that looked like me. A dark flame had entered my soul and devoured it.

From now on there is no soul, so self. Only a number, tattooed on the left arm. A–7713.

The treatment of A–7713 involves dehumanization. Occasionally there is a kind word, and A–7713 tries to respond to it. But chiefly there are curses, intimidations, beatings, lines of numbers standing rigidly at attention . . . all night . . . in the snow . . . naked . . . Numbers are not supposed to have emotions, and although the number that is A–7713 tries to keep close to a father who has also become a number, and to protect a father progressively enfeebled, the father who is now a number becomes a liability and a burden to A–7713. It is the greatest triumph of the survival of the self that A–7713 retains a concern for the father, and has the self-incriminating honesty to say, when the father is bludgeoned before his eyes and later removed, that he feels a sense of freedom for the moment and of shame forever.

When the camp is evacuated in the face of the Russian offensive, A–7713 and all the other numbers can walk forty-two miles through the snow in a single night, not because they are selves any longer but because they have become machines, literally able to walk mechanically in their sleep. A–7713 and all the other numbers can walk over living bodies and corpses to find shelter in a shed, because in their eyes the living bodies and corpses are now only other numbers like themselves. The number who had once been a rabbi's son can abandon in the snow the number who had once been a rabbi, glad to be rid of the hindrance. In the ten-day trip in the snow in the cattle-cars, the number who had once been the son of Meir can kill the number who had once been Meir for the sake of a piece of bread, and in turn be killed before he can get the piece of bread to his lips, by other numbers who at one time had been fathers, sons, brothers, husbands, and whose lips had gently whispered the sacred words of the Torah.

To reduce persons to numbers is an efficient way to shatter a self.

The victim's future is shattered. The culmination comes at the end of *Night*. But before we can look at endings, we must look at beginnings.

Wiesel says that the beginnings of his novels are crucial: if he gets the first sentence right he knows that the rest will follow, and the reader will have an essential clue to the theme of the book.

> They called him Moché the Beadle, as though he had never had a surname in his life. (*Night*)
>
> Somewhere a child began to cry. (*Dawn*)
>
> The accident occurred on an evening in July, right in the heart of New York, as Kathleen and I were crossing the street to see the movie *The Brothers Karamazov.* (*The Accident*)
>
> Outside, twilight swooped down on the city like a vandal's hand: suddenly, without warning. (*The Town Beyond the Wall*)
>
> He had no name, so he gave him his own. (*The Gates of the Forest*)
>
> The tale the beggar tells must be told from the beginning. (*A Beggar in Jerusulem*)
>
> No, said the old man. I will not speak. (*The Oath*)
>
> *Je n'ai jamais ri de ma vie* [I have never laughed in my whole life]. (*The Testament*, as it begins in the French edition)

But if beginnings are crucial, endings are even more so. Often, the meaning of the tale is not clear until the last pages, the last sentences, even the last line. A stage direction on the last page of *The Trial of God* reveals, with devastating impact, the identity of Sam. Only with the last eight words of *The Accident* is the full poignancy of Eliezer's plight brought home to us. In the six books we are examining, the endings indicate the measure of progress—or lack of it—that has taken place.

In *Night*, the culmination of the shattering of the victim's world, belief, and self, is the shattering of the victim's future. Six million futures were shattered beyond recovery. So were the futures of those beyond the six million who survived. One need not be killed to be a victim; one can be killed and still be alive.

In Latin, *victima* is "an animal offered in sacrifice," which Webster's *Dictionary* amplifies to read, "a person or animal killed as a sacrifice to a god in a religious rite." That is an accurate definition of the victims of the Nazis, for in the most fundamental sense Nazism was a "religion," a collective obeisance before the god of race, blood, and soil, and deeds done in the name of that god were the exercise of a "religious rite," in which persons, reduced to the status of nonpersons, were offered up to appease the greed of the idol being worshipped.

To be fully victimized is not only to be dehumanized in the present by the removal of world, God, and self, but to be denied a future. That is true death, whether physical life is terminated or not.

At the end of *Night,* Buchenwald has been liberated, but in the wake of liberation A–7713 has contracted food poisoning and is in the hospital hovering between life and death. He finally summons enough energy to get out of bed and look in a mirror.

The book closes with the words:

> From the depths of the mirror, a corpse gazed back at me.
> The look in his eyes, as they stared into mine, has never left me.

A–7713 confronts himself. And death is all he finds. The future is destroyed as well.

Darkness has eclipsed light.

Executioner

Is there any place to go beyond the world of the victim? Is that the best that can be managed in the presence of monstrous evil?

There is another option. Rather than being victims, we might be executioners—better to kill and survive than be killed and succumb. The alternative is explored in *Dawn*, Wiesel's second book and first novel.

There is a similarity between the two alternatives. The victim has no choice: the role is imposed by another. The executioner, it might seem, does have a choice. True, the executioner is at least free enough to be held accountable. But the matter is more poignant. In addition to being dependent on each other—there can be no victim without an executioner, no executioner without a victim—the two share a further fate in common:

> What matters is the fact that each of them is playing a role which has been imposed on him. The two roles are the extremities of the estate of man. The tragic thing is the imposition.

If the limits of human possibility are victim-executioner, then Wiesel tells us that a heavy hand is laid upon the destroyer as well as the one destroyed. We must later ask if there is a choice beyond the polarity; but within it, a tragic necessity is at work.

As the tragic necessity unfolds, Elisha (the name means "God will save") is a victim, a former inmate of Buchenwald, living in Paris after the war. He enrolls to study philosophy at the Sorbonne, "because I wanted to understand the meaning of the events of which I had been the victim." He plans to press his questions about God, suffering, rebellion, human nature, purification, bestiality.

So far the story parallels Wiesel's. But whereas Elie Wiesel did pursue philosophy, his fictional counterpart never gets the chance. For a "messenger" intervenes, one who in Hasidic tradition is a *Meshulah*, "the mysterious messenger of fate to whom nothing is impossible." The messenger's name is Gad. The name is not a play on the word "God." Wiesel writes in French, and the words "Gad" and "Dieu" have no common linguistic ancestry. But Gad does possess a Biblical name and both Gad and his scriptural counterpart are warriors. The earlier Gad is commissioned by Jacob to take military initiatives; his tribe will have the east side of Jordan, an outpost subject to attack by pagan nations. When Moses gives his blessing to the tribes of Israel, he calls for the tribe of Gad to increase—the Gaddites are mighty warriors, and Gad himself is a brave leader.

The modern Gad lives up to his heritage. He has come to persuade Elisha to join the guerilla forces in Palestine, so that they can drive out the British and create a homeland for post-Holocaust Jews. Jews, he says, with fire in his eyes, will be victims no more. Rather than being fearful themselves, they will instill fear in others. If it is necessary to kill, they will kill. Since no one else has ever looked out for them, they will now look out for themselves. Elisha is enthralled:

> This was the first story I had ever heard in which the Jews were not the ones to be afraid. Until this moment I had believed that the mission of the Jews was to represent the trembling of history rather than the wind which made it tremble.

Elisha and Gad talk until dawn, a Parisian dawn, described as "a pale, prematurely weary light the color of stagnant water." Elisha accepts Gad's invitation, full of promise that there will be more vibrant dawns: "Here," Gad says, "the dawn is gray; in Palestine it is red like fire."

The student of philosophy becomes a terrorist. Instead of studying Plato and Spinoza, he studies the use of machine guns, hand grenades, and daggers; instead of learning aesthetics, he learns the fine arts of strangulation and prison escape. It is inhuman, Gad acknowledges, but no other choices are left; being more just than those who speak in the name of justice led to the abandonment of Jews in Hitler's camps.

> We can rely on ourselves. If we must become more unjust and inhuman than those who have been unjust and inhuman to us,

> then we shall do so. We don't like to be bearers of death; heretofore we have chosen to be victims rather than executioners. The commandment *Thou shalt not kill* was given from the summit of one of the mountains here in Palestine, and we were the only ones to obey it. But that's all over, we must be like everybody else. Murder will not be our profession but our duty. In the days and weeks and months to come you will have only one purpose: to kill those who have made us killers. We shall kill in order that once more we may be men. . . .

His training completed, Elisha takes part in a commando raid. A convoy is blown up and a whole truckload of British soldiers is machine-gunned to death; they run "like rabbits, sotted with wine and sorrow."

A blow for the cause of freedom. There is only one problem: "I imagined that I was in the dark gray uniform of an SS officer." Elisha is suddenly back in the Polish ghettos, where SS guards slaughtered the Jews, and where the Jews ran "like rabbits sotted with wine and sorrow." The script is the same: only the roles have been changed.

The British announce that they will hang David ben Mosche, caught during another guerrilla raid. The guerrillas retaliate by capturing a British officer, John Dawson, and announce that they will shoot him as a hostage if David ben Mosche is hanged. A perfect symmetry of reprisal. Neither side will back down; to do so, both affirm, might be interpreted as a sign of weakness. Both men will die.

Who is to murder John Dawson?

Elisha . . .

He is not thrilled by the assignment. Killing others in guerrilla combat is one thing, killing a single defenseless human being in cold blood is another. The role of executioner is imposed on him, just as the role of victim is imposed on John Dawson.

An eighteen-year-old boy waiting for dawn, which will make him a killer, has various things with which to cope. He has to cope with *the intervening moments*, and he is helped in that by his friends, Ilana, Gad, Gideon, Joab. They rally around and share stories of how they were saved from death. Elisha too has been saved from death, but he realizes in retrospect that it is quite possible that he has "died and come back to earth, dead."

He has to cope with *the past*. The ghosts of his boyhood return and almost choke the atmosphere. Why have they come? As reminders that one never kills alone. When Elisha kills, he will make killers of them as well. Those who shaped and formed him will be re-shaped and re-formed by him. He feels judged by their presence; Jewish history has never glorified bloodshed and murder. His act will betray them, for there is no present without a past, and the past cannot be shed.

He has to cope with *John Dawson,* the man he is to kill. Considerably before the appointed hour of execution he goes down to the prison cell, "as if," he remarks with prescience, "I were going to my own execution." He realizes that it will be easier to kill John Dawson if he can hate him, if he can see John Dawson as a villain whose death will be a gift to humanity. They talk. And he finds to his dismay that he cannot hate John Dawson. In any other situation they would have been friends. "There was harmony between us; my smile answered his; his pity was mine." (Wiesel comments almost in passing that the inability to hate may have been the presence of God in the prison cell.)

A tragedy: the lack of hatred makes it more difficult to kill. A greater tragedy: in spite of the lack of hatred, to have to kill anyway.

In spite of the lack of hatred, he has to kill anyway. Precisely at 5 A.M. he pulls the trigger, while his name is still on the dying man's lips. The episode is over. "That's it," Elisha says to himself, preparing to go back upstairs. "It's done. I've killed."

But he does not say, "I've killed John Dawson."

He says, "I've killed Elisha."

At the beginning of *Dawn* Elisha tells how a beggar once taught him to distinguish night from day. "Always look at a window. . . . If you see a face, any face, then you will be sure that night has succeeded day. For, believe me, night has a face."

At the beginning of *Dawn* Elisha does look out a window. And he sees a face, his own. So he knows two things: he knows that it is still night, and he knows that the face of night is his own face. And we know one thing: we know that Elisha is still in the kingdom of night. The beginning of *Dawn* is the same as the end of *Night.*

At the end of *Dawn,* Elisha goes to the window to see the Palestinian dawn—a dawn that will not be like the gray dawn back in Paris, like the color of stagnant water, but, as Gad had promised, "red like fire." But the Palestinian dawn he sees has "a grayish light the color of stagnant water."

It is still the tired dawn of Paris. Worse, it is not even dawn at all. For as Elisha looks through the window, he reports, "Fear caught my throat. The tattered fragment of darkness had a face. Looking at it, I understood the reason for my fear. The face was my own."

The title *Dawn* is ironic. It is still night. The road to emancipation through becoming an executioner has been a cul-de-sac, for murder is only another form of suicide. A corpse is meeting the gaze of this beholder, too, and the beholder can see nothing else.

Darkness is still eclipsing night.

Flight

But do the roles of victim and executioner exhaust the alternatives? Could we decide (in the title of an essay by Albert Camus that strongly influenced Wiesel) to be "neither victims nor executioners"? Camus broke with his friends of the French resistance who decided after World War II that they could continue to justify collective violence for political ends. In "a world where murder is legitimate, and where human life is considered trifling," Camus responds that there are two questions we must face:

> Do you or do you not, directly or indirectly, want to be killed or assaulted? Do you or do you not, directly or indirectly, want to kill or assault?

Those like himself who answer "no" to both questions must face some consequences. Pacifism, he feels, is unrealistic. But he insists: "People like myself want not a world in which murder no longer exists (we are not so crazy as that!) but rather one in which murder is not legitimate.

Wiesel would agree. And having discovered that we must be "neither victims nor executioners," he searches for other options. They do not come easily, and most of them are unsatisfactory. But the search is a consuming passion.

The ghosts that haunted Elisha momentarily in *Dawn* obsess Eliezer unendingly in *The Accident*; how to deal with a destructive past, which is what the ghosts represent, forms the theme of the book. How could one deal with a destructive past? One might seek to run away from it, deny it, keep distanced from it. Common to all of these is the notion of *flight*. Conventional criticism describes *The Accident* as a testing of the option of suicide—the extreme instance of flight—but the book is also a series of variations on the overall theme.

This time the scene is New York City. The narrator is a newspaper correspondent at the United Nations. Crossing Times Square to go to a movie, he is hit by a taxicab and almost killed. He is closely linked to the protagonists of the two previous books, sharing the history and deprivation of those who physically survived the death camps but remain psychically scarred. The wounds creating those scars are more clearly discerned by Eliezer than by either of his predecessors; areas of anxiety surface for him that were only latent in Elie and Elisha. Symptomatic is his sense of guilt that he survived while others did not, and his consequent sense of moral obligation to the dead, on whose unfinished lives he must impose a meaning. It is the sense of the impossible odds thus created, and the power of a destructive past to wipe out the possibility of a creative present, that is at the heart of his struggle.

Up to this point the story is autobiography as well as fiction, and the fact that the fictional counterpart is called Eliezer (Wiesel's own name), suggests the degree of identification he has with the creation of his pen. But further details in *The Accident*—that there was a girlfriend, and that "the accident" was not quite . . . an accident—are points at which autobiography has moved over into fiction.

Eliezer is taken to the hospital, and Dr. Russel, the surgeon, saves his life. After a few days, Kathleen, his girlfriend, begins to visit him, and most of the book is a series of flashbacks from the hospital bed—several extended ones with Kathleen, many brief ones with the dead but pervasively present grandmother, and one (which we will consider in a later chapter) with Sarah, who at the age of twelve was the sport of Nazi officers.

Eliezer's self-understanding poses the spectre of the past most graphically. He defines himself as "a messenger of the dead among the living," and is convinced that all he and those like him are capable of doing is to pour the filth of their own past on those around them. They are the living-dead. They may look like others, but they are not. Their lives are pretense: "Anyone who has seen what they have seen cannot be like the others, cannot laugh, love, pray, bargain, suffer, have fun, or forget." They have been "amputated," not of their limbs but of "their will and their taste for life."

At the beginning Wiesel draws on Kazantzakis' *Zorba the Greek* for an image:

> Man's heart is a ditch full of blood. The loved ones who have died throw themselves down on the bank of the ditch to drink the blood and so come to life again; the dearer they are to you, the more of your blood they drink.

And the problem is whether or not one can survive such an assault. The incinerated forebears of Holocaust survivors had no burial place; the living thus become "a grave for the unburied dead." They rob the living of what little was left to them: "Our dead take with them to the hereafter not only clothes and food, but also the futures of their descendents." After such pillage, nothing is left to the survivors. Others may speak of love, or justice, or freedom, but "they don't know that the planet is drained [by the dead] and that an enormous train has carried everything off to heaven."

Fated with such a legacy, survivors feel that all they do is contaminate others with their suffering. They provide a sour taste and incur animosity. One night on shipboard, Eliezer, after prodding from a stranger, pours out his story.

The listener appears sympathetic, but at its conclusion he takes Eliezer's measure and responds, "You must know this. . . . I think I'm going to hate you."

Who would not flee a past that so shuts one off from other human beings? Who would not flee even from oneself, as Eliezer does when the nurse wants him to look in a mirror, and he vehemently refuses?

Another image for the destructive and immobilizing past is the image of Grandmother. Grandmother wears a black shawl. She has no burial place; she too was wreathed in smoke exhaled from tall chimneys. She left her grandson on the station platform when her train left and mounted the skies to heaven. She is always present. Eliezer cannot be rid of her. She is there when he makes love to Kathleen, and when he does not. In his post-operational delirium he cannot disentangle the two. When Gyula tries to destroy Eliezer's past, it is Grandmother he is destroying for a second time. She is a constant rebuke. To affirm the living is to deny her. She compounds guilt. She opens wounds that do not heal.

Under whatever imagery, the past is a curse. How can one flee from its ongoing power to work evil?

There are many possibilities. Eliezer tries them all.

The simplest is to acknowledge that the destructive power of the past makes it impossible to share with those who were not there, and *exist alone*, cutting oneself off from others, acknowledging that real companionship is impossible. "A man who has suffered more than others, and differently, should live apart. Alone."

But one cannot really exist alone. The next best thing is to keep one's own world barred against invasion by others, and *live a life of pretense*. Eliezer's most frequent response to others is to employ deception as a means of survival. If the truth can only lacerate, perhaps falsehood can make relationship endurable. So Eliezer tells Dr. Russel what Dr. Russel wants to hear when the latter accuses him of having no desire to live. He tells Kathleen what Kathleen wants to hear, assuring her of a love he does not actually feel. When she urges Eliezer to forget the past and exorcize its demons with the help of their mutual love, he promises to do both things, all the while realizing that both are pretense: he cannot forget the past, and even her love will be impotent to exorcize its demons. Confirmation of the pretense: it is the day after making the false promises that "the accident" occurs.

Sometimes Eliezer tries *to thrust the past on someone else*. This also fails to work. The man on shipboard solicits this, and ends up hating. Kathleen solicits it; she wants to "know everything," to wallow in the misery of another, asking for more and more horror. Eliezer tires to comply: "I bared my soul. My most contemptible thoughts and desires, my most painful betrayals, my vaguest lies. I tore them from inside me and placed them in front of her, like an impure offering, so she could see them and smell their stench." It does not seal the relationship; without loving her, he "makes love" to her, trying to hurt her.

One can respond by *suicide*: admit total defeat, stop trying, succumb. The "accident" was really a conscious decision not to step out of the way of the taxi while there was still time. There is little to say about this option. Those who succeed are not available for comment, and those who fail, like Eliezer, do not often repeat the experiment.

The ways so far explored are negative. There are other ways that appear to hold promise.

Dr. Russel's way, for instance. Dr. Russel counsels *struggle*. Seize the initiative against whatever is threatening one. In Eliezer's case it is the spectre of the past, in Dr. Russel's case it is the spectre of death. The two spectres are finally one. Dr. Russel confronts death every time he approaches the operating table. Sometimes he wins, a heady wine. But his is finally a loser's game: "My victories can only be temporary. My defeats are final. Always." The option is reminiscent of Albert Camus, so influential in Wiesel's life, and especially Dr. Rieux in *The Plague*, who likewise fights against evil, even though he too can ultimately know nothing but defeat. But for Eliezer, the magnitude of ongoing defeat negates the possibility of tiny, temporary victories.

Kathleen has a second proposal more dignified than simply soaking up Eliezer's filth like a vicarious sponge. She truly believes that *love can conquer a loveless past*, and that two can share burdens redemptively in ways that are impossible for one alone. She refuses to believe that the dead, lacking love, are more powerful than the living, possessing love. She proposes to take the place of Eliezer's fate. But the contest between Grandmother with the black shawl and Kathleen with the good intention is not an even match. Grandmother wins every time.

A final proposal is presented in the closing pages of the book, by Gyula, a Hungarian portrait painter, whose name means "redemption." He appears only in the final episode, and dominates it totally. Gyula knows the burden of the past. He too had fought such demons. As a result, he "had an obsession: to pit himself against fate, to force it to give human meaning to its cruelty." He sets out to share the obsession with Eliezer. His advice, nay, his command, is clear: *you must choose the present over the past, the living over the dead, and do so by whatever means are necessary.*

Gyula comes to Eliezer's hospital room every afternoon, having made a typically unilateral decision to paint the patient's portrait. When he finally shows it to Eliezer, a moment of truth occurs, for Gyula has penetrated Eliezer's inmost being. There follows "a silent dialogue" between the two. The gist of it:

Gyula's mandate to Eliezer is unequivocal: "Maybe God is dead, but man is alive. The proof: he is capable of friendship. . . . You must forget [the dead]. You must chase them from your memory. With a whip, if necessary. . . . The dead have no place down here. They must leave us in peace. If they refuse, use a whip."

Although Eliezer responds that he can't use a whip, Gyula is adamant: "Suffering is given to the living, not to the dead. . . . It is man's duty to make it cease, not to increase it. One hour of suffering less is already a victory over fate."

Eliezer acknowledges the importance of this insight. Gyula continues: "If your suffering splashes others, those around you, those for whom you represent a reason to live, then you must kill it, choke it. If the dead are its source, kill them again. . . ."

Eliezer is not sure it can be done. And rather than pretending to do it, rather than lying, he would prefer lucidity.

Gyula is not for lucidity. "Lucidity is fate's victory, not man's. It is an act of freedom that carries within itself the negation of freedom." Lucidity stands for easy answers, finding ways to explain suffering, determining who God is, and other impossible things. Gyula prefers active questioning; indeed, it is the source of hope he offers: "Man must keep loving, searching, weighing, holding out his hand, offering himself, inventing himself." It means choosing the living over the dead. "Only the living can [suffer]. Kathleen is alive. I am alive. You must think of us. Not of them."

This is the choice Gyula forces on Eliezer: will he choose the living or the dead? Will he choose (and it is the same thing) day or night? Eliezer will be leaving the hospital tomorrow, on crutches. He is to lean (quite literally) on Kathleen. "She'll be happy if you lean on her. Receiving is a superior form of generosity. Make her happy. A little happiness justifies the efforts of a whole life."

Is this the breakthrough we have been waiting for? We must move to the very end, for, as we have already seen, only at the very end of a Wiesel novel is the story complete.

At the end of *Night*, Elie Wiesel looks in a mirror and a corpse looks back at him.

At the end of *Dawn*, Elisha looks at a window and his own face stares back at him, which is the face of night, which is the face of death.

At the end of *The Accident*, Eliezer looks at a portrait of himself, and it too is the face of death, for in its eyes Gyula has captured the fact that "the accident had been an accident only in the most limited sense of the word." It is the face of death doubly, for in its eyes Eliezer also sees Grandmother, promising that next time she will take her grandson with her into the land of the dead.

When that twin revelation has registered on Eliezer's mind, Gyula lights the canvas with a match and it is consumed by the flames. It is Gyula's way of saying: destroy the past, flee from it, burn away your desire to die in front of a taxi or on a station platform with Grandmother, choose to live, choose the living over the dead, begin again.

It is the moment of greatest hope in all of Wiesel's writing thus far: a creative choice is offered that promises to overcome the destructive power of the past, in the name of friendship and love.

It is the moment of greatest despair in all of Wiesel's writing thus far. The book ends with words about Gyula's exit: "He had forgotten to take along the ashes." The experiment does not work. The past cannot be destroyed. The ashes remain. Grandmother's ashes are on the hospital floor just as they still float over all of Europe. Eliezer's face is still the face of death.

Wiesel has said that the entire book was written for the sake of that final line.

The title of *The Accident* in the original French is *Le Jour*, *Day*. Like the title *Dawn*, it, too, is ironic. Day has not come. A false dawn and a false day are all that have intervened since the kingdom of night.

Darkness is still eclipsing light.

Spectator

Victim, executioner, flight—nothing works. Could one, therefore, simply disengage, refuse to get involved, remain on the sidelines? Could one become a spectator?

The option is explored in Wiesel's fourth book, *The Town Beyond the Wall*. The book as a whole is a turning point in his series of responses to monstrous moral evil, and it will engage us for the rest of this chapter and the first part of the next, for it confronts us with three further possibilities.

Michael, a post-Holocaust Jew like Elie, Elisha, and Eliezer, returns to the boyhood home, Szerencsevàros (a name which means "the city of luck"), from which he had been deported by the Germans during World War II. Since Szerencsevàros is now behind the Iron Curtain, the visit involves considerable risk. He is not sure what he is looking for, but he is convinced that whatever he needs to find can only be found in the town of his youth.

Once over the border and within the precincts of the town, Michael wanders about, gazing longingly at the old family home, visiting the shop his father had owned, and going to the site of the synagogue, which has been destroyed and replaced by a modern four-story building—symbol of the plight of Jews from Warsaw, Sighet, Szerencsevásros.

Without warning a memory surfaces: on the day of the deportation he had seen a face in a window of the town square, watching the scene with utter indifference. The face of a spectator.

In a later conversation with Pedro he says, "Do you understand that I need to understand? To understand the others—the Other—those who watched us depart for the unknown; those who observed us, without emotion, while we became objects—living sticks of wood—and carefully numbered victims?"

The reason for his return—a reason he had not previously been able to articulate—is now clear:

> This, this was the thing I had wanted to understand ever since the war. Nothing else. How a human being can remain indifferent. The executioners I understood; also the victims, though with more difficulty. For the others, all the others, those who were neither for nor against, those who sprawled in passive patience, those who told themselves, "The storm will blow over and everything will be normal again," those who thought themselves above the battle, those who were permanently and merely spectators—all those were closed to me, incomprehensible.

The man in the window represents another way to deal with monstrous moral evil: "He was neither victim nor executioner; a spectator, that's what he was. He wanted to live in peace and quiet."

The spectator did not fill Michael with hatred. He felt only curiosity.

> How can anyone remain a spectator indefinitely? How can anyone continue to embrace the woman he loves, to pray to God with fervor if not faith, to dream of a better tomorrow—after having seen *that*? . . . Between victims and executioners there is a mysterious bond; they belong to the same universe; one is the negation of the other. . . . The spectator is entirely beyond us.

Michael goes to the spectator's apartment explicitly to humiliate him. The spectator remains impassive, even as Michael splashes two glasses of wine in his face. He felt nothing then, he reports, he feels nothing now.

During an extended conversation, the ground shifts only when

Michael, responding to a question, makes clear that he does not hate the spectator:

> "No," I said. "I don't hate you." A pause; then: "I feel contempt for you. That's worse. The man who inspires hatred is still human; but not the man who inspires contempt. . . . Hatred implies humanity. . . . But contempt has only one implication: decadence."

Here, at last, is something the spectator cannot handle. Four times he insists that he will not accept such humiliation, and insists on being hated. Four times Michael refuses him the humanity such an emotion would confer.

But as Michael leaves, the spectator says, "I feel sure you'll hate me," and within minutes Michael is picked up by the police. Sitting in the front of the police car is the spectator, sure that his act of betrayal will move Michael from contempt to hatred. Michael refuses the offer.

The episode is disturbing. It reminds us of the strange bond between victim and executioner ("one is the negation of the other"), both of whom at least belong to the same universe—a universe from which the spectator is excluded. It reminds us further that none of the categories are mutually exclusive. When the man in the window disavows the spectator role by summoning the police, Michael must conclude, "He had become human again. Deep down, I thought, man is not only an executioner, not only a victim, not only a spectator: he is all three at once." Michael, sitting in the police car as victim, remains a spectator of the other's pain, thus acting as his executioner.

It is lack of relationship, indifference, that characterizes the spectator, and it is the most dehumanizing of all human acts, for it destroys both the observer and the one observed. Martin Buber, whose influence is apparent in *The Town Beyond the Wall*, comments in *I and Thou*: "Whoever hates directly is closer to a relation than those who are without love and hate."

Spectators are without love and also without hate, and this makes the spectator the most morally culpable of all, even more than the executioner. For spectators, unwilling to do the dirty work themselves, consent to letting others do the dirty work on their behalf, encouraging them by silent complicity. "Go ahead. We will watch. And while we will not participate, neither will we condemn. You get our vote by default." So the spectator is not really neutral. The spectator sides with the executioner. Such a pose, masking silent support of evil, is worthy only of contempt.

The indictment of a spectator in Szerencseváros is a microcosm of the indictment of a generation, and a God. Indifference, as far as Wiesel is concerned, is the greatest sin. The title of his first book, *And the World Has Remained Silent*, encapsulates the concerns of every subsequent book. In later essays he reminds us that it was the spectator attitude of the western world that emboldened the Nazis to take the next step, and the next . . . (see *Legends*). He finds it "strange" (to use a neutral word) that "the civilized world waited until it was too late before expressing its moral indignation." Not only were principles betrayed, so were persons. One of his most poignant paragraphs:

> At the risk of offending, it must be emphasized that the victims suffered more, and more profoundly, from the indifference of the onlookers than from the brutality of the executioner. The cruelty of the enemy would have been incapable of breaking the prisoner; it was the silence of those he believed to be his friends—cruelty more cowardly, more subtle—which broke his heart.

Is God also a spectator? In the first quotation cited above, reference to "the other," the spectator, is followed by extending the description to include "the Other." God, too, is described as One who "watched us depart for the unknown," One "who observed us, without emotion, while we became objects—living sticks of wood—and carefully numbered victims." This is what Michael could not understand. Seen on the face of a human being, such indifference inspired only contempt. Seen on the face of God . . .

Could God, too, be worthy only of contempt?

Darkness is still eclipsing night.

Madness

No matter where he turns—whether his name is Elie, Elisha, Eliezer, or Michael—he finds nothing but darkness surrounding him. Why should he expect light to dawn? Why not surrender to the darkness? Why not sink into its arms? Why not acknowledge its sovereignty? Why not . . . go mad?

The epigraph of *The Town Beyond the Wall* signals the importance of this option. It is from Dostoievski's *The Possessed*: "I have a plan—to go mad." On a few occasions it is a potential agenda for Michael and on many occasions it is an actual agenda for others.

The sanest thing to say about madness is that it is complicated, and we must tentatively distinguish two interrelated kinds of madness that are operative in Wiesel's novels. One of these is what Abraham Heschel calls "moral madness," the madness of the Hebrew prophets, and what Wiesel calls "mystical madness." It characterizes those whom the world calls "mad," since they live by a different vision and challenge the existing order in the name of that vision. They are spokespersons for the divine and purveyors of a truth all persons need to hear. They offer a creative, indeed essential, contribution to human well-being, and we will explore their positive contribution in chapter 7.

But there is another kind of madness, sometimes called "clinical madness," which consists of being so out of touch with one's surroundings as to be unable to function within them, cut off from the ability to respond or communicate. When one's surroundings are threatening and destructive, it is a great temptation to deny the existence of what is threatening and destructive and substitute a secure and unthreatening world of one's own creation.

After his arrest, Michael is subjected to torture. The occupying powers have developed an exquisitely refined method for getting prisoners to talk; they simply stand them before a wall eight hours at a stretch until they break. During the first "prayer," as the sessions before the wall are ironically labeled, Michael recalls boyhood experiences in the town in which he is now imprisoned, a series of reminiscences that conjure up varieties of madness.

There is Martha. Ugly, obscene, insulting; the town drunk who flings her skirts up, and her curses out, to any who will come within seeing or hearing. Her life is submission to impulse, her organizing principle is chaos. She invites young Michael—eight, nine, ten years old—to make love with her. He runs home terrified. Actually, Martha doesn't need him. She sleeps with Satan, and the result of their union is the world itself, which therefore is not clean and pure, as its inhabitants think. "You stink of my blood, you're tangled in my guts," she tells all listeners.

Madness. And yet, perhaps that *is* the world? The post-Holocaust world?

There is Moishe. We have met Moishe before and will meet him again. He is in most of Wiesel's novels. Moishe is a bridge between the two kinds of madness. He sees—perhaps even dwells—in a world inaccessible to those around him. Michael's father thinks the madness may be a protection for Moishe's friends rather than for Moishe, since seeing what he sees would be too dangerous for the others. Moishe asserts that "in this base world only madmen know." In Hitler's world, Moishe's credo goes, "These days honest men can do only one thing: go mad! Spit on logic, intelligence, sacrosanct reason! That's what you have to do, that's the way to stay human, to keep your wholeness!"

Michael comes to the disturbing conclusion that Moishe is not crazy. But if he is not, then the others are. And where does that leave Michael? With Moishe or the others?

There is old Varady. Old indeed. Over a hundred, and on record as having said—in the temple—that he would live forever. Varady preaches a human strength greater even than the strength of God. For such blasphemy Varady is ostracized, and accepts isolation as his lot. But whenever there is a death in the community, Varady's longevity becomes a disrespectful reminder of the mortality of others. He is disturbingly present in his very absence.

When the Germans come to deport the Jews, Varady kills himself.

Finally there is Kalman, who has three students, Hersh-Leib, Menashe, and Michael himself. If Varady wants to outwit death, Kalman and his protégés want to force the hand of destiny. Through prayers and asceticism they will hasten the time of Messiah's coming. He failed to come this week? Maybe by next week they will be strong enough. It is too great a strain. Hersh-Leib loses his mind first, then Menashe. Kalman must be mad as well, the townfolk say.

Michael alone is saved from madness . . . by the Germans, who thoughtfully occupy Szerencseváros in time to save him. (Of all the episodes in *The Town Beyond the Wall*, Wiesel says, this is the only one with an autobiographical base; he was the third student, the one the Germans "saved.")

They were all mad, Michael reflects later on to Pedro. Mad to think that people had any control over their fate, mad to imagine any possibility of redemption. There was no rational basis, in Hitler's world, for believing in God or humanity or any reconciliation between the two. So they defied the world, in their various ways, making an almost Promethean decision to assert themselves against all the outside forces—the world, death, God, evil.

And who is finally to say whether that is moral or clinical madness?

Out of the tutoring of his youth, Michael later faces the possibility of madness himself. He comes closest to it after the war in Paris, while waiting out the slow, agonizing death of Yankel. In the camps, Yankel had been a *pilpul*, a child whom fate had chosen as the darling of the Nazi guards, and who as a result had extraordinary power over the fate of fellow prisoners, a power he often exercised cruelly. He had been present at the death of Michael's father and had observed that Michael had been unable to cry. Yankel is Michael's alter-ego; Michael is afraid, as he tells Yankel, "of the bit of me that's part of you." As Yankel is dying, after being run over by a truck, Michael, outraged at the injustice in the world and looking for something to destroy, finds his hands around the boy's throat. He squeezes involuntarily, not so much to kill Yankel as "to strangle his own despair," which Yankel, vivid reminder of the past, represents to him. He is jolted out of his trance just in time by the entrance of a doctor.

Later, talking about the episode with Pedro, Michael twice acknowledges, "I was on the verge of madness." Trying to justify his own existence, he was creating a universe in which the one absolute value was the death of Yankel, which he saw as "the death agonies of a future that was, at bottom, mine too." Out of this, he says, "I wove a universe of hallucinations, I blended the past with the future. All the men on earth bore a single face: that of my dying friend. Their destinies were measured by his."

The temptation to enter this world is almost overpowering. Even as Michael recalls the episode, he feels its attraction once again. It would have provided entrance into a world without fear, release from misery. And it would have been so easy: "Just to say yes, to acquiesce with a nod, would have been enough; to roll on the floor, stick out my tongue, break into song, howl like a hurt dog; safety was there within reach, and detachment, deliverance."

Michael resists. He realizes that while it is true that "the choice of madness is an act of courage," it is also true that "it can't be done more than once. It's an end in itself. An act of the free will that destroys freedom." So he resists.

But such victories are never final. The temptation recurs, and must be resisted again. Michael and Pedro are walking along the waterfront in Algiers, where an old man drowned the night before. From the depth of his being Pedro shares an account of the rape—thirty-seven times—of the woman he loved, who died even before the multiple assault was over. Love and death, Pedro reflects grimly, can only be understood together. The story pushes Michael to the verge of madness. He wants to shake the universe, to dig up all the graves in Spain until her body is found, to create a world where one can make love . . . to a corpse. It is all he can do "to keep from dashing to join the waves and the man they had swallowed up the night before."

Later, in the prison cell, Michael is confined with two madmen—the Silent One, living in a world so withdrawn that he is totally out of reach, and the Impatient One, living in a world where the only "truth" is a conviction that his cellmates are hiding a letter from him. Michael's almost uncontrollable impulse is to follow their example and enter a world not answerable to forces outside himself, a world in which all is permitted and all is possible.

> There A does not precede B, children are born dotards, fire produces cold, and snow becomes the source of desire. There, animals are gifted with human intelligence and demons display a

> sense of humor. There, all is impulse, passion, and chaos. There, the laws are abolished and those who promulgated them removed from office. The universe frees itself from the order in which it was imprisoned. Appearance snaps its ties with reality. A chair is no longer a chair, the king no longer king, the fool ceases to be a fool, or to cry.

Michael ponders: why not enter that world? Read the Impatient One the letter that doesn't exist. Construct a system all his own and nobody else's, where nobody can intrude and bother him.

He becomes furious as he remembers King Lear, who resists going mad, "who preferred suffering at the hands of men to flight into a trackless desert." He could have protected himself from friends who betray as well as from cowardly enemies, "and yet [he] chose the least easy solution: he faced them directly." What folly, Michael feels, when there is such an easy way to avoid pain and injustice, by resigning from the struggle, by going mad.

But the old king refuses Michael's advice, so does Michael.

Darkness is still eclipsing light.

But could such refusal, after gazing into the deep darkness, be the forerunner of light?

COLIN DAVIS

The Conversion to Ambiguity (Early Works)

Chapter 2 illustrated a change in Wiesel's practice as a storyteller from the autobiographical témoignange to the parabolic narrative of *Le Mendiant de Jérusalem.* By examining Wiesel's early texts, specifically *La Nuit* (1958), *L'Aube* (1960), *Le Jour* (1961), and *La Ville de la chance* (1962), this chapter shows how the origins of the ambiguity of his later fiction can be seen in tensions that appear in the early texts.

LA NUIT

More than thirty years after its first publication, *La Nuit* is still a shocking and remarkable book. It also occupies a unique and ambiguous position in the corpus of Wiesel's work. It is the only text in which Wiesel talks at length about his experiences in the concentration camps. At the same time it can be read as integral to Wiesel's fictional corpus. It constitutes the nonfictional basis of Wiesel's subsequent fiction, it is the center around which his later works revolve and to which they always implicitly refer.

Critics have implied that *La Nuit* should be *read*, but not *interpreted.* Robert McAfee Brown and Ted Estess, for example, both preface their commentaries on *La Nuit* with disarming remarks on the inappropriateness of critical analysis: "Of all Wiesel's works, [*La Nuit*] is the one that most cries out not to be touched, interpreted, synthesized. It must be encountered at first hand." "One is reluctant to apply the usual conventions of literary analysis to the book, for by doing so one runs the risk of blunting the impact of its testimony by too quickly speaking of secondary matters. Against the horror of the story, literary considerations seem somehow beside the point."

Some readers have nevertheless insisted that *La Nuit* should be read as a literary text. Denis Boak describes it as "a highly conscious literary artifact," and Zsuzsanna Ozsvath and Martha Satz argue that "the power of [*La Nuit*] as a document of the Holocaust owes much of its intensity to its literary quality." Moreover, despite the scruples of Wiesel's readers, interpretation does inevitably take place, and the text has been interpreted in a variety of ways. Particularly fruitful readings have been generated by the expedient of comparing the text with biblical stories. *La Nuit* has been read as an inversion of the story of the Exodus and as a version of the story of Abraham and Isaac, the sacrificial drama of father and son played out against the silence of God. And one critic, adapting a phrase from Martin Buber and justified by a reference in *La Nuit* itself, describes Wiesel as the "Job of Auschwitz."

La Nuit can be read both as a historical document and a reenactment of biblical stories "by the opaque light of the Night of Auschwitz." There is no contradiction here. Wiesel's account of the Holocaust gives signs of adherence to the belief—essential to the Jewish tradition—that history is not just a random sequence of events; as Paul Johnson puts it, "no people has ever insisted more firmly than the Jews that history has a purpose and humanity a destiny." In the Jewish tradition past and present are linked by the continuing spiritual drama that is enacted through history, and also by a dialectic through which individual experience and biblical story reciprocally illumine one another. Wiesel expresses this view in his *Célébration biblique*, a work in which he constantly uses episodes from the Bible as a means of reflecting on recent history:

> In Jewish history all events are linked. It is only today, after the whirlwind of fire and blood of the Holocaust, that we can read of the murder of a man by his brother, the questions of a father and his disturbing silences. It is by recounting them now, in the light of certain experiences of life and death, that we can understand them.

The interlinking of historical and spiritual dramas is reflected in the second and third paragraphs of *La Nuit*:

> Physically, [Moché the Beadle] was clumsy like a clown. He raised smiles, with his orphan's shyness. I loved his large dreamy eyes, lost in the distance. He spoke little. He sang; or rather he murmured tunes to himself. The snatches that one could hear spoke of the suffering of God, of the Exile of Providence that, according to the Kabbalah, would await its redemption in that of man.
>
> I got to know him toward the end of 1941. I was twelve. I was deeply religious. By day I studied the Talmud, and, at night, I ran to the synagogue to cry over the destruction of the temple.

Both of these paragraphs show the same development from factual description to spiritual meaning. Moché's songs introduce the themes of exile, providence, and deliverance; Eliezer's piety forges a link between the Europe of 1941 and Jerusalem at the time of the destruction of the Temple. Moché sings of exile; Eliezer longs for return.

There is no place for arbitrariness in this world. When Moché comes back to Sighet to describe Nazi atrocities against the Jews, we are told twice that he has escaped "by miracle." The choice of the word *miracle* reflects the belief according to which individual actions or events are providential manifestations of a higher order of meaning. Moché's survival, in as far as it is miraculous, confirms the continuing intervention of God in human affairs. However, while adopting verbal and narrative forms that suggest the union of historical event and spiritual meaning, Wiesel's text describes their effective separation. Moché escapes "by miracle," but what he experiences is brute historical reality. The divine order implied by the word *miracle* does not operate when it is most needed—God does not intervene to prevent the massacre of the Jews. The initial fusion of literal and spiritual realities has now been shattered. What Moché sees has no link with the sacred drama: "He no longer spoke to me of God or the Kabbalah, but only of what he had seen." Complementary aspects of the same truth have been torn apart, and the rest of the narrative sets out—and fails—to heal this rift.

La Nuit can be read as an attempt to achieve existential self-recognition, as the narrator attempts to understand himself and his place in history. This is emblematized—and its failure underscored—in the final lines of the text when he looks in a mirror and sees a corpse looking back at him. *La Nuit* does not offer unmediated, uninterpreted realities. Events are filtered through the eyes of a narrator, Eliezer, whose primary function is to seize their meaning as he organizes them into a coherent narrative. He exhibits considerable control in his organization of material. The nine short chapters divide the text into manageable units that can be summarized as follows:

Chapter 1. In Sighet. Buildup to deportation.
Chapter 2. In train. Arrival in Birkenau.
Chapter 3. First experiences of Auschwitz. Transfer to Buna.
Chapter 4. Life in Buna. Hangings.
Chapter 5. Selections. Evacuation of camp.
Chapter 6. Evacuation through snow. Arrival in Gleiwitz.
Chapter 7. In train to Buchenwald
Chapter 8. Death of father.
Chapter 9. Liberation of Buchenwald.

Throughout *La Nuit* Wiesel uses the past historic tense as part of a retrospective narrative. He is "telling a story" in a way that becomes more problematic in his later, more formally sophisticated fiction, with its changing narrative voices, shifting time scales, and unstable tense systems. In *La Nuit* the past historic gives the narrator retrospective command over his material. This allows him to organize and underline its significance, as well as to calculate and control its effect on the reader. Since this narrative mastery is important to the central tension of *La Nuit*, it is worth briefly describing some of the means by which it is achieved.

Direct comment. The narrator interrupts his description of events and comments directly; for example, while life for the Jews in the ghetto is still relatively tolerable, the narrator shows the wisdom of hindsight:

> It was neither the German nor the Jew who reigned over the ghetto: it was illusion.

Reader's knowledge of history. Much of *La Nuit* is written in a terse, telegraphic style. Eliezer avoids commentary or explanation when the reader's knowledge of history can be expected to fill in gaps. The use of place names provides a clear example:

> But we arrived at a station. Those who were near the windows told us the name of the station:
> - Auschwitz.
> No one had ever heard that name.
>
> In front of us, those flames. In the air, that smell of burnt flesh. It must have been midnight. We had arrived. At Birkenau.

Warning and premonition. The Jews of Sighet are constantly being warned of what will happen to them. Moché recounts the atrocities of the

Nazis, but is not believed. In the train to Auschwitz Mme Schächter has a premonitory vision ("—A fire! I can see a fire! I can see a fire!"), but she is bound, gagged, and beaten up by the other Jews. Later, the Jews are told what will happen to them:

> Sons of dogs, do you understand nothing then? You're going to be burned! Burned to a cinder! Turned to ashes!

Eliezer's direct comments also have a premonitory function:

> From that moment everything happened with great speed. The chase toward death had begun.

Retrospective viewpoint. Related to the latter point is the way in which the narrator can explain what he did not know at the time of the events being described due to knowledge acquired in the period between experiencing and describing. He uses phrases like "Later we were to learn," "I learned later," "I learned after the war," "Many years later."

Repetition of themes. One of the central concerns of *La Nuit* is Eliezer's relationship with his father and his ambiguous sense of guilt and liberation when his father dies. Eliezer's feeling that he has betrayed his father is reflected in other father-son relationships that he compulsively describes. Bela Katz, seconded to the *Sonder-Kommando*, places his own father's body into the furnace at Birkenau; the narrator refers to a child who beats his father; during the long march from Buna to Gleiwitz, Rabi Eliahou is left behind by his son, who has run on ahead, Eliezer believes, "in order to free himself from a burden that could reduce his own chances of survival"; and on the train to Buchenwald, a man murders his own father for the sake of a piece of bread.

Preparation of effects. Eliezer introduces striking or unexpected details that seem out of place at first, but that reinforce the impact of what comes later. After the first execution that he witnesses, Eliezer seems unmoved: "I remember that that evening I found the soup excellent . . ."; later, the cruel execution of a young boy is interpreted as reflecting the death of God, and Eliezer picks up his words from the previous page: "That evening, the soup had the taste of corpse." In Buna the treatment of the children seems to indicate a more humane attitude than we had been led to expect:

> Our convoy contained several children of ten, twelve years of age. The officer took an interest in them and ordered that some food be brought for them.

A page later, a more sinister explanation for the officer's interest is suggested as a new character is introduced:

> Our block leader was a German [. . .] Like the head of the camp, he liked children. Immediately after our arrival he had had some bread, soup and margarine brought for them (in reality, this affection was not disinterested: children here were the object, amongst homosexuals, of a real trade, as I was to learn later).

Through these devices, the narrator filters, interprets, and assimilates the experience of the Holocaust. Wiesel adopts a form and techniques that seem to confirm the Jewish expectation of the meaning of history and the interpretability of experience. The essential problem of *La Nuit* derives from the tension between the formal coherence and retrospective authority of the narrative, and the subject-matter of the work. Wiesel has always emphasized that the Holocaust can be neither understood nor described; it is a unique event without precedent, parallel, analogy, or meaning. This results in a problem of communication, and the survivors' predicament is particularly acute. They must, and cannot, recount the experience of the death camps: "Impossible to speak of it, impossible not to speak of it." *La Nuit*, then, is written in the knowledge of its own inevitable failure: the survivor must tell his story, but will never communicate the truth of his experience; what is kept silent is more true than what is said, words distort and betray, the Holocaust cannot be understood or described, the constraints of *vraisemblance* ensure that the story will always fall short of *vérité.* As Wiesel writes in *Un Juif, aujourd'hui*, "In order to be realistic [*vraisemblables*], the stories recounted less than the truth."

The failure of narration to command belief is reflected at the very beginning of *La Nuit* in the incredulous reaction encountered by Moché the Beadle. Moché is disbelieved, his story dismissed as imagination or madness, utterly contrary to *vraisemblance*. Finally, he chooses silence rather than futile narrative. Later, Eliezer meets with a similar reaction when he goes to warn a friend of his father's about the liquidation of the ghetto: "—What are you talking about [*Que racontes-tu*]? [. . .] Have you gone mad?" Eliezer is reduced to silence: "My throat was dry and the words were choked there, paralysing my lips. I couldn't say another word to him"; and paradoxically it is this silence that convinces the father's friend: "Then he understood." In its opening pages the text describes an anxiety about its own status and its communicative capabilities. The messenger is unwelcome and his story disbelieved or dismissed. The narrative process itself is interrupted. Eliezer's father is recounting a story when he is called away to be told of the deportation of the Jews: "The good story that he was telling us would remain unfinished." The father's "good story" is unfinished and supplanted by the less pleasant story that the son will now recount.

The failure of narrative represented at the beginning of *La Nuit* by these incidents is reflected in the writing of the text as a whole. The retrospective stance of the narrator and the control he exhibits over the presentation of his material put him in a privileged position of authority and understanding; at the same time, what he describes is the destruction of all points of certainty, resulting in the collapse of the interpretative authority that his stance as narrator seems to arrogate. *La Nuit* is above all a narrative of loss; in the course of the text, family, community, religious certainty, paternal authority, and the narrator's identity are corroded or destroyed. The theme of loss also has consequences for the validity of the narrative. The narrator constantly expresses the desperate hope that what he is witnessing is not real; thereby he draws attention to the desire to deny the truth of his own experience, to subvert the credibility of his own narrative:

> Wasn't all that a nightmare? An unimaginable nightmare? [. . .] No, all that could not be true. A nightmare [. . .] It was surely a dream.

This does not mean that narrated events did not take place; but it does disclose a reluctance within the témoignange itself to accept the validity of experience. While *La Nuit* never discredits the authority of its narrator, significant aspects of the text seem to resist acknowledging what Eliezer nevertheless knows to be true. Like the man in *Le Mendiant de Jérusalem* who believes himself mad rather than accepting that what he has seen—the consequences of the Holocaust—can be true, the narrator of *La Nuit* seeks to deny the evidence of his senses. The witness simultaneously suggests "this is true" and "this cannot be true."

This tension is compounded by a mistrust of language, which, Wiesel has suggested, was corrupted by the Holocaust: "The absolute perversion of language dates from that period."

> If our language is corrupted it is because, at that time, language itself was denatured. Innocent and beautiful words designated the most abject crimes [. . .] The first crime committed by the Nazis was against language.

This corruption of language is reflected in the course of *La Nuit*. The book begins in a world of confident speech: Moché the Beadle teaches Eliezer the mysteries of the Kabbalah; the father gives paternal advice; Eliezer narrates his childhood. However, the precariousness of this confidence in language is signaled by Moché's story of Nazi atrocities, which is true but discredited and disbelieved, and the father's never-finished anecdote. The rest of the text, and indeed all Wiesel's texts, fall under the shadow of these failed narratives. In Auschwitz language itself is devalued and stripped of its conventional meanings. Only one word retains its significance:

> The word "chimney" was not a word empty of sense here: it floated in the air, mixed with the smoke. It was perhaps the only word here that had a real meaning.

The degradation of language is shown most clearly in the use of direct speech in the course of *La Nuit*. The advice and teaching of Eliezer's father and Moché are supplanted by the curt imperatives of the concentration camp guards. "Everyone get out! Leave everything in the wagon! Quickly!"; "—Men to the left! Women to the right!" The dialogue between Eliezer and his father acquires a surreal, futile quality as the son repeats the father's imperatives—now devoid of all imperative force—and begins to usurp his father's authority:

> —Don't let yourself be carried off by sleep, Eliezer. It is dangerous to fall asleep in the snow. You can fall asleep for good. Come, my little one, come. Get up.
>
> Get up? How could I? How could I get out from this good covering? I heard the words of my father, but their meaning seemed empty to me, as if he had asked me to carry the whole hangar in my arms . . .
>
> —Come, my son, come [. . .]
>
> —Come, father, let us get back to the hangar . . .
>
> He did not reply. He was not looking at the dead.
>
> —Come, father. It's better over there [. . .]
>
> —There's nothing to fear, my little one. Sleep, you can sleep. I will stay awake.
>
> —First you, father. Sleep.
>
> He refused.

As *La Nuit* unfolds the father's speech indicates most dramatically the decay of linguistic authority and the sources of traditional authority in general. Initially, the father is presented as a well-respected figure: "The Jewish community of Sighet held him in the highest consideration; he was often consulted on public affairs and even on private matters." In particular, his authority is reflected in his command of language:

> My father told anecdotes to them and explained his opinion on the situation. He was a good storyteller [*un bon conteur*].

Eliezer first disregards his father's authority (he begins to study the Kabbalah despite his father's warnings), and then in his narrative undermines the validity of his father's views. This is done gently in the early stages of the text; Eliezer's father sees little to worry about in the decree ordering Jews to wear the yellow star:

> —The yellow star? So what? You don't die of that . . .
> (Poor father! What did you die of, then?)

Subsequently, *La Nuit* narrates the degradation and humiliation of the father, who becomes an increasingly unwelcome burden on his son. The growing desire for freedom from his father goes together with Eliezer's increasing sense of guilt. Finally, Eliezer experiences the death of his father as a terrible liberation, bringing freedom from an unwanted burden but also the loss of his self-respect and of his closest link with the values of the past:

> I didn't cry, and it pained me not to cry. But I had no tears left. And, within myself, if I had searched the depths of my enfeebled mind, I would perhaps have found something like: free at last! . . .

As this loss of authority is taking place, the father's speech undergoes a decline from command to incoherence. His first speech in the book underlines his assurance and confidence with language:

> —You are too young for that. It's only when you are thirty, according to Maimonides, that you have the right to explore the perilous world of mysticism. First you must study the basic texts that you are capable of understanding.

This contrasts starkly with the unfinished sentences of his final speeches:

> —Eliezer . . . I must tell you where to find the gold and sliver that I buried . . . In the cellar . . . You know . . . [. . .] I'm wasting

> away . . . Why do you behave so badly toward me, my son . . . Water . . . [. . .] My son, water . . . I'm wasting away. . . My guts . . .

The fundamental double bind at the core of Wiesel's writing lies in the fact that he must and cannot write about the Holocaust. His experiences during the war are at the source of his urge to narrate and to bear witness; at the same time, those experiences corrode the foundations of his narrative art as they undermine faith in mankind, God, self, and language. *La Nuit* is a work sustained by its own impossibility: the need to tell the truth about something that entails a crisis of belief in truth. The tension of *La Nuit* lies in its simultaneous assertion that what it narrates is true and that it cannot be true; such events cannot be perpetrated or seen or described. The narrator wants to believe he is mistaken at the very moment when he claims to be most brutally honest. So *La Nuit*, despite its apparent simplicity, is a deeply paradoxical work; a first-person narrative that recounts the destruction of identity, a témoignange in which the narrator wants most urgently to undermine his own credibility, a coherent account of the collapse of coherence, an attempt to describe what the author of the text insists cannot be described.

In the opening pages of *La Nuit* Eliezer's narrative suggests the unity of historical event and spiritual meaning; his stance as narrator shows retrospective command and interpretative authority over his material. In this respect, then, *La Nuit* has—paradoxically—a *reassuring* aspect in as far as it preserves the norms of narrative coherence and authorial presence. But the narrative order is shadowed by a counternarrative that denies the foundation of order. The text draws attention to its own impossibility as the narrator describes his own death; when Moché returns to Sighet it is, he says, "to recount my death to you," and when at the end of the text Eliezer looks in a mirror he sees a corpse: "From within the mirror a corpse was looking at me." Most crucially, and despite the narrator's strategies for conferring order on his experiences, *La Nuit* describes the origins of disjunction between historical and spiritual dramas, between history and its significance. The story of Auschwitz can no longer be assimilated to the story of exile and providence introduced in the second paragraph of the book. The narrative attempts to establish a command over meaning that the counternarrative negates; Eliezer tries to understand, but his story does not make sense.

At the beginning of *La Nuit* Moché is saved from death "by miracle." The miracle suggests a divine intervention that the circumstances of the event belie. *La Nuit* is written in this same tension between the establishment of order in the narrative and the description of order in process of collapse. The miracle does not take place, though the narrative forms and strategies that Wiesel adopts in his first work indicate the continuing desire for the miracle, for the restitution of the union of event and meaning. Perhaps it would be impossible for him to write without the presumption of order, so that in writing he is bound to affirm values that his texts nevertheless show to be without foundation. In his later fiction Wiesel experiments with ambiguous, fragmented narrative forms more appropriate to the collapse of meanings that is at the source of his writing. This entails a growing lucidity on Wiesel's part to the broader implications of narrative technique and an explicit rejection of the attempt to inscribe historical events within a scheme of miraculous intervention and divine providence:

> But there was a miracle. Sorry, I withdraw that term: the war broke out and, if it saved me from prison, it cost twenty million men, women and children their lives and, we now know, it allowed the annihilation of six million of my people . . . No, it wasn't a miracle.

L'AUBE AND *LE JOUR*

La Nuit describes the collapse of coherence from a deceptively stable standpoint that is itself implicated in and threatened by that collapse. Like *La Nuit*, Wiesel's subsequent texts *L'Aube* and *Le Jour* are retrospective first-person narratives that use the past historic tense. The narrators look back on their lives and are able to give their experience a degree of order. Despite the wandering memory of its narrator, *L'Aube* even preserves the dramatic unities of time, space and action: the text describes the events of one night in a house in Palestine. However, the material of *L'Aube* and *Le Jour* continues to strain against the semblance of coherence conferred by the retrospective narratives. The progression implied in the titles of Wiesel's first three works (*La Nuit*, *L'Aube*, *Le Jour*) is not borne out by the texts themselves; there is no unambiguous movement from darkness to light, despair to hope. Wiesel's "trilogy" appears to set itself a teleological program with which it fails to comply.

The ambiguity of Wiesel's writing after *La Nuit* is compounded by the fictionalization of the narrative voice. The force of *La Nuit* as a témoignage depends upon the reader's identification of the author Elie with the narrator Eliezer. The claim of the text that "all this really happened," and hence also its moral urgency, flounder if we refuse to invest the narrative voice with the authority of a witness. Interestingly, it is the narrator not the author of *La Nuit* who bears the "proper name" of the historical protagonist, since Elie is a French version of the name given to the child at birth. In a sense then, Wiesel is already playing with his own name by indicating a possible distinction between the victim of the concentration camps (Eliezer) and the author of the text (Elie). Such a distinction does not deny the autobiographical status of the text, though it may indicate the author's desire to dissociate himself from his narrator, while also being identified with him. This process of dissociation continues in *L'Aube* and *Le Jour*, the titles of which suggest a connection with *La Nuit*, with the consequence that Wiesel's first text belongs to a cycle that combines an autobiographical work with two overtly fictional narratives.

The fictional status of *L'Aube* and *Le Jour* is acknowledged on their title pages, which describe the texts respectively as a *récit* and a *roman*. Nevertheless, the divorce between fictional narrator and "real" author remains incomplete; Wiesel names his principal characters Elisha ("I am called Elisha [. . .] Elisha was the disciple of Elijah [*Elie*],") and Eliezer ("I am called Eliezer, son of Sarah,"), and thereby invites some degree of identification between author and narrator (in the same way that Proust does by suggesting that his narrator may be called Marcel), even though the texts in which they appear are presented to the reader as fictional.

The status of the texts is problematic: in as far as they are fiction, we are discouraged from regarding them as historically truthful; in as far as the narrators are, *at least to some degree*, identifiable with the author, we are encouraged not to disregard their value as témoignage (this is reinforced with respect to *Le Jour* by the fact that Wiesel himself was hit by a taxi in 1956). Rather than recording real lives and real selves, Wiesel now begins to explore potential serves that are related to, but not entirely identifiable with, himself. The fictionalization of the narrative voice can be seen as a sort of self-fictionalization. Eliezer becomes Elie, and is refracted, particularly in the recurrence of the constituent /el/ (Hebrew for God), which occurs twice in the name Elie Wiesel, in the names of numerous subsequent fictional characters: Dr. Russel, Avriel, Azriel, Michael, Paltiel, Raphael, Malkiel, Elhanan.

Wiesel's fictional texts constantly reflect upon their own status as fiction. This is already apparent in *L'Abue*. At one point in the *récit* telling stories is described as equivalent to doing nothing at all:

> —What did you do afterward? she asked, suddenly anxious.
> [. . .] —Nothing [*Rien*]. He told me stories.

Earlier in *L'Aube*, however, the implication is that storytelling and the process of fictionalization may have a therapeutic aspect. Ilana describes to

Elisha a future time when the telling of stories will enable the forgetting, and facilitate the overcoming, of present anxieties:

> You will get married. You will have children. You will tell them stories. You will make them laugh. You will be happy because they will be happy [. . .] And long ago you will have forgotten this night, this room, me and all the rest. . .

Storytelling is possible when the present can be forgotten, and it may even contribute to the process of forgetting; it may help to liquidate the memory of a traumatic past. "I am Eliezer, this happened to me," claims the author of the autobiographical *La Nuit*; "I am not Elisha, this never happened," suggests the author of the fictional *L'Aube*.

Disguise, concealment, the swapping of names, and the assumption of false identities are central motifs in Wiesel's writing; the creation of illusions and the telling of lies appear as essential strategies of survival (see in particular *Les Portes de la forêt*). There is a curious discrepancy between Wiesel's public image as a man of impeccable moral integrity (Berenbaum, for example, refers to "Wiesel's compelling honesty as a writer") and the prominent theme of dissimulation in his fiction. Thematically at least, language is not used as a medium of truth, but as a screen to hide what the speaker does not wish to say. The emptiness of language is described on the first page of *Le Jour*:

> I had barely finished my work: a five-hundred-word cable. Five hundred words to say nothing [*pour ne rien dire*]. To mask the void of the day that passed [. . .] To say in five hundred words that there was nothing to say [*rien à dire*] was not an easy matter.

The text itself is at a further remove from the narrator's insistence that he has *rien à dire* (nothing to say). It revolves around an initial text, the journalist's report, which has nothing to say, and it repeats and comments on that absence of message. The use of *rien* (nothing) here recalls the equation of storytelling with doing nothing in *L'Aube* (see above), and is developed in Wiesel's next novel, *La Ville de la chance*. In the course of *Le Jour* the theme of empty language is reinforced by the narrator's decision to tell lies: "I will have to practice lying, I decided."

> I will have to learn how to lie, I thought again. Even for the short time I have left. To lie well. Without blushing.

The question of lying is related to the status of literature in general, as Wiesel indicates in the anecdote recounted in *Entre deux soleils*, when the rabbi equates fiction with a masking of the truth: "you write lies." As I suggested in chapter 2, Wiesel's evasive response fails to disarm the rabbi's accusation. Eliezer, the narrator of *Le Jour*, also attempts to make an unconvincing defense of lying:

> I was lying. I was going to have to lie. A lot. She was suffering. It is permissible to lie to those who are ill.

In *L'Aube*, as we saw, *raconter des histories* (to tell stories) is equated with forgetting the past and being happy; a similar equation is established on the final page of *Le Jour*, though here *raconter* is replaced by *mentir* (to lie):

> Kathleen will be happy, I decided. I will learn to lie well and she will be happy. It's absurd: lies can give rise to real happiness. Happiness that, as long as it lasts, seems real. The living love lies, like they love to acquire friendship.

The change from Eliezer mark one, in *La Nuit*, to Eliezer mark two, in *Le Jour*, signals the transition from autobiography to fiction; and this also marks the shift from a sincere idiom based on individual experience ("Yes, I had seen it, seen it with my own eyes . . .") to a self-consciously false discourse ("I will learn to lie well,"). This entry into fiction develops out of the desire of the narrator of *La Nuit* to discredit and disbelieve the evidence of his senses: "That could not be true." Nevertheless, particularly in Wiesel's early fiction, the presumption of intelligibility has not been overcome. This is shown in *L'Aube* and *Le Jour* by the attempts of the respective narrators to assume authority over their narratives. Elisha in *L'Aube* presents himself as someone in search of meaning: "Philosophy attracted me: I wanted to understand the meaning of the events of which I was the victim." Elisha lives in anticipation of meaning, and he seems justified in his anticipation when he abandons philosophy in favor of direct intervention in the struggle for the foundation of Israel: "I entered a messianic world [. . .] in which no act was lost, no look was wasted." When Elisha kills John Dawson, he hopes to find in his act "a meaning that transcends it." Nevertheless, such a meaning is never revealed. John Dawson turns his failure to understand the meaning of his death back onto Elisha: "I don't even know why I am dying [. . .] Do you know why?" The question remains unanswered, and thereby the text refuses to confirm the authority over meaning for which the narrator is searching.

An illustration of this potential loss of meaning is also given in *Le Jour* through the contrast between the narrator's two operations, the first of which took place when he was twelve, the second after his accident in New York. At the time of his first operation, while he is under the anaesthetic, he dreams of a meeting with God. He thinks of all the questions he might ask, and God gives him all the answers he wanted: "God had answered all my questions and many others besides." When the child awakes, he has forgotten God's response, but his dream nevertheless stands as evidence of hope in the revelation of ultimate meaning. At the time of the second operation, the dream is not repeated:

> And you see, Doctor, this time, stretched out on your operating table, deeply asleep, I did not see God in my dream. He was no longer there.

Paul Russel, the surgeon during the second operation, seems to expect "a hidden meaning [*un sens caché*]" in the narrator's story; but the story concerns the withdrawal or eclipse of transcendent meaning rather than its revelation.

The final page of the novel shows that this loss of intelligibility is at work within the text itself. Gyula has finished his portrait of the narrator, in which the latter sees his grandmother; recognizing the narrator's morbid thoughts, the artist burns his work. This has been read as an important step forward in Wiesel's "choice of life"; but the passage is too enigmatic and ambivalent to fit easily with any such interpretation. The burning of the portrait appears as a second Holocaust in which the grandmother is destroyed once again ("Don't burn Grandmother a second time!"); and as Gyula leaves he does not take the ashes with him ("He had forgotten to take the ashes away,"), suggesting perhaps that the traces of the past remain despite the desire to efface them. And the "choice of life" is deeply ambiguous if it involves a destruction that can be compared to the Holocaust. What is certain is that this final page does not offer any unequivocal solutions to unresolvable questions. The retrospective first-person narrator seems to promise a control over meaning that remains elusive. Intimations of significance are not fulfilled; and the reader of Wiesel's fiction is increasingly put in the same position as his narrators: confronted with uninterpreted signs and portents that do not quite make sense.

LA VILLE DE LA CHANCE

The narrators of *La Nuit*, *L'Aube*, and *Le Jour* attempt to maintain an interpretative command over experiences that threaten to undermine the foundations of intelligibility. The tension between coherence and incoherence, narrative authority, and narrative subversion come to a head in Wiesel's next novel, *La Ville de la chance*. I suggest that this novel is a watershed between the tensions of the early texts and the ambiguities of the later fiction.

The central issue of *La Ville de la chance* is the return to origins, and its principal character, Michael, reflects on the motivation and viability of such a return:

> —Since the end of the war, Michael continued, I have done nothing except look for Szerencsevàros. I thought that it was everywhere, except where geography situates it. I told myself that like me it had been deported, transplanted elsewhere, to Germany or to heaven. Now, I would like to go back. To see if it exists, if it has remained similar to itself.

Michael is convinced of the value of return: "Me, I know, the truth is to be found in Szerencseváros." His journey has a purpose, even if he is not fully aware of it himself; Pedro's question "why this desire to go back?" turns out to have a precise answer, which is revealed toward the end of the novel when Michael begins to realize why he has returned:

> Suddenly, I understood that of all the reasons behind my return, this one was linked to a precise aim, to a specific idea. I was looking for something, but did not know what; someone, but did not know whom.

When Michael recalls the face of a man who dispassionately observed the deportation of the Jews, the meaning of his return is revealed:

> At last! Everything became clear, laid bare. So this was the reason, the real reason, the one that motivated all the others. So my acts, my desires were obeying a logic that was contained within them.

Michael's meeting with the man who witnessed the deportation of the Jews in indifference does not end the novel, but it does ensure the coherence and success of Michael's quest. His return now makes sense; and the encounter with the indifferent witness prepares his conversion to a humanist ethic of responsibility. In the final pages of the novel he rejects the temptation of madness and undertakes to restore his cell mate, *le Silencieux* (the Silent One), to the world of human relations. Toward the end of the novel a distinctly moralistic tone is adopted as narration gives way to prescription:

> It is within man that we find both our question and the strength to delimit it or, on the contrary, to make it universal. To take refuge in a sort of Nirvana—whether it be reasoned indifference or pathological apathy—is to oppose man in the most absurd way, the most futile, the most comfortable way. Man is only man amongst other men. It is more difficult to remain a man than to attempt to go beyond oneself [. . .] Don't stay at the window. Leave your nest but don't attempt to reach the heights by distancing yourself from the children who are thirsty and the mothers who don't have a single drop of milk left in their breasts. The true heights are like the true depths: they are to be found at your own level, in the pure and simple dialogue, in a look full of being.

When the young Michael begins to study Kabbalism, he discovers a world suffused with the meaningful designs of God:

> Suddenly all acts had a meaning, occupied a definite place in that immense mosaic of which even the contours escape our understanding. God was presence. He could be seen in every object, behind every gesture.

It is this sense of pervasive meaningfulness that *La Ville de la chance* attempts to recover. It is partly provided by the theme of return and Michael's final ethical conversion, which give the novel a degree of coherence; but there is also another aspect to the text that shadows this search for meaning and threatens its success. This is indicated when Michael's father denies the unity of reality sought by the mystics and describes life as "made of laughter, foolishness, daily hopes, childish illusions, adventures without future [*adventures sans lendemain*]!" The novel contains further examples of the denial or absence of intelligibility, or of incoherent stories and messages that fail to arrive. Pedro waits to hear the end of a story that is in fact already completed; the narrator's father dies murmuring "unintelligible words"; in prison Michael meets *L'Impatient* (the Impatient One) who is awaiting a letter that never arrives. When Michael is reunited with Yankel, a fellow concentration camp survivor, he cannot make sense of his story:

> [Yankel] began to recount to him his life in Paris. Michael, despite his efforts, could not follow the thread of the story [*le fil du récit*].

Later Yankel dies without giving the elucidation expected by Michael:

> [Michael] thought: if Yankel could speak now, he would help me unveil mysteries [. . .] But Yankel could not speak. He kept his mouth open, his eyes open: no word, no message came out of them.

Michael encounters the prototype of the coherent narrative when he listens to an Arab storyteller in Tangiers. The pleasure of the story derives from its familiarity; the audience gets what it knows, expects, and wants: "In the market place, the old storyteller, as he did every evening, was reciting the same story, which caused the same enthusiasm in the listeners as if they were hearing it for the first time." This pleasure in repetition reaches its climax in the security of a known ending:

> Michael guessed that the story would soon be reaching its end. The happy ending—the merciful intervention of Allah, the miracle—was close. The Arabs were waiting for it avidly, impatiently, to greet it with a deafening roar. All's well that ends well. Up above someone is watching, someone is smiling.

The coherence of the story depends upon a divine presence, the guarantor that actions are not arbitrary, that a transcendent eye oversees and approves human activity and governs its significance. The story persuades its audience of the connection between the teleology of the narrative, where the ending is crucial to the conferment of meaning, and the teleological order of the universe. The end assures the meaning and meaningfulness of what precedes. The conversion to humanistic responsibility at the end of *La Ville de la chance* reflects the Arab storyteller's aesthetic of "all's well that ends well [*tout est bien, tout finit bien*]." The bond of communication that unites storyteller and audience is assured by the familiarity of the story's conclusion. The Arab delivers what is expected of him and leaves his audience deeply satisfied. In the less coherent world of "adventures without future," the father dies with only "unintelligible words" on his lips, Yankel dies leaving "no message." Michael, on the other hand, succeeds in delivering his message, as he proclaims the storyteller's version of *veni, vidi, vici*: "I came, I saw, I delivered the message: the cycle is closed. The act accomplished."

The end of *La Ville de la chance* is not, however, as straightforward as this presentation would suggest. The final page of the novel recounts a legend in which man and God exchange places; taking advantage of his omnipotence, man then refuses to return to his human condition (see *Ville*). This legend and it relation to the main text are enigmatic: does it suggest that man has now acquired the powers of God, hence endorsing Michael's attempt to redeem *le Silencieux*, or does it imply that man's usurpation of God's power is an abuse, an illusion based on a world order that no longer makes sense ("so neither God nor man was any longer what he appeared to be,") or a betrayal of the initial bargain between man and God? In the latter case the legend might indicate that the redemption of *le Silencieux* is less assured that it seems. Moreover, the conclusion to Michael's story itself raises problems of interpretation that unsettle the coherent reading of the story that I have sketched so far.

The name of the man whom Michael has undertaken to save from silence and solitude turns out to be Eliezer: "The other [*L'autre*] bore the biblical name of Eliezer, which means *God has answered my prayer*." The name suggests that God has intervened just as Allah's miracle ensured the successful conclusion of the storyteller's tale. However, such an interpretation of this sentence fails to account for some of its most striking and strangest features. Wiesel gives *le Silencieux* his own forename, drawing a connection between the autobiographical Eliezer of *La Nuit* and the fictional Eliezer of *Le Jour*. At the end of *La Ville de la chance*, then, he suggests that the man who does not speak is another fictionalized version of himself. Michael's role, it might seem, is to rescue his own author from silence. And the introduction of the name Eliezer at the end of the novel indicates once again the duality of an identity that is torn between silence (*le Silencieux*) and writing (Wiesel the novelist), and between real and fictional selves. Eliezer is described as "L'autre" (the other), reminding us that he is both Wiesel and other than Wiesel. Like *La Nuit*, *La Ville de la chance* ends with the author reflecting on himself; and as in that first text, the mirror reveals the author as other than himself.

The meaning of the name Eliezer is given as "*God has answered my prayer* [*prière*]," and the use of the word *prière* here contributes to the strangeness of this final sentence. *La Ville de la chance* is divided into four sections, each of which is called a prayer: "Première prière," "Deuxième prière," "Troisème priere," "Dernière prière." and the word *prière* acquires ironic force because it is used to refer to the form of torture adopted by the Hungarian police in their interrogation of Michael:

> So that's the prayer, the famous prayer, thought Michael. Given this name by an erudite torturer, the torture consists in breaking the resistance of the prisoner by obliging him to remain standing until he passes out. It is because Jews stand up when they pray that this torture is now called the prayer.

The pious assertion "*God has answered my prayer*" has, then, a bitter ring when *prière* refers to a form of torture; and the coherence of the conclusion to the novel, suggested in the reference to a fulfilled prayer, is undercut by the presence of elements with multiple and contradictory resonances: Eliezer (fictional character/real author, silence/writing) and *prière* (pious prayer/cruel torture). In consequence, the sentence itself has an excess of meaning that resists simple explanation and undercuts the reader's anticipated pleasure in the predictable rediscovery that "all's well that ends well." Michael's ethical conversion does not satisfactorily tie up all the loose ends of the novel; and the intervention of Allah, bringing coherence guaranteed from above, has not unambiguously taken place.

What is at issue here is the degree to which *La Ville de la chance* fulfills the anticipation of intelligibility, of which the model is the tale of the Arab storyteller. In this respect there is a revealing difference between *La Ville de la chance* and Wiesel's essay "Le Dernier Retour," in which he describes his first return visit to Sighet in 1964, two years after the publication of *La Ville de la chance*. Wiesel himself makes the connection between the novel and the essay:

> I lived my return a long time previously. I tried to describe it in *La Ville de la chance*. Afterward, reality confirmed the fiction.

Wiesel, like Michael, anticipates some event or revelation that will justify his return:

> What have I come to do in Sighet, so late at night, so late in life? [. . .] Night is advancing and I am looking for a sign.

Unlike Michael, however, he finds no hidden purpose that explains his journey: "I came to do something, I still do not know what." This is Wiesel's "dernier retour" (final return)—not because he will never visit Sighet again (he has in fact been back since 1964; see *Qui êtes-vous?*), but because the return journey confirms the impossibility of authentic return. The quest for origins culminates in the knowledge of loss:

> Sighet is no longer Sighet [. . .] I had no home any more [. . .] That town they spoke to me about, it no longer existed [. . .] No possibility of returning again [. . .] For the town that, previously, had been mine, never existed.

No revelation, other than the revelation of the futility of return, takes place;

and Wiesel leaves Sighet after only twenty-four hours. In the novel, Michael seems to be afforded the positive revelation of purpose that is denied to Wiesel: "so that is the reason, the real reason, the one that motivated all the others." Michael discovers, if not the answers to his questions, at least the faith in the sense of the question and the possibility of an answer: "The depth, the meaning, the salt of man, is to attempt to ask the question in a more and more internal way, to feel in a more and more intimate way the existence of an answer that he does not know."

This conclusion makes it possible to read *La Ville de la chance* as a larger-scale version of the tale of the Arab storyteller—a coherent story of return and revelation, depending upon the existence of a meaningful universe in which all actions imply one another; the audience belongs to an established community in which each member reacts in the appropriate way at the appropriate moment. All this depends upon a miracle—"the merciful intervention of Allah, the miracle." This miracle gives the whole story its meaning, the end explains the beginning, everything coheres thanks to the divine eye that watches over human affairs. But we have seen already, in relation to *La Nuit*, that Wiesel's texts are written in the absence of the redemptive miracle that confers meaning on history and gives wholeness to the story. Michael would like to be a storyteller: "Michael said to himself that if he were to return to earth, he would like to be a teller of legends [*conteur de légendes*]"; but he realizes that his life and story do not conform to the aesthetics of the legend and the assurance of order that it gives to its audience. Michael's insight into the exclusion is shown by his eagerness to avoid witnessing the audience's ecstatic reaction to the divinely inspired dénouement to the story; and as he hurries away from the scene, he also turns his back on the aesthetics of the legend and the unified community of listeners: "Dreading this scene of collective emotion, Michael got up and departed as fast as he could."

Michael's reaction to the Arab storyteller and his relationship with his audience involves, then, both envy ("he would like to be a teller of legends") and rejection ("Michael got up and departed as fast as he could"). In its formal aspects *La Ville de la chance* reflects this ambivalence toward the aesthetics of the coherent narrative. *La Ville de la chance* contains more formal innovation than Wiesel's earlier books. In *L'Aube* and *Le Jour*, and to a certain extent in *La Ville de la chance*, Wiesel continues to employ narrative forms that give a semblance of coherence to experience. At the same time, *La Ville de la chance* is a more fragmented work. It does not rely exclusively on a first-person retrospective narrative; it oscillates between first- and third-person narrators, between real and imaginary conversations (such as the final conversations with Pedro); and, beginning a practice that Wiesel would adopt more extensively in his later fiction, passages in italics stand apart from and comment on some of the main issues in the principal body of the text. Wiesel's novel begins to adopt formal strategies that disrupt the anticipation of coherence. The first page gives a good illustration of this. It begins by describing the town at dusk:

> Outside dusk has fallen onto the town, like the heavy fist of a malefactor. Rapidly, without warning. Onto the low houses with red and grey roofs, onto the living wall of ants surrounding the cemetery, onto the dogs with anxious looks. No light anywhere. All the windows are dark. The streets: almost deserted.

The narrator seems in full command of his description. A quasi-divine eye surveys the whole town and describes the darkness everywhere, in every window, without exception. The details given are not arbitrary. The comparison of nightfall to "the heavy fist of a malefactor" prepares us for the most satisfying of literary events: a crime perpetrated under the cover of darkness, a mystery waiting to be explained. The ants encircling the cemetery and the dogs "with anxious looks" reinforce the reader's sense of anticipation: something strange is afoot, something is about to happen. The scene is pregnant with anticipated meanings; we are drawn into the narrative by its promise of an imminent event. In short, we have here a classic beginning to a novel—reminiscent of Roquentin's parody in Sartre's *La Nausée*. "'It was night, the street was deserted.' The phrase is proffered causally, it seems superfluous; but we aren't deceived and we put it to one side: it's a piece of information of which we will understand the value by what follows. And we have the impression that the hero experienced all the details of that night like forewarnings, like promises, or even that he experienced only those which were promises, deaf and blind to everything that didn't announce the coming adventure."

The opening paragraph of *La Ville de la chance* is rich with such promise. This is no disconnected assortment of facts, but the preparation of an event, the advent of meaning. As "old Martha, the accredited drunkard of the community" begins her drunken dance, the narrative raises its stakes to a universal level of meaning, which unites protagonist and audience in the same joyful anticipation of significance: "Happy, she performs before the universe, as if before an audience, her mirror."

This opening is followed, however, by what I call a textual stutter, as we realize that the first paragraph was a false start:

> —What did you say?

> Michael opened his eyes. The voice was that of a man who did not live in the town. It brought no memory, no richness.
>
> —Nothing [*Rien*], he said. I said nothing [*Je n'ai rien dit*].
>
> He returned to his images.

The first paragraph turns out to have been only masquerading as narration. The present tense ("All the windows are dark") does not correspond to any observed reality contemporaneous with the time of description. Michael's mind is wandering, and the narrator's command over his material is now revealed as a deception. Michael's "I said nothing" describes what the text itself is doing as it undercuts the validity of its own utterances. What the text has said—its first paragraph—is shown to be *rien* (nothing): the description of something that does not exist.

One of the characteristics of modern self-conscious literature is its tendency to foreground disjunctions between intention, utterance, and world. A clear example of this is given in the final lines of Beckett's *Molloy*, which draw attention to the conscious falsehood of fiction: "Then I returned home and I wrote: It is midnight. The rain is lashing the windows. It was not midnight. It was not raining." The opening paragraphs of *La Ville de la chance* adopt the same self-canceling effect as the passage from Beckett, though it is more elaborately and deceptively prepared. The text speaks, but then declares that it has said nothing to an understandably confused interrogator-reader. The text is an infelicitous speech act aware of its infelicity. As Michael returns to his imagination ("He returned to his images,"), the description acquires an apocalyptic dimension: "It was as if it were [*On dirait*, literally: One would say] the end of the world." The condition implied in "On dirait" is fulfilled in the same sentence: as the text suggests that one *might* say "the end of the world," it *does* indeed say it, but this realization of its own prophecy is trivially linguistic rather than properly apocalyptic. And this again provokes the disclosure that the text has nothing to say:

> It was as if it were the end of the world.
>
> —What did you say?
>
> —Nothing, replied Michael. I said nothing.
>
> —I heard you mutter something.
>
> —I said it was the end of the world.

Michael's "I said nothing" is reflected in the course of *La Ville de la chance* in a range of similar formulations. For example, when Michael meets his friend Meir:

> —What are you going to tell me now?
> —Nothing, Meir. Nothing. I said nothing.

Later, when he meets Meir again:

> —How did you get in this state? said Meir. Tell me.
> —There is nothing to tell.

In a story recounted by Michael about a man hiding Jews from the Germans in the back of a cart:

> "What are you hiding under the hay?"
> "Nothing. Nothing at all. I swear to you. I have nothing to hide."

And in the surprise of an interrogating officer at Michael's refusal to speak when he has nothing to say:

> —The idiot, said the colonel. To keep silent, to play the hero, when you have nothing to say, what an imbecile.

A humorous version of this "nothing to say" occurs in the episode describing Michael's short-lived career as a smuggler. On the outward trip Michael is so terrified by the customs officer's question "Anything [*Rien*] to declare?" that Meir decides to send him back without contraband. On the return journey Michael discovers the joy of the smuggler who has nothing to declare:

> Michael returned the following day. At the frontier, when the customs officer asked him what he had to declare, Michael retorted, with a smile, in a proud and loud voice:
> —Nothing, sir. Nothing at all!

"I said nothing," "nothing to recount," "nothing to hide," "nothing to say," "nothing to declare": the response to the question is "rien," nothing, the absence of substantive reply. This is reminiscent of the journalist's "five hundred words to say nothing" at the beginning of *Le Jour*. And on a more somber note, it is also reflected in Michael's reaction to the death of his father:

> —Tell me, Yankel, what was I doing whilst my father was dying?

—I've just told you. Nothing. You did nothing. You watched.

This repeated insistence that there is "nothing to say" can be related to the theme of the unanswered question in Wiesel's novel. The importance of the question and the primacy of the question over the answer in Wiesel's writing are well known. At the end of *La Ville de la chance* we are given the clearest expression of Wiesel's thinking on the subject: "The essence of man is to question and the essence of the question is to be without answer." The ontological openness of the question is crucial to what I would call the "official" Wiesel: it brings with it a moral commitment to enquiry, reflection, and receptivity to others. However, in the main part of *La Ville de la chance* the theme of the unanswered question does not have the moral and intellectual respectability that this account would give it. Indeed, the unanswered question forms a disruptive countertext to the ethical thrust of the novel. It marks the refusal to answer, the interruption, deferment, or avoidance of dialogue. Pedro is able "to elude all questions concerning his identity," and Michael also "skillfully eluded" questions. Numerous other examples could be quoted from *La Ville de la chance*, illustrating the prohibition on questions: "It is forbidden to ask questions." The most sustained passage that highlights this theme is the nondialogue between Michael and Yankel:

> —You haven't answered me! said Yankel.
> —What did you say?
> —I asked you a question.
> —A question? What was it?
> —You didn't listen to me.
> —Yes, Yankel. I did pay attention. I didn't hear everything, but I did listen to you.
> —Why don't you answer me then? [. . .]
>
> —. . . How can you speak like that? After all that you did for my father? Do you think that I've forgotten?
> Yankel left the question unanswered. [. . .]
> —Do you remember Karl? said the boy very gently [. . .] It was Michael's turn to leave the question hanging in the air.

The deferred question—suppressed by the questioner or eluded by the addressee—indicates, in opposition to Wiesel's "official" stance, the impulse to hide, to guard one's own secrets, to reject narrative ("—Recount, he said simply. /—No. Not now. Not yet,") as Azriel does at the beginning of *Le Serment de Kolvillàg*:

> I will not speak, said the old man. What I have to say, I do not want to say it.

The deferment of unwelcome revelations is a crucial aspect of Wiesel's fiction. His texts withdraw into themselves, using their exclusion from the felicity of successful speech acts to disclose an essential secretiveness within the urge to write. Once again it is worth recalling Wiesel's assertion that "the better the story is, the more it seems clothed. The secret must remain in a pure state." Wiesel seems actually to value the secretiveness of the text above its potential for revelation; and the emphasis on the withholding of secrets constitutes a disruptive countertext to the ethical conversion recounted in *La Ville de la chance*.

The difference versions of Michael's "I said nothing," as well as the unanswered, unasked, forgotten, or eluded questions that fill the text, suggest an evasive aloofness from humanist ethics; and this indifference to the ethical concerns that seem so urgent to Wiesel himself (to judge from his nonliterary texts) is reflected in *La Ville de la chance* by the moral neutrality of the man who witnessed the deportation of the Jews from Szerencsevàros. Not surprisingly *le Témoin* (the Witness) is characterized by his negations and the repeated "rien" (nothing) that recalls Michael's "I said nothing":

> —I remember.
> —With shame?
> —No.
> —With remorse?
> —No.
> —With sadness?
> —Not that either. With nothing at all. It's a memory that is associated with no emotion.
> I leaned forward slightly.
> —What did you feel?
> —Nothing.
> The muscles in my face were tightening:
> —Outside, children were dying of thirst: what did you feel?
> —Nothing.
> —Outside, men turned away their eyes to avoid seeing their children writhing in pain: what did you feel?
> —Nothing.
> A silence, then:
> —Absolutely nothing. My wife was crying in the kitchen. Not me. She was sad and depressed. Not me.

Michael discovers that his purpose in returning to his hometown was to confront the witness. This turns out to entail an element of self-confrontation, since the "nothing" of the witness is an uncanny reflection of Michael's "I said nothing." And this may also reflect the moral neutrality of literature, which Michael's ethical conversion at the end of the novel attempts to mute, but which reemerges through the excess of meaning in the text. The witness here is not the survivor-witness of Wiesel's nonfictional writings, on whom it is incumbent to preserve and transmit memories of atrocity. He is, on the contrary, an entirely indifferent figure, characterized by negation, signaling the temptation of indifference by which Wiesel's fiction is fascinated, even while it attempts to elude or condemn it. Wiesel's committed literature—like that of his prominent literary forebears in the French tradition, Malraux, Sartre, and Camus—can perhaps be characterized by the tension between the desire for an art freed from moral constraints and the need to resist such a desire. The witness rejects the moral concerns of Wiesel's text; so, in staging the confrontation between Michael and the witness, *La Ville de la chance* also confronts and gives voice to the obverse of its own ethical imperative:

> The witness eludes us completely. He sees without being seen. He is there without being conspicuous. The lights protect him. He does not applaud, does not protest: his presence is evasive, it commits him less than his absence. He says neither yes nor no, nor perhaps. He says nothing [*Il ne dit rien*]. He is there, but he acts as if he weren't there. Worse: he acts as if we weren't there.

Wiesel's text pursues a prolonged and partly concealed meditation on the "nothing" of the witness as it discloses and explores his ambiguous, uncommitted stance. Ambiguity is depicted as both fascinating and dangerous: a thematic illustration of this is provided by the establishment and disruption of barriers and oppositions in the novel. As a child, Michael is intrigued by the bond between his father, a rationalist and humanist, and Moishe the Madman: "The young boy had never fully understood the bond between these two men, one of whom believed only in the power of reason, whilst the other refused all clarity." This bond between opposites is reflected in the marriage of Michael's parents:

> They are strange, my parents: my mother is a fervent follower of the Hassidic movement. Her actions and thoughts are devoted to God. My father is a worshipper of reason. He spends his time putting everything into question.

Michael observes a link between clearly differentiated positions: madness and reason, religion and skepticism. The boundaries appear distinct, but Michael is put in an intermediary position, simultaneously drawn to both poles of the opposition as those poles are also drawn to one another. Michael's role is to reconcile opposites and to become the living embodiment of the bond between conflicting positions. He mediates between the inclinations of his parents in his choice of a future course of study: "To make peace between them, I promised them that I would study both philosophy and religion." On a more theological level God is also characterized by Michael's father as the paradoxical mediation between opposites: "God is God because he is a link [*trait d'union*]: between things and beings, between the heart and the soul, between good and evil, between the past and the future." The keyword here is *entre* (between), repeated four times in the sentence: God is between, he is defined by his in-betweenness. If Michael is to succeed in his role as mediator, he must—like God—become the "link" that makes possible the union of opposites.

Opposites, however, remain separate despite the bond that keeps them together. The importance of separation is foregrounded in the theme of the wall, which is acknowledged in the English translation of Wiesel's novel as *The Town Beyond the Wall. Mur* (wall) and related words—*muraille, clôture, rempart, rideau*—appear frequently in *La Ville de la chance* with a variety of literal and nonliteral senses. *Mur* refers to the wall by which Michael stands while being tortured, the wall that separates the vision of the madman from that of the sane, the barrier between man and God, a barrier between men. *Muraille* has this latter sense, and it also refers to the boundary between madness and sanity. *Remparts* must be overcome for mankind to liberate its free will and conquer death; and Western and Eastern Europe are separated by a *rideau de fer* (iron curtain). The barrier separates, but also marks the proximity of what is kept apart. And the barrier invites transgression. Michael crosses the iron curtain illegally in order to return to Hungary; he is tempted to cross the boundary between sanity and madness; and he attempts to break down the wall between himself and *le Silencieux*.

This transgression of boundaries also involves disobedience. As a boy, Michael becomes intrigued by Vàrady, an ancient neighbor toward whom Michael's parents exhibit an unexplained hostility. They refuse to answer the boy's questions concerning the old man, and the prohibition that they set up ("What is the meaning of this prohibition, of this mystery?") is described as a protective wall: "the wall that his parents raised to protect him from the old man." The prohibition is compounded by the literal *clôture* that separates Vàrady's garden from that of Michael's parents:

> Vàrady lived in the next house. The two gardens were separated by a wooden fence [clôture]. Varady's property was declared a "forbidden zone" for the young boy.

Obedience to the parents would involve respect for the barriers, both literal and metaphorical; Michael's disobedience involves the breaking of the fence that separates the forbidden garden from his own. Michael sees the old man "through the gap in the dividing fence," and Wiesel's text emphasizes the relationship between crime, destruction, and the crossing of boundaries: "His heart beating like a thief, he removed the nails from a plank, forced an opening and slid through to the other side of the fence [*de l'autre côté de la clôture*]." The phrase "de la'autre côté de la clôture" has resonances that exceed its literal meaning in the context of Michael's crossing into the forbidden garden. Michael is acting out a version of the Talmudic story, frequently mentioned in Wiesel's writing, of the four sages who enter the garden of esoteric knowledge. Only one of the sages leaves the garden with his faith intact; and Michael, through his conversations with Vàrady, is reminded of Elisha ben Avuya, who lost faith in the garden, and whose name recalls that of the narrator of *L'Aube*.

The encounter with Vàrady entails, then, at least three transgressions: Michael disobeys his parents, breaks through the *clôture* into the forbidden garden, and faces a trial in which the desire for knowledge endangers both faith and reason. Vàrady, however, does not sanction these transgressions; on the contrary, he alerts Michael to the dangers involved in the confusion of what should be separate. Vàrady's use of the phrase "de l'autre côté de la cloture" (which was first used to describe Michael's entry into the garden) underlines its symbolic significance; and Vàrady denies the viability of Michael's desire to make peace between his mother's faith and his father's doubt:

> —It's dangerous, the old man repeated. To swear loyalty to light and to darkness, that's cheating. There are not several paths that lead to the truth. For each man, there is only one. In this sense, the atheist is like the mystic: both go right to their goal without turning aside. Of course, at the end they come together. But if their paths cross in the middle, they risk destroying each other. You can't be both inside and outside. Man is too weak, his imagination is too poor to enter the garden and remain at the same time on the other side of the fence [*de l'autre côté de la clôture*]. I know what I'm talking about . . .

According to Vàrady, Michael cannot be both *dedans* (inside) and *dehors* (outside); there is no deconstructed position outside the binary opposition. The *clôture* can be crossed or transgressed, but not abolished; and the transgression of barriers involves danger, not erasure.

Michael occupies an intermediary position between religion and doubt, faith and reason, past and present, madness and sanity; but this in-betweenness is qualified by Vàrady as untenable, even dangerous. Michael must occupy one pole of the opposition or the other, there is no third option; so his in-betweenness is manifested as instability, a continual changing of positions, rather than the consistent espousal of a fixed third position. The desire to reconcile opposites falters, as the young Michael studies Kabbalistic mysticism in defiance of his father's authority: "Michael had to overcome strong opposition from his father in order to join the disciples of Kalman." One option triumphs over another, but only temporarily. The German occupation of Hungary puts an end to Michael's mystical endeavor: "Michael left his master." This also saves him for the first time from the path of madness in that he does not follow the same route as his two fellow students. (The text comments, somewhat ironically, "The Germans saved him.") Nevertheless, the temptation of madness remains, and the text adopts an array of shifting attitudes. Confronted with the madwoman Martha, Michael feels the draw of madness: "There is no reason not to follow her into madness." After the death of Yankel, he is tempted but refuses to succumb: "I resisted, I said no."

In prison he begins to lose his sanity: "Michael could feel his reason dying away." He seems inclined to give in to madness: "Go mad: why not?" He recovers his lucidity through his attempts to save *le Silencieux*, but the need of the novel leaves him, perhaps, on the point of succumbing again to the temptation of madness: "Michael was reaching the limit of his strength."

The alternations of temptation and resistance are accompanied by shifting views of the relationship between madness and freedom. At one moment madness appears as the negation of freedom: "A free act that destroys freedom"; but later it appears as a route to freedom: "For Michael, madness always represented a doorway into a forest, into freedom where everything is allowed and possible." This view is in turn contradicted shortly afterward: "It is wrong to see freedom only in madness: liberation, yes; freedom, no." *La Ville de la chance* constantly adopts different positions; and if at the end of the novel Michael seems to choose reason over madness, there is no ground for thinking that this choice could or should be definitive. The conclusiveness of the ending is made precarious by the unease and instability that have characterized the text up to this point. The desire, at the final moment, to arrive at firm conclusions is resisted by the constant fluctuations in the preceding narrative and, as I argue, by the persistence of ambiguity in the final pages of the novel.

The madness/reason opposition has a particular importance in respect to the necessity of choosing between contradictory positions. Madness is not simply the radical alternative to reason, because—once its attraction has been felt—it threatens to invade reason and undermine the certainties of the rational subject. Madness is the extreme pole of an opposition that threatens to negate the very existence of its opposite; it confounds the categories upon which reason relies. So, the fear of the spread of madness comes to haunt Wiesel's novel, taking the form of an anxiety over the limits of madness and the possibility of distinguishing with confidence where madness begins and ends. (I discuss this further in chapter 4). The anxiety is first expressed when it occurs to Michael that Moishe the Madman may not be mad:

> That's his secret, Michael thought. He isn't mad. But in that case, the others are. And what about me, then? Who am I: Moishe or the others?

Someone who believed himself to be rational could not know that he was mad; hence, the crucial question: "—Are you sure that you are not already mad?" And once this doubt has been raised, nothing is preserved from the spread of madness:

> I have the impression that the whole universe has gone mad. Here and everywhere.

Vàrady expresses the necessity of choosing between opposites, of being either inside or outside, but not both. Madness, however, confuses oppositions and distinctions, and thereby threatens the possibility of choice. It also endangers the values that *La Ville de la chance* attempts to establish. Moishe insists that nothing is genuine; madness corrodes value as it proclaims the falsehood of everything, including itself. There is only falsehood, with no reassuring polar opposite:

> —I am not happy, he exclaimed in fury as he threw the bottle against the wall. Wine brings no joy to my heart. What is written in books is false! Just like wine! Wine is also false! Just like the heart! The heart is false as well!
>
> Suddenly, tears began to flow and disappeared into his dense beard.
>
> —You, he said, you, you know nothing. You are too small. Too young. Me, I know. I am mad and in this low world only the mad know. They know that everything is false. Wine is false, the heart is false, tears are false. And perhaps the mad are also false.

Madness confuses and confounds; the madman describes a universal falsehood that sits uneasily with those aspects of Wiesel's novel that attempt to establish positive values and the possibility of meaningful ethical conversion. The text resists madness, as does Michael. Moishe is described as someone who "refused all clarity," whereas, in his hometown, Michael experiences a revelation that seems to make sense of his return: "Everything became clear, laid bare." Nevertheless, *La Ville de la chance* does not entirely cast off the temptation of madness. The form of the novel is itself influenced by the instability and confusion that endanger the rationalist's desire for clear boundaries.

The deliberate strategies of confusion adopted on the opening page of the novel continue as the text shifts between different time periods in a way that is calculated to disorientate. Indeed, readers are warned from the beginning of the novel of the effect that this is likely to have:

> How many hours have already passed? These leaps from one world to another have killed all notion of time. No longer any reference point [*point de repère*].

The novel exploits the disorientation and ultimately tries to overcome it by a gesture of regrounding: the foundation of ethical action "on the fragile terrain of the human." However, it is no coincidence that Moishe includes the written text in his account of universal falsehood: "What is written in books is false." *La Ville de la chance* is haunted (but perhaps also made possible) by the knowledge that literature belongs to the realm of the inauthentic, neither témoignage, nor history, it discloses the emptiness of its language by qualifying its own statements as "nothing": "I said nothing." The text is drawn to and horrified by madness, which represents the freedom to say anything, but also the knowledge that nothing will be taken as true. This madness endangers the ability of Wiesel's text to make even straightforward affirmations:

> Is Yankel still there? Yes. Has he left? Yes. He is there and he is not there.

La Ville de la chance is, then, a crucial novel for Wiesel: the tensions inherent in his earlier writing emerge with an insistence that cannot be overlooked. From the coherent narrative of experiences that undermine coherence in *La Nuit*, *L'Aube*, and *Le Jour*, Wiesel comes closer to a mode of writing that matches his subject: the collapse of the intelligible world narrated in an ambiguous text. Wiesel withdraws from the full consequences of this by giving his novel a "conclusion" that appears to resolve some of the preceding confusions. But Wiesel is now approaching his mature aesthetic, as the thematic failure of understanding is mimicked by an ambiguous practice of writing that exposes the reader more directly to the incoherences of the text.

ORA AVNI

Beyond Psychoanalysis: Elie Wiesel's Night *in Historical Perspective*

Night is the story of a young boy's journey through hell, as he is taken first to a ghetto, and then to Auschwitz and Buchenwald. It is a story of survival and of death: survival of the young narrator himself, but death of the world as he knew it. It is therefore a negative *Bildungsroman*, in which the character does not end up, as expected, fit for life in society, but on the contrary, a living dead, unfit for life as defined by his community.

Its opening focuses not so much on the boy, however, as on a foreigner, Moshe the Beadle, a wretched yet good-natured and lovable dreamer, versed in Jewish mysticism. When the town's foreign Jews are deported by the Nazis to an unknown destination, he leaves with them; but he comes back. Having miraculously survived the murder of his convoy, he hurries back to warn the others. No longer singing, humming, or praying, he plods from door to door, desperately repeating the same stories of calm and dispassionate killings. But, despite his unrelenting efforts, "people refused not only to believe his stories, but even to listen to them."

Like Moshe the Beadle, the first survivors who told their stories either to other Jews or to the world were usually met with disbelief. When the first escapees from Ponar's killing grounds tried to warn the Vilna ghetto that they were not sent to work but to be murdered, not only did the Jews not believe them, but they accused the survivors of demoralizing the ghetto, and

From *Auschwitz and After: Race, Culture, and "the Jewish Question" in France*. © 1995 by Routledge Inc.

demanded that they stop spreading such stories. Similarly, when Jan Karski, the courier of the Polish government-in-exile who had smuggled himself into the Warsaw Ghetto so that he could report the Nazis' atrocities as an eyewitness, made his report to Justice Felix Frankfurter, the latter simply said, "I don't believe you." Asked to explain, he added, "I did not say that this young man is lying. I said I cannot believe him. There is a difference." How are we to understand this disbelief? What are its causes and effects, and above all, what lesson can we learn from it.

Shoah Narratives and the Scene of Narration

In this episode, the actual tales of Nazi atrocities occupy only a fraction of the narrative. Most of the section deals with Moshe the Beadle's easy manners and deep faith *before* his ordeal, and his desperate and obsessive storytelling *after* his return. This section mirrors the narrator's account in reverse: while the boy's account of his adventure is the actual story of death and survival with no "before" or "after," the opening section calls our attention precisely to the difference between "before" and "after," when after means both *after the event* and *after the telling of the event.* It thus steers us towards the scene of narration (all but absent from the main story of the boy's experience), that is, not only *what* actually and factually happened, but *how it affects* those who come in contact with the story of what happened. In so doing, it moves us towards the scene of narration of all *Shoah* narratives, towards the effects these narratives had and still have on their readers and listeners, and, in turn, towards the narrator's reaction to these effects. We may thus say that the opening episode of *Night* stages the performing or performative aspects of survivors' narratives, their effectiveness, and the consequences they may entail.

We must also note that Moshe the Beadle's narrative does not only *open* the boy's narrative as it first appears, but frames it on both ends: once the reader is aware of the consequences of telling such a story, he or she extends this awareness to the story told by the boy. The opening episode thus invites the reader to read beyond the abrupt end of *Night*, all the way to the moment absent from *Night* proper, when the newly freed boy tells his own tale of survival: will this story, too, meet with hostility, disbelief, and denial? (And who better than the reader knows that the boy did eventually tell his story, and that this tale constitutes the very text he or she is reading?) The scene of narration of the opening episode thus prefigures the scene of reading of *Night.* It is a pessimistic *mise en abyme* of the novel's scene of reading; as such, it warns the reader of the consequences of disbelief no less than it warns the town folks.

Shoah narratives have given rise to a host of false problems. Faced with the horror of the *Shoah* and the suffering of its survivors, some have felt overwhelmed and, overcome with a sense of simple human decency, have questioned their right to examine an extreme experience in which they had no part. These scruples are, I think, misplaced: no one questions the right, or even the need of survivors to sort out their experience, or to bear witness. We readily concede survivors' wish and right to bear witness, to leave a historical account of their ordeal for posterity. But what about this posterity (ourselves), what about the recipients of those narratives? We—the latecomers to the experience of the *Shoah*—shall never be able to fully grasp the abysmal suffering and despair of the survivors. And yet, not only do we share with them a scene of narration, but our participation in this scene of narration may have become the organizing principle of our lives and our own historical imperative. How, then, are we going to face up to this task? Like the town folks, we have gone through disbelief and denial. But today, two generations later, we have rediscovered the *Shoah*, as the numerous publications on the subject will attest (some even claim that we have trivialized the *Shoah* with excessive verbiage). How, then, are we to dispose of the knowledge conveyed by survivors' narratives? How can we integrate the lesson of their testimonies in our historical project—at least, if ours is a project in which there is no room for racial discrimination, genocide, acquiescence to evil, passive participation in mass murder; a project in which "get involved" has come to replace "look the other way"?

Wiesel often mentions Moshe the Beadle in other works. Invariably he insists on Moshe's need to commune with the town folks. In *One Generation After*, for example, Wiesel writes that upon his return, Moshe:

> was unrecognizable: gone were his gentleness, his shyness. Impatient, irascible, he now wore the mysterious face of a messenger pursued by those whose message he carried. He who used to stutter whenever he had to say a single word, suddenly began to speak. He talked and talked without pity for either his listeners or himself . . . he alone survived. Why? So that he could come back to his town and tell the tale. And that is why he never stopped talking. But his audiences, weary and naïve, would not, could not believe. People said: Poor beadle, he has lost his mind. Finally he understood; and fell silent. Only his burning eyes reveal the impotent rage inside him. His muteness bordered on madness.

On the one hand, Moshe's distress is undoubtedly Wiesel's. Like Moshe, Wiesel came back; like Moshe, he told his story; and like Moshe, he told it again and again. It is therefore not merely a question of informing others (for information purposes, once the story is told, one need not tell it again). Like Moshe, Wiesel clearly does not set out to impart information only, but to tell the tale, that is, to share a scene of narration with a community of readers. This explains why, while the *Shoah* is in fact the subject of all his texts, Wiesel, wiser than Moshe, never recounted his actual experience in the death camps again. Like the opening episode of *Night*, his other works deal with "before" and "after": before, as a premonition of things to come; after, as a call for latecomers to see themselves accountable for living in a post-*Shoah* world. The opening episode thus encapsulates Wiesel's life project, in that it invites us to reflect not only on the nature of the *Shoah* itself, but first, on living historically (that is, on living in a world of which the *Shoah* is part), and second, on transmitting this history from one person and one generation to the other.

I suggest therefore that we read the first episode for its exemplary value, as a beacon guiding our reading from the horror of the past to the imperatives of the present, all the while illuminating the Charybdis and Scylla of *Shoah* narratives: excessive distrust, as well as easy empathy; resentment of those who cannot let bygones be bygones, as well as a morbid and voyeuristic obsession with *Shoah* details; impatience with survivors' pain, as well as glib recognition of the alienating effect of the survivors' experience that frees us from partaking in their burden; an excessively inclusive approach that leads to an undiscriminating identification with *Shoah* participants ("We are all German Jews" of Cohn-Bendit), as well as excessive exclusiveness that frees all non-Jews (or even post-*Shoah* Jews) from deeming the *Shoah* experience relevant to one's being–in-the-world today; trivializing the *Shoah* with a host of comparisons, as well as insisting on its uniqueness so much that it becomes alien and irrelevant to our reality.

To what, then, does this episode owe its exemplary value? Why has Moshe, the ultimate *Shoah* survivor-narrator, come back? Why does he feel compelled to endlessly repeat his story? Why does he no longer pray? On the other hand, why are his listeners so recalcitrant? Why do they not believe him? Why do they accuse him of madness or of ulterior motives? Why do they all but gag him? That this episode illustrates widespread attitudes towards all accounts of Nazi atrocities and Jewish victimization is unquestionable. We shall therefore focus on the *self-positioning* of the subject (teller or listener, knowledgeable or uninformed) in the face of accounts of the *Shoah*, be it at the dinner table, in the classroom, on the psychoanalyst's couch, in academe, or in the morning paper. It is at once a positioning vis-à-vis one's self, one's interlocutors, and one's community.

Therapeutic explanations

Attempts to account for failed communication of survivors' experience follow roughly two major lines, the first psychotherapeutic, the second cognitive. Among the first, we can cite collections of case studies of survivors who went through some form of extended therapy and, perhaps more interestingly for our purpose, of similar case studies to their children. The problems may vary from case to case, but certain themes prevail: denial, fear, survivor's guilt, psychic numbing, derealization, depersonalization, paranoid attitudes, shock, identification either with a lost loved one or with the perpetrators, inability to mourn. These analyses are predicated on a strong belief in the healing virtue of therapy and in its ability to resolve the post-*Shoah* anxieties. In a now-classic collection of such case studies, the writer-editors state:

> Elie Wiesel has repeatedly stated that survivors of the Holocaust live in a nightmare world that can never be understood. Although his opinion has its stark and bitter truth, *we believe that the nightmare can be dispelled*; that, through words, analysis can penetrate the shadowy inner world of the patient, which operates in metaphor, and, *by illuminating it, diminish pain, and heal.* Furthermore, analysis can demonstrate *how* the tragedy of one generation may be transmitted to the next, and then *break the chain of suffering.*

I doubt that healing the victims or their children will heal the wound inflicted on our vision of man and society. The *Shoah* has shaken our vision of man so profoundly that, half a century later, we are still grappling with its aftermath, with our urgent albeit terrifying need for a radical reevaluation of our concept of man-in-the-world. And, as the reluctance to believe the stories or even to listen to them shows, this reevaluation does not befall only those who were the subjects of the event or their children (victims, perpetrators, or even bystanders). It extends to an entire generation. As Terence des Pres rightly notes, "the self's sense of itself is different now, and what has made the difference, both as cause and continuing condition, is simply knowing that the Holocaust occurred." There is no denying that this "difference" may take the various forms inventoried by psychoanalysts—but it would be a mistake to reduce the aftermath of the *Shoah* to those forms alone.

I shall therefore focus on approaches that do not regard the survivor in the privacy and intimacy of his or her personal experience only, but contextualize this experience in a community (and its modes of representation), in a narrative, and in a multi-generational culture. Now, since clinical therapy deals mostly with individuals, few therapists have adopted this path, and even fewer have done so with either rigor or consistency. Among the most interesting, and the most representative of the strengths and the limitations of individual therapy, I shall briefly mention two essays, one by Dori Laub and Nanette Auerhann, and the other by Martin Wangh.

Laub and Auerhann focus on the second generation—but on children of people not directly affected by the *Shoah*, Jews and non-Jews alike. They make two points: The first is that the *Shoah* has provided a handy metaphor, a linguistic mold subsequently used by patients to couch their non-*Shoah* related hostilities and violence. The second point goes further, in that it suggests that the patient cannot help but notice that his so-called metaphor is in fact quite literal: it denotes a past reality. This unavoidable literalization of the metaphor then grafts an external referent onto an internal conflict. Furthermore, in using such a metaphor, the patient (who is after all the author of the fantasized violence) finds himself identified with the Nazi perpetrators and, consequently, guilty of much more serious crimes than he would have been, had he used a more literal language to describe his limited experience.

We may wish to infer from these two points that the cumulative effect of *Shoah* narratives, its historic and referential effect on the representations by which a community defines itself, is such that not only would it determine the linguistic and cognitive tools available to the patient, but, going beyond the patient's personal experience, it would impose on his experience a different referent which it would force him to appropriate, thus invading the space of his subjectivity and robbing him of what was previously his own experience or fantasy. The patient would thus be projected outside his own life narrative into a different one, shared by his community; but one in which he would play a role at which he balks (since it exceeds his fantasies) and, more importantly, into one in which he could no longer recognize himself or his fantasy. Ultimately, the *Shoah* metaphor would become a wedge driven into the relationships that constitute the conscious self, threatening to split the neatly bundled relationships on which the self is built: first, between the patient and his community, and second, within the subject himself, by substituting the *Shoah* narrative (and its terrifying effects) for the patient's experience (or fantasy) of limited violence.

At this point however, that is, at the point in which they might have drawn the conclusions I have just suggested regarding the relationship between the individual and the historico-cognitive and linguistic molds through which that individual lives his inner experience and couches its expression, the authors stop short of examining the social and philosophical implications of their analysis and, shunning generalizations that might take them beyond the four walls of their offices and the pragmatics of their trade, prudently withdraw to the safety of their clinical experience:

> Our point of view is no way intended to replace the centrality of psychic reality or of psychosexual developmental themes. Rather, our purpose is to supplement them *by acknowledging* the significance and permanence of the permeating metaphors and images in which these themes are couched and take shape in the post-Holocaust era. It is to appreciate, too, the extent to which reality may confirm fantasy and to *recognize* that whenever fantasy is given reality reference, an *acknowledgment* of the reality is required before one can analyze its use as defense. If such *acknowledgment* does not take place—that is, if profound, conflict-laden perceptions of the patient are ignored or regarded as fantasy only—then the patient will feel that his sense of reality is assaulted. He will need to protect himself from feeling crazy by closing off communication and insight all together.

The individuated cognitive approach suggested here—unorthodox as it may be from a strictly Freudian viewpoint—still falls short of addressing the collective dimension of the problem: "acknowledging" in the privacy of one's confrontation with one's self or one's analyst hardly suffices when the root of the problem is not the self but the *dynamics* between the self (already partly constructed through its interaction with others) and its community (or its community's narratives).

Wangh's essay goes Laub and Auerhann one better, in that it does not stop at patients in treatment, but attempts to sketch a broader social pattern. Like Laub and Auerhann, Wangh does not limit his study to *Shoah* survivors: since Nazi atrocities are public knowledge, since they constitute a chapter of our shared stories and history, since, today, we have to integrate that knowledge into this shared history in and by which we define our social and ethical selves, the conflicts of those who were directly affected and of those who were not "differ only in magnitude." Like Laub and Auerhann again,

Wangh points out that the past pervades the present, and that, unless its effects are properly worked through, it may surreptitiously confuse present stimuli with the past trauma. Eventually, writes Wangh, "crises may spring from judgments that were correct for past experience but which, applied in the here and now, impede clear sight of present reality."

Unlike Laub and Auerhann, however, Wangh does not stop at case studies, at patients in need of a cure. The kind of "working through" he recommends does not befall a few deviant individuals only, prime candidates for the analyst's couch. It applies to a whole culture: the *Shoah* was an event of such magnitude that we all need to work through the shattering of our values and our world. The task is difficult, however, since the intensity of the trauma is such that any subsequent violence is perceived and reacted to in terms of the past, as if it were a reenactment of the initial horror. Hence, whereas the passing of time is normally beneficial, in this case, the present's misperceptions perpetuate the lingering pain of the past and exacerbate all-too-real anxieties. If working through is the solution to this catch-22, what, then, should this working through consist of?

In comparison to the complexity of his analysis, Wangh's solution is surprisingly simple:

> For any kind of curative relief that aims at keeping a rational stance in an irrational world, the sensitizing past trauma *together* with the stimulating present-day residue have to be simultaneously lifted into full consciousness, and separated out from each other.

In other words, he adds a pragmatic, quasi-behaviorist twist to the cognitive approach advocated by Laub and Auerhann: once we become aware of the pervasiveness of the past, we should be able to keep past- and present-related affects distinct, and to impose some order on our chaotic world. Therapy is, of course, privileged ground for the recommended "lifting into full consciousness" and "separation" of the intertwined time sequences, but it is not the only one. The classroom is another: "The nexus of past-present sequences, their facts and affects, should be taught as a basic sociological principle from every cathedra in history, philosophy, and political science and conveyed from every pulpit. Eventually, this teaching would thus reach everyone: "the psychohistorian hopes that such knowledge of, and alertness to, this intertwining circuitry [of past and present] can help the social scientist, the people at large and thence the decision-making politician to obtain self-understanding and thus get a clearer vision of present day reality."

I find it surprising that, having convincingly demonstrated the psychoanalytic intertwining of the time sequences, and having given pointed examples illustrating the grasp of the past on the present, Wangh concludes with such a positivist invitation to sort them out. Is it so simple? I doubt that one can put the past to rest simply by labelling it "past." We can no more know the past without seeing it through all the subsequent experiences of our life (all the subsequent "presents"), than we can know the present without submitting it to the lessons of the past: if we did not know from past experience that the sun would rise in the morning, we might be terrified anew by its disappearance every night. The solution is therefore not to separate out the past from the present. Past and present are irremediably intertwined. Whereas Wangh recommends an excessive and unrealistic *analysis*, what we need is a *synthesis*, that is, a balanced integration of past and present, one that projects the lesson of the past on the present, without obfuscating this present. This too, of course, may sound like wishful thinking, but a synthetic approach has at least the advantage of reflecting normal (that is, sometimes successful) processes of assimilation of past into present and vice versa—including all cognitive learning processes—and thus has a better chance of identifying the difficulty when these processes are hampered.

The Subject in History

Our critique of the psychoanalytic approach relies on our view of the subject's self-positioning in history, at once in the privacy of his inner world, in the limited exchange set with one's interlocutor (say, a therapist), and mostly, in the larger context of stories we tell ourselves versus stories into which we are born. The exemplary value of *Night*'s opening episode hinges upon its containing the narrative of the boy, and by extension of any survivor, within the problems raised by this self-positioning.

Prior to his own encounter with Nazism, the boy asks Moshe: "Why are you so anxious that people should believe what you say? In your place, I shouldn't care whether they believe me or not. . . ." Indeed, in comparison with the ordeal from which he has just escaped, there seems to be little reason for Moshe's present distress. What, then, hangs upon the credibility of his story? Why do the town people refuse to listen to the beadle? What effect does their reaction have on the *project* that brought him back to town? Somehow tentatively, Moshe answers the boy's query:

> "You don't understand," he said in despair. "You can't understand. I have been saved miraculously. I managed to get

> back here. Where did I get the strength from? I wanted to come back to Sighet to tell you the story of my death. So that you could prepare yourselves while there was still time. To live? I don't attach any importance to my life any more. I'm alone. No, I wanted to come back, and to warn you. And see how it is, no one will listen to me. . . ."

Moshe's anguished insistence on being heard undoubtedly illustrates the well-known recourse to narrative in order to impose coherence on an incoherent experience (a commonplace of literary criticism), to work through a trauma (a commonplace of psychoanalysis), the laudable drive to testify to a crime (a commonplace of *Shoah* narratives), or even the heroics of saving others (a commonplace of resistance literature). Although such readings of *Night* are certainly not irrelevant, I do not think that they do justice to the gripping urgency of his unwelcome and redundant narrative, unless we read the text literally: Moshe came back "to tell you the story."

We must rule out simply imparting knowledge, since Moshe's undertaking clearly does not stop at communicating the story. A scenario in which the town folks gather around him to listen to his story, and then go on about their business would be absurd. In this case, to "believe" the story is to be affected by it. Moshe's story is therefore a speech act. Allow me an example to clarify this last point: Paul Revere tearing through the countryside and screaming "The British are coming!" His message was immediately understood. No one suspected him of either madness or excessive need of attention. Unlike Moshe and the town folks, and unlike *Shoah* survivors and ourselves, Paul Revere and his New Englanders lived in the same world, a world in which British might and probably would come; a world in which that would be a very bad thing indeed; and a world in which should they come, clear measures must be taken. If the story is to realize its illocutionary force, not only does it have to be integrated into its listeners' stock of "facts they know about their world," but it must also rely on a known formula (a convention) by which an individual reacts to such knowledge. For example, one has to know that if the British are coming, one is expected to arm oneself and prepare for resistance (a clean shave would be a highly inappropriate reaction to Paul Revere's message). Revere could therefore speedily spread his message while never dismounting his horse, and still secure its uptake. In short, to be a felicitous speech act, the story must affect its listeners in an expected, conventional manner (that is, following clear precedents). Until it does, its force is void.

Speech act theorists unanimously agree on the conventional aspect of a speech act, that is, on its reliance on a preexisting convention shared by the community of its listeners. But sometimes, such a precise convention does not exist. It has to be inferred and activated out of the stock of beliefs and conventions that both utterer and listeners find workable, plausible, and altogether acceptable. In invoking their shared beliefs, the felicitous speech act thus becomes a *rallying point* for the utterer and the listeners. It binds them together. A community is therefore as much the *result* of its speech acts as it is the necessary condition for their success. In other words, if, as he claims, Moshe came back to town in order to tell his story, and if indeed he is determined to secure the felicitous uptake of his narrative's illocutionary force, then this determination reveals yet *another project*, one that is even more exacting in that it affects his (and his fellow villagers') being-in-the-world: his return to town is also an attempt to reaffirm his ties to his community (its conventions, its values), to reintegrate into the human community of his past—a community whose integrity was put into question by the absurd, incomprehensible, and unassimilable killings he had witnessed. Through his encounter with Nazism, Moshe has witnessed not only the slaughter of a human cargo, but the demise of his notion of humanity—a notion, however, still shared by the town folks. As long as they hold on to this notion of humanity to which he can no longer adhere, he is, *ipso facto*, a freak. Coming back to town to tell his story to a receptive audience is therefore Moshe's way back to normalcy, back to humanity. Only by having a community integrate his dehumanizing experience into the narratives of self-representation that it shares and infer a new code of behavior based on the information he is imparting, only by becoming part of his community's history, can Moshe hope to reclaim his lost humanity (the question remains, as we shall see, at what price to that community). It is therefore not a question of privately telling the story (to oneself, to one's editor or to one's analyst) as of having others—a whole community—*claim* it, *appropriate* it, and *react* (properly) to it.

The closing scene of *Night* echoes this concern. Upon his liberation by American troops, the narrator first rushes to a mirror to look at himself. Is he still himself? Can the mirror show him unchanged since the last time he looked at himself in the mirror, before he was taken out of his village? Can he reintegrate into himself? Will the mirror allow him to bridge over pain and time, and reach the cathartic recognition that will bracket out the horror of the death camps and open the way for a "normal" life; or will it, on the contrary, irreparably clinch his alienation not only from the world but from the supposed intimacy of his self-knowledge? Like Moshe then, the boy leaves it to a third party (a willing community or a mirror) to mediate between his present and past selves, and cancel out the alienating effect of his brush with inhumanity. Just like the town folks, however, the mirror does not cooperate. Instead of the familiar face that would have reconciled him with his former self (and consequently, with a pre-*Shoah* world), his reflection seals his alienation: "From the depth of the mirror, a corpse gazed back at me. The look in his eyes, as they stared into mine, has never left me."

Night is the story of a repeated dying, at once the death of man and of the *idea* of man. The final recognition never obtains. Instead, the subject is propelled out of himself, out of humanity, out of the world as he knew it. It is a double failure: both Moshe and the boy fail to recover their selves' integrity and to reintegrate into the community of the living; both fail to assimilate the traces left by their experience (either in a narrative or in a physiognomy) into a coherent picture to be accepted by the other(s) they so wish to reach. But the story goes on: *Night* is a first-person narrative. Like Moshe, the boy will try again to reintegrate the human community, this time, by telling his story (and many others). Like all survivors' narratives, *Night* is thus yet another plodding from door to door to solicit listeners, so as to reclaim one's ties to the community of the living by inscribing oneself into its shared narratives.

On Communities

Night's opening episode thus raises two major questions, stretched over the two ends of the communication process: Why did Moshe so desperately need to be listened to; and why do the town folks obtusely refuse to take in his story (at the risk of their lives)? Clearly, something crucial must be at stake for both parties, something that defies storytelling, "lifting to consciousness," or literalized metaphors. Whether we address the question from one end of the scene of narration or from the other, I suggest that the answer is one and the same.

We may approach it through two often-overlooked truisms: on the one hand, whatever horrible trauma an individual may have experienced, he or she remains an individual, no more, no less. That person will retain and exercise all or any of the psychological and psychoanalytic processes by which one normally sorts out experiences or fantasies. So much for the idiosyncratic treatment of psychic traces, however, since, as we have seen, no individual lives in a vacuum. Our second truism is, therefore, that we live in society, that is, we are born into a world in which our options are predetermined and limited: we are born into an already existing language, into social, ethical and legal codes; we are born into a world rife with events, narratives, histories—in short, *memories*—which are as constitutive of our selves as are our fantasies or experiences. Moreover, as education and the media have tightened their grip on our lives, societies have become increasingly permeable to each other; we share more stories, more myths, more histories than ever before. And as Robinson Crusoe illustrates, should we try to escape to a desert island, these social norms are so deeply imprinted on us that we necessarily reproduce the absent society within ourselves and our solitude.

The two truisms I am describing underlie Saussure's well-known distinction between *langue* and *parole*. On the one hand, I am free to choose my expression, my words, my metaphors. Each of my utterances indisputably reflects my free will and psychological profile. On the other hand, however, *langue* is the limit of my personal freedom and expression, since whatever I say will be governed by and limited to what is accepted by the community, that is, determined by the usage of that *langue*. A private language is no language. I am not free to rename objects, for example; nor am I free to change syntax. Or, rather, I am free to do so only within the limits of communicability: despite irregularities and agrammaticalities, I have to retain enough of the lexical and syntactical rules in place in my community to ensure communication. Furthermore, unless my interlocutors plug their ears or turn away from me (which is exactly what the town folks did), my sentence will bridge my subjectivity and theirs: no longer mine alone, it will have become the object of our shared attention. "My" expression is therefore never mine alone. It is "ours." It connects and binds me, first, to my immediate interlocutor, of course, but more importantly, to the community for and in which my language and my utterance are intelligible. Every sentence I utter confirms this bond, just as any historical narrative would confirm my historical bond with my community, and would transform "my" narrative into "our" narrative.

Now, the dynamics of *Night*'s opening episode may be clearer: Moshe and the town folks occupy two opposite ends of a transaction. Moshe wants the community to assimilate his story, to take it in and learn its lesson, in the hope that it will allow him a way out of the unbearable solitude into which his experience has cast him, and bridge over the tear that his encounter with the dispassionate force of evil has introduced in his life. In other words, he wants the agrammaticality of his experience, his odd and deviant *parole*, to become part of their *langue*. The town folk, however, do not want to take up this horror, to make it theirs, to make this story the *rallying point* between themselves and the narrator, since if they did, his burden would become theirs: it would then behoove *them* to mend the tear, and to assimilate an unassimilable experience (an experience that is not, but would become, theirs, should they be forced into a shared scene of narration with Moshe). To integrate Moshe's *parole* into their *langue* would demand such an extensive review of the rules of the *langue* by which they live that it could put its very structure and coherence in question. They would rather risk their lives than tamper with their cognitive framework. Moshe's compulsion can thus be understood only within the dynamics of his interaction with his community, just as the denial of each member of the community can only be understood as an attempt to maintain the integrity of this community.

It is in this respect that psychotherapeutic approaches are the most vulnerable to criticism: by treating the individual who steps into a therapist's office as if the problem were contained in him or her, as if this trauma was merely personal (like any other trauma), as if it did not partake in a whole culture's convulsion and the ensuing need for a cognitive overhaul on a scale unmatched in world history, the therapeutic practice (especially psychoanalysis) risks taking part in yet another variant of the generalized denial illustrated by the town folks. In accepting an individual for treatment, a therapist implicitly recognizes that the burden of dealing with the *Shoah*'s legacy falls upon this individual—otherwise, why should he or she be treated in private? Consequently, this therapist (and his ailing and trusting patient) releases the community (and the historical consciousness of each "normal" individual in this community) from having to alter its shared narratives and representations and from integrating the incompatible lesson (our capacity for indifference, cowardice, stupidity, moral detachment, cruelty, and so on) into its historical project.

Conclusion

It has often been said that *Night* is the gloomy story of a loss for which no solace, no solution is offered. Indeed, "Elie Wiesel has repeatedly stated that survivors of the Holocaust live in a nightmare world that can never be understood. . . ." But it should also be noted that, although *Night* is the only novel in which he dealt directly and explicitly with his experience of the *Shoah*, Wiesel's whole life has been dedicated to its ensuing moral and historical imperatives. Moshe the Beadle (Wiesel's spokesman) thus offers a critique of facile answers to post-*Shoah* difficulties—narrowly individualized answers that, despite their limited usefulness, nonetheless overlook the collective dimension and its impact on the individual's self-positioning. Excessive separateness of past and present is yet another form of repression, another defense mechanism. The historical imperative today is not to "sort out" but, on the contrary, to find a way of *taking in* the reality of industrialized killing, knowing fully that this reality contradicts every aspect of our historical project, everything we would like to believe about ourselves.

To date, we have not resolved this incongruity. If we are to deal with the legacy of the *Shoah*, we must make room in our project for the disturbing truths of the *Shoah*. Our historical imperative is to go beyond this contradiction and to integrate the lesson of the *Shoah* into the coherence of the stories and histories by which we define our sociohistorical project (by "project" I mean the future we wish upon ourselves as a society, and according to which we shape our present perception and representations of ourselves). None of us, therefore, escapes the need to "deal" with the *Shoah*; but none of us can do it alone, or be led to believe that he or she can.

Yes, we want to "heal." Society wants to heal; history wants to heal. But no, a simple "life goes on," "tell your story," "come to terms with your pain," or "sort out your ghosts" will not do. It will not do, because the problem lies not in the individual—survivor or not—but in his or her interaction with society, and more precisely, in his or her relationship to the narratives and values by which this community defines and represents itself. It would be more optimistic, indeed, to think that each hurting person could solve his or her problem privately, with or without a therapist's help, so that the sum of the healed parts will eventually bring about a newly healed whole. Although there is some undeniable value (and sometimes even a measure of success) in attempting to help each part, in attempting to alleviate individual suffering so as to restore a semblance of normalcy (but precisely, "normalcy" is hurting; it is no longer normal), neither "healing" nor "breaking the chain of suffering" will ensue. The *Shoah* legacy remains a case in which the whole does not amount to the neat sum of its parts. A "successful" analysis will still leave the patient to deal with the integration of the lesson of the *Shoah* into the project he or she shares with his or her community. On the whole, despite the laudable optimism of its practitioners, psychotherapy cannot heal the historical, shared dimension of this wound. History is not psychotherapy's proper field of application. This misconception is a moving and tragic testimony to the urge of therapists themselves to wrestle with the evil of the past, and negate the nefarious effects of the *Shoah*; but it misses the historical imperative of our times.

SIMON P. SIBELMAN

Victims to Victors: The Trilogy

Dire l'indicible est presque impossible
—Elie Wiesel

The existence and significance of the *univers concentrationnaire* occupy a central position in the history of the twentieth century. Prior to the rise of Hitler and the creation of his unique hell on earth humanity had never faced such barbarity, depravity, or abject terror where existence was a crime punishable by death. Merely to remember those horrors is not sufficient. As Paul Thibaud believes, we must forge new modes of thought and art to assist in responding to the two most obsessive questions arising from the Holocaust: How did the event occur, and how shall we think and act after the fact? As in a crystal, Auschwitz stands as the focal point through which all facets of contemporary civilization and culture pass. It constitutes the delicate fulcrum on which human history currently shifts. Auschwitz is likewise to be viewed as central to Wiesel's attitudes toward life and philosophy. Moreover, in his earliest novels, Wiesel demonstrates an affinity for the nucleus of preoccupations to which he would subsequently gravitate throughout his career: Silence. Through *La Nuit* (*Night*), his first novel, this event, Auschwitz, encounters the phenomenon of silence, together forming the epicenter of his literary creation.

LA NUIT

The text of *La Nuit* represents the survivor's cautiously painful attempts to set down a record of the horror and incarnate evil that was the *univers concentrationnaire* and about which David Rousset has proposed several interesting notions: "The camps were inspired by the world of Ubu. . . . Camp inmates inhabited a world torn from the imagination of Céline with the haunting obsessions of Kafka." Rousset's proposal suggests a most striking metaphor, for in relating to the reality of the camps, his language fails and he has been obliged to resort to literary references as if they offer the only means by which he can properly hope to define the *univers concentrationnaire.* More explicitly, Rousset alludes to three writers—Jarry, Céline, and Kafka—each of whom presents chilling, nightmarish visions of the world and of humanity. Yet, even allusions to particular literary figures and their deformed view of the world can only approximate the full reality.

Against this phantasmagorical decor, the sixteen-year-old Wiesel witnessed the destruction of the world he had known, that peaceful existence of the Jewish shtetl where the changing seasons had been celebrated by the pious joys of the Jewish holy days and festivals. That unique pre-Holocaust world had undeniably suffered the poverty and deprivation of two millennia of prejudice, pitting against them the light of Jewish life and learning. This distinctive culture had nurtured in Wiesel "a respectful, almost reverential attitude toward language." Neither the traditional strengths nor the word itself could stave off the onslaught of this particular "Night." If one accepts part of A. Alvarez's definition of Judaism "not as a narrow orthodoxy but as a force working perennially on the side of sanity," *La Nuit* would then appear to announce the advent of ungodly insanity.

La Nuit is a *témoignage*, a *document vécu* that mercilessly projects the reader into Hitler's inferno. Eugene Heimler suggests that "you can only create from something which is negative," and it does seem that Wiesel has used the *nihil* of the Holocaust as the generative material for a work that recounts the deportation and destruction of a single Hungarian Jewish community and details the loss of the witness's identity, who is reduced to a physical and spiritual cadaver at the novel's denouement. As shall be demonstrated, this text is written in ever more negative layers of silence.

In *La Nuit*, silence combines with sparse, tautly concise prose in which the naked horrors of the *univers concentrationnaire* infrequently appear, and from which hysteria and disingenuous sentimentality are banished. If the Holocaust as macro- /micro-experience reflecting on the human condition cannot be properly expressed, then one must shroud those unspeakable elements. Wiesel has stated that uttering the ineffable is almost impossible.

His idea elicits a paradox common to Holocaust literature. As noted in the previous chapter, the survivor must bear witness to what has been; yet aspects of that reality cannot be told. Despite this, the author/survivor must strive to achieve what he or she can. Wiesel's acceptance of the need to speak, in spite of the imposed silence of Auschwitz and of the impotence of words to describe the event, highlights his personal quest for a sense of truth.

In *La Nuit,* one is faced with silence in its most negative forms. It exists firmly as the novel's core. In referring to silence, I am not alluding to the high frequency of the word silence itself, but to those other structural features previously described and employed by Wiesel to evoke silence, notably *la page blanche* and *le grand silence typographique-respiratoire.* Within the space of this slim volume, Wiesel interrupts the text with such *blancs* eighty-two times. Elsewhere, the author himself emphasizes the importance such bits of white space signify when he writes: ". . . in the universe Auschwitz, everything is mystery. . . . White spaces themselves have their importance." Clear evidence of this abounds in this *document vécu.*

The theme of silence found in *La Nuit,* however, extends far beyond such textual elements of words and blanks. If this *témoignage* represents the absolute negative pole attainable by silence, we must undertake to seek out its cancerous growth within other elements as they are drawn into the vortex of the *nihil.* The primary level at which one discovers this negative silence is the utter destruction of the self. "Silence in its primal aspect, is a consequence of terror, of a dissolution of self and world that, once known, can never be fully dispelled." This loss of identity effectively silences the image that constitutes human essence. "One literally became a number: dead or alive—that was unimportant; the life of a "number" was completely irrelevant." This destruction extends beyond simple identity as it seeks to silence the unique world of childhood and innocence. One must therefore seek to trace the evolution of the antithesis of all human values, in general, and the Jewish ethos, in particular, an action that is achieved by a painful silencing of words by words as readers are conducted into the chaos of silent, destructive negativity. Proceeding a step beyond, one must subsequently seek the ultimate denial of God, humanity, and the word in order to arrive at the heart of the *nihil ani mundi.*

The first element of life that must be silenced is time. Time lies at the heart of existence, a principle particularly true in Jewish thought and teachings. Abraham Joshua Heschel notes that "Judaism is a religion of time aiming at the sanctification of time." So it is that at the beginning of *La Nuit,* time meticulously and meaningfully guides the young protagonist through life, through his studies and prayers. Time is represented as a creative force, a bridge linking man to eternity.

The first incursion of night into the harmonious passage of time is the deportation and subsequent return of Moché-le-Bedeau. The destructive silence of the Jewish tragedy has taken its toll. "Il ferma ses yeux, comme pour fuir le temps"; "He closed his eyes, as though to escape time." More importantly, this silencing of time brings with it other startling transformations. "Il avait changé, Moché. Ses yeux ne reflétaient plus la joie. Il ne chantait plus. Il ne me parlait plus de Dieu ou de Kabbale. . . ."; "Moché had changed. There was no longer any joy in his eyes. He no longer sang. He no longer talked to me of God or the cabbala." As time is silenced, creativity ceases, and negative silence descends over life.

Moché's return not only marks the initial transformation of time, but it evokes a curious response from the Jewish community of Sighet. Moché (whose name is Moses), the prophet who has seen the advancing night, is viewed as being a madman. The Jews would prefer to purchase his silence, to erase his message. Ironically, Moché's purchased mutism only permits the Jews of Sighet to resume life behind a protective facade of silence that descends. But this brief contact with the night has unquestionably altered life. Though the Allied broadcasts offer a degree of hope, Wiesel underlies the text with a bitter irony: The utter silence of the Allies concerning the fate of Europe's Jewish population.

Though metamorphosing, time persists in its existence. With its natural passage the Nazis arrive. The course which would lead to Birkenau has been set into motion. Ghettos were established where life sought to maintain a degree of normalcy. Stories, part of the fabric of Jewish life, continued to be told. But, in medias res, the good stories being told are silenced and will remain forever unfinished. Words have lost their positive creative powers. The only remaining significant communication becomes nonverbal. Whereas time had previously stimulated creativity, it now stifles the word/Word. Time comes to represent a negative force, and even the "ongoing tale" is tainted by it.

Religious traditions whose foundations rest on the positive nature of time are effectively altered. "Nous avions fait . . . le repas traditionnel du vendredi soir. Nous avions dit les bénédictions d'usage sur le pain et le vin et avalé les mets sans dire mot"; "We had the traditional Friday evening meal. We said the customary grace for the bread and wine and swallowed our food without a word." The traditional Jewish Sabbath meal, which inaugurates the day of rest, is a time of joy and song. The table is literally considered an altar to God around which special Sabbath songs, *zmirot*, are sung. Family and friends join together in peace and speak of God, the Sabbath, and the joys of life. These elements are pointedly absent. Wiesel's use of the French verb *avaler* likewise imparts a sense of haste foreign to the Sabbath table, as well as presenting connotations of animal-like behavior, both notions sadly lost in the English translation.

Wiesel's use of the Sabbath in this context is essential, for if the silencing of time is to be absolute, the element of *kdusha* (holiness), which first appears in the Bible with reference to time—"And God blessed the seventh day and made it holy" (Genesis 2:3)—must be removed. Holiness is lodged in time, most notably on one particular day: the Sabbath. The Talmud explains that the Sabbath represents *m'en olam ha'ba*, something akin to the world to come. Heschel believes the Sabbath is:

> The microcosm of spirit. . . . The seventh day is a reminder that God is our father, that time is life and the spirit our mate. . . . For the Sabbath is the counterpart of living; the melody sustained throughout all agitations and vicissitudes which menace our conscience; our awareness of God's presence in the world.

As the final blow, therefore, the Sabbath, replete with its holiness, is silenced. "Samedi, le jour de repos, était le jour choisi pour notre expulsion"; "Saturday, the day of rest, was chosen for our expulsion." The synagogue where Sabbath prayers had previously been offered is transformed into a scene of desecration.

> La synagogue ressemblait à une grande gare. . . . L'autel était brisé, les tapisseries arrachées, les murs dénudés. Nous étions si nombreux que nous pouvions à peine respirer. Epouvantables vingt-quatre heures passées là. Les hommes étaient en bas. Les femmes, au premier étage. C'était samedi: on aurait dit que nous étions venus assister à l'office. Ne pouvant sortir, les gens faisaient leurs besoins dans un coin.

> The synagogue was like a huge station. . . . The altar was broken, the hangings torn down, the walls bare. There were so many of us that we could scarcely breathe. We spent a horrible twenty-four hours there. There were men downstairs; women on the first floor. It was Saturday; it was as though we had come to attend the service. Since no one could go out, people were relieving themselves in a corner.

Not only has the Sabbath been stilled, but with this act of unholiness, universal *menuhah* (rest; repose) has been destroyed. In the ensuing timeless silent void, there is no place for the Jews of Sighet.

The final rupture of time occurs with the arrival of the deported Jews at Birkenau-Auschwitz. After a seemingly endless night in the stinking confines of the cattle cars, time ceases to exist as they enter the kingdom of night where all the imagined horrors of two millennia of Christian iconography become real.

> Non loin de nous, des flammes montaient d'une fosse, des flammes gigantesques. On y brûlait quelque chose. Un camion s'approcha du trou et y déversa sa charge: c'étaient des petits enfants. Des bébés! Des enfants dans les flammes.

> Not far from us, flames were leaping up from the ditch, gigantic flames. They were burning something. A lorry drew up at the pit and delivered its load—little children. Babies! Yes, I saw it—saw it with my own eyes . . . those children in the flames.

Such a vision cannot be real; it cannot exist within a normal temporal framework. "Je me pinçai le visage: vivais-je encore? Etais-je éveillé?"; "I pinched my face. Was I still alive? Was I awake?" Moral time, creative time, that dimension in which humanity exists and in which it discovers traces of the living God has been abrogated. "J'avais complètement perdu la notion du temps. . . . C'était sûrement un rêve"; "I had lost all sense of time. . . . Surely it was a dream." The coup de grace is finally dealt by the camp code of hairlessness. All vestiges of age disappear as young and old are reduced to naked, hairless beings. With the erasure of time, little remains of the protagonist.

This argument has merely attempted to point to the silencing of time within the Wieselian universe. In *La Nuit*, time ceases to have a creative dimension and enters the realm of pure negativism. As Wiesel's work evolves, time will remain fragmented as he passes from the world of the living to the domain of the dead. This particular feature produces a unique literary structure that will facilitate the blending of the past, present, and future, and will reinforce the notion of the instantaneous multiplicity of various levels of perception and significance.

Wiesel's use of time and fragmented structure firmly entrench his oeuvre within the traditions of contemporary writers, most especially the *nouveaux romanciers*. The role of the writer has been radically altered. Beliefs in former literary dogmas, which had propounded a faith in the unshakable nature of civilization, can no longer be supported. As a result, chronological time as a traditional aspect of storytelling can no longer be viewed as an ally; it has become a menacing shadow. Time had been equated to man's perception of reality. Moreover, after Auschwitz, reality could no longer be viewed as before. For Jean Cayrol, this fact represents perhaps the most influential element in the creation of modern literature. He discerns aspects of the *univers concentrationnaire* within all men. The fragmentation of linear time permits the past inexorably to become part of the future. Thus one can view Wiesel's use of this technique as representing his adherence to current literary trends, as well as serving as a universal reminder of those events that produced the initial rupture. Moreover, one must also view Wiesel's perception of time as being reflective of his own Hasidic background. Hasidic stories do not adhere to occidental conventions of temporal exigencies, but create notions of time that are subordinated to the message of the tale. Metaphysics and mystery reign, and the storyteller manipulates past and present to enhance particular moral themes.

As time is closely related to our understanding of reality, its silencing must therefore effect the existence and perception of truth. As previously noted, when Moché-le-Bedeau returned from his deportation and sought to warn the Jews of Sighet about the existence of the *univers concentrationnaire*, no one would believe him. His vision of truth could not be accommodated within a traditional temporal framework. This attitude is strengthened when, during the journey to Auschwitz, Moché's words are echoed and even intensified in the frightening prophetic ravings of Mme. Schächter.

Within the timeless world of the sealed cattle cars that serve as the bridge between Sighet and Auschwitz, between life and death, the journey becomes a metonomy of existence in the *univers concentrationnaire*. In this environment, Mme. Schäcter's voice painfully reiterates the horrific reality Moché's had announced earlier, and which their current journey represents. The others react to her much as they had to Moché: They attempt to silence her. Nothing, however, is capable of stifling her violent, prophetic outbursts.

This action possesses intense irony as Wiesel here expresses a particularly Jewish element: The desire of a community to silence or drive away any bad tidings. Such behavior can be traced to the manner in which many prophets of the Old Testament were treated when pronouncing their visions. Wiesel has stated that the people of Judah rejected the prophet Jeremiah in much the same way as the Jews of Sighet spurned Moché and Mme. Schächter:

> One feared his words, therefore one rejected the person. They called him false prophet, madman. They pushed him aside, tormented him in public, they threw him into the dungeon: in short they did everything possible to discredit him.

Nevertheless, Mme. Schäcter's prophecies, like those of Jeremiah, become unbearable reality as the sealed train arrives at Birkenau.

Eliezer has come to exist within a timeless void from which truth has been either exiled or deformed. In this silent wasteland, he will suffer the destruction of his own beliefs in a just and true God, as well as in the goodness of fellow human beings. Wiesel accomplishes this annihilation of Eliezer's essence within the space of seventeen pages as the devouring black flame of the *anus mundi* rapidly erases the being who had existed. Within the text, silence becomes the method by which Eliezer is reduced to a cipher. This silence is evoked by several techniques. Sparse dialogue couples with terse, journalistic language, and *le grand silence typographique-respiratoire* to create a taut, fearful atmosphere. The word *silence* and its synonyms do not recur frequently, a choice that saves them from becoming meaningless clichés. Wiesel does, however, strike upon another technique: Punctuation. The use of punctuation accentuates the rapid respiration of the text and creates a feeling of impending doom. The text progresses haltingly, tripping and falling on its descent to hell.

Another striking feature is the absolute lack of gruesome detail, or even the mention of death. For the reader, these elements exist, but only in the meta-silence that Wiesel imposes and which forms the background of the story. The language of the *univers concentrationnaire* is one which cannot be expressed in common terms. "Languages have great reserves of life," states George Steiner. "They can absorb masses of hysteria, illiteracy and cheapness. . . . But, there comes a breaking point." Wiesel does relegate certain realities of the *anus mundi* to silence. And yet, unexpressed elements do eventually rise from the depths to extinguish the voices of the living.

Roland Barthes believes that the voice is the symbolic substance of human life. As a symbol of life, the voice has no rightful place in the kingdom of death and is therefore methodically silenced. First, the protagonist's father's voice is stilled, then Eliezer's. Gradually, language itself is silenced. Life as it has been perceived ceases to exist.

With time and creative language silenced, the spirit of the *anus mundi* proceeds to invade Eliezer's soul and crushes his spiritual identity. One of the most painful acts is the demolition of the protagonist's view of God. The young talmudic student deeply believed in God, and had always nurtured the notion of the unique convenantal relationship between the Jews and God. Man would supplicate; God would respond. To those faced with the reality of Auschwitz, God reveals Himself as an impotent entity who has been robbed of His attributes of justice and mercy by the Angel of Death. For Wiesel, the God of the yeshiva student has abdicated His Throne.

The pious Jew prays three times daily. During the morning prayers, psalms are chanted to the Creator of the Universe. Within the horrific kingdom of night such psalms would prove to be ironically blasphemous or utterly senseless. So it is that Wiesel composes a new psalm, one which reflects the negativity of Auschwitz and the eclipse of God. Its form and message offer the antithesis of Psalm 150, the culmination of the Psalter, a psalm which is an ecstatic exaltation in the Divinity. The French text alone is considered here:

> Jamais je n'oublierai cette nuit, la première
> nuit de camp qui a fait de ma vie une
> nuit longue et sept fois verrouillée.
> Jamais je n'oublierai cette fumée.
> Jamais je n'oublierai les petits visages des
> enfants dont j'avais vu les corps se
> transformer en volutes sous un azur muet.
> Jamais je n'oublierai ces flammes qui
> consumèrent pour toujours ma Foi.
> Jamais je n'oublierai ce silence nocturne qui
> m'a privé pour l'éternité du désir de
> vivre.
> Jamais je n'oublierai ces instants qui
> assassinèrent mon Dieu et mon âme, et
> mes rêves qui prirent le visage du désert.
> Jamais je n'oublierai cela, même si j'étais
> condammé à vivre aussi longtemps que Dieu
> lui-même.
> Jamais.

Each line of Psalm 150 commences with the word: Hallelujah. The short flowing verses positively direct and enjoin humanity to exalt in God's presence. They resume the aspiration of Israel's mission. In contrast, Wiesel's lugubrious eight lines negate that message while openly accusing God of complicity in the creation of the *anus mundi* and in the murder of His "Chosen People." The Francophone reader would also hear in Wiesel's anti-psalm a more secular echo: the resounding "*J'accuse*" of Emile Zola. Stylistically akin to Zola's controversial piece of 1898, Wiesel hammers out the message of his inability to forget what he had witnessed. The driving rhythm accentuates that the author will force God to remember what He had permitted to occur. This striking text similarly signifies the protagonist's utter disillusionment with God. Former beliefs possess no validity. Eliezer has found that his God is lost amid the negative silence of the *univers concentrationnaire.* And God's own silence amid such incarnate evil indicts and condemns Him. Yet despite such a challenge to his beliefs, Eliezer never rejects the existence of God. The silence of Auschwitz has submitted the omnipotent God of Eliezer's youth to the test of truth, only to find Him wanting.

Not only is God called to the bar in this silence; the very notion of humanity, the enlightened being to which Mauriac makes reference in his Preface to the novel, is likewise examined and found to be wanting. The vision of the human race has radically altered. On "planet Auschwitz," human moral responsibilities are silenced and deformed into indifference. Humankind blindly and mutely accepts the events of the Holocaust. Human guilt is first evidenced while the Jews of Sighet are still in their ghetto. The "others" in the town indifferently accept matters, and eventually witness the deportation of their Jewish neighbors. Their silence condemns them and, by extension, all humanity. As Cynthia Haft concludes: "Non-activity, passivity, for Wiesel . . . is equated with negative activity; therefore the man (*i.e.*, the Other in *La Ville de la chance*) is guilty of collaboration." The very fact that the Jewish population could so easily be deported destroys Eliezer's innocent illusions about human goodness and justice. Thus, for the protagonist, the corrosive, negative mentality of the concentration camp philosophy, that of every person for himself/herself and every person being your enemy, evolves and assumes primacy. The view of humanity, created in the image of God, is shattered and banished. The last shreds of respectful human dignity fall away under the cries of camp guards. The ultimate silencing blow to human identity occurs when Eliezer is stripped of his name and thereafter becomes A–7713.

By the conclusion of this third episode, the silent backdrop of Auschwitz has annihilated the voices of the pre-Holocaust world. The remainder of the narrative merely serves to supplement this initial silencing. The voice that is bound up with life and in life is strangled and muted. Only the chaotic, destructive silence of the *nihil* remains.

Each of the various episodes comprising the story of *La Nuit* reflects the omnipresent scenic silence of Auschwitz. Wiesel's use of the morphological, syntactic, and semantic aspects of silence permit the novel to descend into the depths of depraved negativity. And the principal question raised by the theme of silence emerges as: Where was God? This becomes the central issue about which silence and all other themes come to revolve.

In the opening episodes, Eliezer had been transported from the light of learning and truth to the blackness of the void as experienced at Auschwitz. Prayer and praise were cut off before a silent God. The only force to which one could respond, the only source of potency, was the SS, whom David Rousset defines as: "In the high places of a merciless cult of punishment, the SS were the frenzied sacrificial priests dedicated to the service of an output-hungry Moloch and to a sinister, burlesque justice. Ubu was their god" [my translation]. God no longer controls His creation. The SS decide who shall live and who shall die; it is they who direct the fate of the Jewish prisoners. Throughout the book, the fiery cloud created by the Nazis compels the Jews to move on. When the Jewish remnant is starving, sadistic workers—emanations of this *Ubu-Dieu*—cast stale bread into the open railway cars, a scene serving as the antithesis of God's gift of manna in the wilderness. (Exodus 16:13–17) Each step, every example, emphasizes the absence of the divine and the presence of evil. Akiba Drumer, another character whose faith is shattered, poses this most serious question: "Where is God?" Those three words, like the four opening notes of Beethoven's Fifth Symphony, pound out the single most urgent question against which Eliezer and all humanity must struggle. Where was God? At the public hanging of a young boy that obsessive question arises from the meta-silence before uneasily dissolving again into it:

> —Oú donc est Dieu?
> Et je sentais en moi une voix qui lui répondait:
> —Oú il est? Le voici—il est pendu ici, à cette potence. . . .
>
> "Where is God now?"
> And I heard a voice within me answer him:
> "Where is He? Here He is—He is hanging here on this gallows. . . ."

According to André Neher, this scene echoes the Crucifixion:

> A strange evocation of the Passion, with the difference, deep as an abyss, that it was not, however, God who was hanging on the cross but an innocent little Jewish child, and that after three days he was not to rise again.

This particular scene reflects the final silencing of the young protagonist's faith and hopes in the God of his youth. The powerful God of his religious studies possesses no meaning in Auschwitz. How could one maintain belief in the majesty and justice of God in the face of such debasement and depravity? The overwhelming silence of God generates a spiritual revolt within Eliezer, so that on Rosh Hashana, he refuses to pray or to bless God's Name. God stands in the dock, accused by Eliezer of silent indifference. This rebellion casts the protagonist into the depths of a void where he is painfully alone in a world whence God has been exiled. This bitter estrangement culminates ten days later on Yom Kippur when Eliezer abandons the obligatory fast and stresses: "Je n'acceptais plus le silence de Dieu"; "I no longer accepted God's silence."

As Eliezer no longer possesses faith in God, he must seek strength and life elsewhere. In the context of traditional Jewish life, such a source of comfort and renewal can be found within the family. Yet the family unit Eliezer had known was forever ruptured upon his arrival in the *univers concentrationnaire* when his mother and sisters had been marched off to the gas chambers. His only hope lies in his father whose hand he tightly holds. The remainder of *La Nuit* reflects the relation of father and son within the *anus mundi.*

Wiesel demonstrates a particular fondness for introducing biblical stories and characters into his oeuvre. In *La Nuit*, the tale he evokes is that of the *Akeda*, the story of Abraham and Isaac and God's demand for sacrifice. *La Nuit* becomes a rewriting of this story; and, Eliezer's question "Where is God" stands as the antithesis to Isaac's question in Genesis 22:7: "Where is the lamb?"

The *Akeda* is a principle central to Judaism, as it clearly demonstrates the faith and fervor of both Abraham and Isaac in their service to God's commands.

> Few chapters of the Bible have had a more potent and more far-reaching influence on our people than the story of the binding of Isaac. It has fired the hearts of countless generations of Israel with an indomitable spirit and with unwavering steadfastness to the principles of our faith, however great the sacrifices involved.

The Akeda's influence resides in the fact that it offers a brief outline of the entirety of the Jewish experience of *Leidensgeschichte*, while also posing several difficult and perhaps insoluble questions for human beings.

The rewriting and reversals of the *Akeda* in *La Nuit* underscore how radically the original has been transformed, how much more painful is God's silence, and how the miracle that saved Isaac's life cannot transpire in this particular story where death reigns supreme. The reversal is further highlighted by the fact that though father and son walk to the sacrifice together, only the son will survive. The father's death signifies the silencing of the past and its meaning. Faith formerly espoused, the legacy of the tale which the protagonist's father had been telling and that had been silenced, can never be transmitted. The Holocaust *Akeda* becomes representative of total negation, of the utter silencing of Eliezer's world and its Jewish ethos. With its evocation, the *anus mundi* achieves momentary victory. Silence in its vilest guise will reign sui generis.

In the universe of death, where the miracle of life cannot occur, the hope and joy of the outcome of the *Akeda* mock man. Faith destroyed, the legends and stories of the past seemingly forever silenced, the only element in Eliezer's existence that has given him the strength to continue, his last vestige of humanity, has been his relationship with his father. They have endured their "test" together, just as Abraham and Isaac had functioned as one, a notion Wiesel stresses in his midrash on the *Akeda*: "Le mot clé ici encore est *yakhdav*, ensemble"; "Once more the key word is *yakhdav*, together." From the moment father and son enter the kingdom of night, they have sought to remain together. This has been Eliezer's overriding desire. Together they are marched to a flaming pit; together they lose all aspects of human dignity and identity; together they suffer the ignominious treatment reserved for *Untermenschen*; together they endeavor to combat the void of the night.

Yet even this element of the *Akeda* of the Night contains a cancerous element that will lead to its being silenced. Walking this path together does not imply life, but death. The philosophy of this kingdom quite simply stated is every man for himself. Each person faces the unutterable pain and loneliness of existence alone. Former relationships, be they father and son, mothers and daughters, brothers, sisters or friends, signified death. This idea produces a state of physical impotence first manifesting itself when his father is beaten and brutalized. The ethos of the *univers concentrationnaire* prevents Eliezer from acting. His conscience weighs the frightening reality of the choice between his moral duty to his father, with whom he walks this frightening path, and his responsibility to preserve his own life at all costs. His body cannot and does not react; he stands paralyzed, his muscles "silenced" before the terrors of Auschwitz. Yet despite this episode, Eliezer remains with his father even while other father-son relationships decay. For example, Rabi Eliahou's search for his own son crystallizes into a chilling realization for Eliezer. He recognizes Rabi Eliahou's son's desperate desire to be rid of the burden his father represents, and thus perhaps to ensure survival for himself. This shocking image more sadistically reveals itself during the transfer from Gleiwitz to Buchenwald, when the starving prisoners fight for bread. From the melee, Eliezer witnesses a son strangle his own father in order to extract a molding crust of bread from the old man's mouth.

Such scenes remain engraved on Eliezer's mind as the life of his own father ebbs. The voice that had come to signify life is gradually silenced.

Without his voice, Eliezer's father effectively no longer exists in this world. The child assumes the role of father, the father the child. And yet, even as his father weakens, even as their relationship together is gradually silenced—a relationship that represents the last vestige of Eliezer's Jewishness—the protagonist refuses to abandon his father. "Ici, il n'y a pas de père qui tienne, pas de frère, pas d'ami. Chacun vit et meurt pour soi, seul"; "Here, every man has to fight for himself and not think of anyone else." This crushing advice is offered by a friendly *kapo* on January 28, 1945. Eliezer's father dies the next morning. Unable to cry, he has but one thought: Free at last! Death has silenced his only link with the past, with the family, with tradition.

Several critics, among them Ted Estess and Ellen Fine, believe that with the death of Eliezer's father the reader has reached the deepest realm of night. I must subjoin a critical subsidiary qualification to their proposal, for this traumatic event only reveals its full power and significance if it is explicitly linked to the *Akeda*. In Genesis, God—albeit through an angel—does intervene, the miracle of salvation does occur. In this instance, however, God is silent and refuses to acknowledge His covenant with the Jews. Hitler alone remained faithful to his covenant: "Il [Hitler] est le seul a avoir tenu ses promesses, au peuple juif"; "He's the only one who's kept his promises, all his promises, to the Jewish people." Elsewhere, Wiesel insists:

> Nous avons connu des enfants qui, comme Isaac, ont subi le sacrifice dans leur chair; et certain, devenus fous, ont vu leur père disparaître sur l'autel avec l'autel, dans un braiser qui incendiait le plus haut des cieux.
>
> We have known children who, like Isaac, lived the Akédah in their flesh; and some who went mad when they saw their father disappear on the altar, with the altar, in a blazing fire whose flames reached into the highest of heavens.

The path that Eliezer has trod with his father is now his alone. His father, his God, his world, are dead. This is his inheritance. "In *Night* I wanted to show the end, the finality of the event. Everything came to an end—man, history, literature, religion, God. There was nothing left." So it is that the protagonist has been swallowed by the silent void of Auschwitz. "Du fond du miroir, un cadavre me contemplait"; "From the depths of the mirror, a corpse gazed back at me." Unlike the biblical survivor, Isaac, who pursued a normal life, Eliezer will always exist in a realm of specters. The cadaverous gaze in the mirror at Buchenwald reflects the paralyzed, mute victim par excellence. He signifies Hitler's victory; and, ironically, he likewise represents the seeds of Hitler's defeat. For if *La Nuit* is the vision of the void, that *nihil* similarly serves as the spawning ground for attempts to break or modify the murderous silence imposed in the *univers concentrationnaire.*

L'AUBE

If *La Nuit* is the foundation of Wiesel's work, *L'Aube* (*Dawn*) constitutes the first degree of commentary. The concentric circle formed by *L'Aube* represents a gray, cold, and silent ashen realm that complements the horror of *La Nuit.* The story is, in fact, drawn in shades of night. The opening and closing passages of the novel echo one another and unite to form a zone that is neither day nor night. Wiesel's literary irony likewise mocks the protagonist's struggle to escape the solitary torment of his Parisian exile where days are drawn in "une lumière pâle, déjà fatiguée, coluleur d'eau moisie"; "A pale, prematurely weary light the color of stagnant water." The character and his tale remain closed within this outer realm of hell; and, just as at the end of *La Nuit* where the protagonist is staring into the mirror, so too is the protagonist of *L'Aube* seeking some reflected image at the beginning of that novel, an image that is only realized with the novel's conclusion: "Je regardais ce morceau de nuit. . . . Le morceau noir, fait de lambeaux d'ombres avait un visage. . . . Ce visage, c'était le mien"; "The tattered fragment of darkness had a face. Looking at it, I understood the reason for my fear. The face was my own." Appearances would suggest, therefore, that the Wieselian circle remains as static and closed as the *nihil* of *La Nuit.* Maurice Blanchot states in *L'Ecriture du désastre* that "Perhaps writing is a means to bring to the surface something of the absent sense, to welcome that passive pressure that is not yet thought, but is already the disaster of thought." Through the medium of writing, Wiesel places his protagonist betwixt and between. Obscured time refuses to progress, forcing the protagonist to wallow in the silent void that rises to engulf him. Questions obsess him. A burning desire drives him to attempt to comprehend the events that had cast him into the role of victim. These various tests resurrect the hidden, muted beast of the Holocaust, without any mention of the event itself. The *poussée passive* Blanchot mentions in the original French text metamorphoses into a tense cloak of silence, which permeates the textual surface and infuses itself into the very essence of writing. *La pensée*, the thought, does not yet exist; only the silence of the preexistent thought. Furthermore, the specially evoked silence of *L'Aube* will stand as a counterpoint to the word and even to the *désastre de la pensée* (disaster of thought) suggested by Blanchot.

The silent elements of *L'Aube* both represent a continuation of the negative silence imposed by the authority of the *anus mundi* and constitute the initial movement away from the *nihil* toward concealed regenerative forms. François Mauriac advances the proposition that "in the most tormented lives, speech counts little. . . . The drama of a living being almost always transpires and comes undone in silence." Mauriac's statement sheds additional light on the general evolutionary course of silence. He perceived everything of importance as passing through a universal atmosphere of silence that molds the destinies of characters, placing them, as M. Parry contends "into a more distant orbit from their fellow men." Parry's observation is equally true with regard to Wiesel's second novel. Though Elisha, the protagonist, has abandoned his Parisian prison for a stiflingly hot, closed room in Palestine, where he is engaged in terrorist activities, he persists in estranging himself from his comrades by his silences. Though he has abandoned his philosophical quest for understanding his situation, and has accepted his role as a maker of historic destiny, silence will continue to open a gulf between him and all he seeks. His silences are negative, destructive. They do not draw him nearer to God or fellow human beings. Thus, the solitary, mute realm in which Elisha exists is not that "sublime world of silence and solitude which is the privileged place of communion with God," which Parry sees in Mauriac's fiction, but rather a silent debate that rages through the night, and will lead, not to God, but cynically back to the ghostly point from which all began. By the novel's conclusion, the negative silences of the Holocaust will again possess him.

Elisha's problem can be defined in Blanchot's words as follows: "It is necessary to cross the abyss, and if one doesn't leap, one will not understand." Blanchot suggests that man must reach out beyond a chasm that separates him from life and others in order to fathom his own existence. Without such an effort to erect a bridge of sorts by which man might attempt to communicate with *l'autrui* (the other), there can be no degree of understanding. Elisha's solitary existence has produced nothing. He must act, for in action he assumes responsibility for his life, his future, and his relations with others. Therefore, he decided to leave Paris for Palestine, exchanging his paralytic impotence for a course of pseudo-Messianic action. But this action achieves nothing. Because of the weight of silence of Auschwitz he bears and which he never honestly faces, any action will result in nothingness, another victory for the negativity of the *anus mundi*, another success for that silence.

From the beginning of the novel, battle lines are plainly delineated for the continued struggle between humanity and God. Placed within the context of silence, the spiritual struggles and physical actions will lead to a further silencing of God's nature in this world, of the past and of the self, thus resulting in a more desperate and pathetic exile for the protagonist—even to the point of rendering his name, Elisha, which means "God will save," useless and redundant.

Before proceeding with an analysis of the role of silence in this novel, a particular element must be mentioned: Gesture. Jean-Jacques Rousseau postulated that gesture represents "an adjunct of speech, but this adjunct is not an artificial supplement, it is a recourse to a more natural, more expressive, more immediate means of communication." Physical gesture possesses the value of a mute linguistic sign, its origins lying in the phenomenon of speech and the human desire to communicate. Rousseau maintains elsewhere that gestures "by their very nature are more expressive. . . ."; they represent humanity's most primordial language, a passionate cry that rises in silence from the depths of the human soul, and as such remain untainted by the ambiguity inherent in the word. It is highly significant, therefore, that Elisha does not gesture to accentuate his state of being during the course of the night's struggle. Vocal articulations are painfully few, gestures freeze in the impotence of the moment. Phenomenologically, it is an absolute, cold, hard silence that results. Again it is Rousseau who in *Les Rêveries du promeneur solitaire* submits that such silences induce sadness serving up an image of death. Despite similarities with those previously expressed views of Brice Parain, Rousseau's evaluation and ideas concerning silence are nevertheless transformed into reality for Elisha. Surrounded by the ghosts of his past, he passes the night in a state of mutism both of word and gesture. Wiesel's ultimate irony lies in the fact that the novel's verbal and gesticular impotence are eventually shattered by a single act: the pulling of a trigger. Rousseau's idea of an image of death indeed metamorphoses into death. Should one accept Emmanuel Lévinas's supposition that "the physical gesture is not a nervous reaction, but a celebration of life," that together with the spoken word it amounts to a creative act, then *L'Aube*, with its gesticular sterility and negative, murderous silences, signifies impotence, lack of creativity, and an act of destruction.

Once again, the textual elements of silence build a particular network of thematic levels where the articulated and unarticulated battle for supremacy transpires. The spoken dialogue remains sparse, taut. The conventional use of interior monologue establishes dramatic tension that erodes the moral character of the protagonist. The living and the dead discover no saving balm in the word. Their only shelter is silence.

From the beginning of the novel, silence is evoked. As the protagonist gazes at the descending night, the city appears more silent than ever. In the confines of the terrorists' cell, physical stillness and metaphysical mutism reign. Each episode, every memory or conversation is intensified by silence, especially those generated by inner reflection that highlight the unspoken. Elisha's first encounter with the Zionist activist, Gad, consists of terse statements whose impact is accentuated by the thoughtful silences that in themselves form a sort of interior monologue, or *sous-conversation proustienne.* Though the unarticulated thoughts may occur within a fraction of a second, they do stress the unsaid, setting those elements into direct contrast with the short, articulated dialogue. Such silent elements also permit us to formulate a composite portrait of the protagonist and his torturous psychological composition.

This technique reaches its climax when Elisha faces his victim, John Dawson, whose life will be taken in revenge for the hanging of a Jewish terrorist by the British. Their conversation gradually becomes unbearable for Elisha, as Dawson's questions elicit cryptic responses pregnant with unspoken meanings. By delving into the words left unsaid, into the silent thoughts themselves, we discover roughly undulating movements and secrets that exist below the surface, silent undercurrents filled with echoes from the past, memories of other victims—whose ghosts stand around Elisha—and of other executioners. All of this directly and tragically links the protagonist to the Nazis. Mental images, prophetic flashes, cascade through the protagonist's mind in a masochistic avalanche as the reader is hurled precipitously toward the moment when Elisha will pull the trigger. Each of John Dawson's questions fuels the silent debate burning Elisha's conscience; every question constructs a new tension between past, present, and future. And, once the deed has been accomplished, the protagonist returns to the stifling room where his comrades await his return. Silence still commands the room when he appears, but it is a radically altered silence. Relief, guilt, indifference? This final silence remains oppressively enigmatic.

A far more frightening aspect of silence haunts the novel: That of the dead who arrive to witness the murder. One-third of the novel consists of a silent debate between Elisha and the dead who represent his past and its ethos. Initially, their silence is frighteningly complete. Elisha's father's specter declines to respond to his son's queries; that of his old master remains mute; and that ghost that represents his own youth threatens him with an impenetrable silence. Elisha comes to recognize that the self he is creating, the future murderer, strikes the ghosts mute. Finally, the ghost of the child he had been speaks, almost in a parody of the Four Questions asked by children at the Passover seder, and accuses him: "Cette nuit est différente; et tu es différent cette nuit—ou plutôt, tu vas l'étre"; "Tonight is different, and you are different also, or at least you're going to be." This remark reflects Wiesel's affinity to Sartre's existentialist views concerning the continuing creation of one's essence. Like Sartre, Wiesel is indicating that whatever one has been can be radically altered by a single action. Thus, in accepting his role as executioner, Elisha becomes a murderer, and I believe Wiesel would argue that, by extension, those people who can be seen as the cornerstones of Elisha's personality would similarly be labeled murderers.

Does the silence of the dead constitute a judgement of Elisha and of the movement he has joined? André Neher views such silences as part of an essential, existential debate: "A life-and-death contestation fought out point by point, scene by scene, between the young unhappy Elisha and these silences embodied in phantoms." The silence of the dead Jews weighs heavily on Elisha, instilling terror and despair. Elisha, the silent, brooding protagonist, stands before these shades: "Lorsque tu nous vois, tu crois que nous sommes là pour te juger. Tu as tort de la croire. Ce n'est pas nous qui te jugeons: c'est le silence qui est en toi"; "When you see us you imagine that we are sitting in judgement upon you. You are wrong. Your silence is your judge." Elisha's silence in accepting the role of executioner judges him, and by extension the movement that commands him to silence God's law and take a life. Ironically, Elisha's silence in accepting this new role parallels God's silent indifference and active collaboration during the Holocaust.

Elisha has freely chosen to enter the terrorist cell, which now demands the taking of a life. The element of silence that drives these young Zionists to this conclusion is precisely God's absolute silence and the bankruptcy of Judeo-Hellenic civilization. Humanity must now seek to play God, to imitate the Creator in whose image human beings were formed. "En tuant, l'homme devient Dieu"; "Why has a man no right to commit murder? Because in so doing he takes upon himself the function of God," a belief that would abolish the ethos of Jewish life. In the face of God's absence, however, humankind feels the compulsion to act in order to affect the course of history. God's laws and commandments, which had framed the pre-Holocaust world, had given it meaning and substance, had constituted and sustained dialogue, now have become superfluous. Thus, when Elisha silences John Dawson's life, he is correct to cry: "J'ai tué! J'ai tué Elisha!"; "I've killed! I've killed Elisha!" His action effectively usurps God's traditional role as the source of all life. The mute God, the impotent Creator of Auschwitz is removed by a human operation. Ironically, the promise of a brighter future merely reduces to another dawn the color of stagnant water. Elisha no longer exists. The dead and all they represent vanish. The understanding so desperately sought remains forever elusive. Only the silence within reaches out to stare back at Elisha from the reflection in the windowpane. Elisha has become one with the night of Auschwitz.

LE JOUR

In *La Nuit*, Eliezer struggled with a silent God, only to lose his faith. In *L'Aube*, Elisha usurped the mute God's primary position in the universe, only to lose his ethical heritage. In *Le Jour* (*The Accident*), a nameless protagonist has no God with whom to contend. He merely seeks Death, the ultimate degree of silence. The entire text evolves as a battleground between life and death.

Viktor Frankl remarks that in the concentration camps

> the prisoner who had lost faith in the future—his future—was doomed. With his loss of belief in the future, he had also lost his spiritual hold; he let himself decline and become subject to mental and physical decay.

Moreover, having survived the *anus mundi* leaves each survivor tainted. "Notre séjour là-bas a posé en nous des bombes à retardement"; "Our stay there planted time bombs within us." Thus, the nameless protagonist's pursuit of death, which in Lillian Szklarczyk's words "represents a refusal to live in a universe that is empty and void," underscores another victory for Hitler. Life, even without the weighty burden of guilt for having survived, presents the anonymous protagonist with no logical reason for existing.

In the first two novels of Wiesel's trilogy, the protagonists have gradually discovered themselves engaged in painful struggles between life and death. In each, the spiritual self is demolished, a notion thematically linking the novels. Yet, despite the violent metaphysical upheavals that destroy the protagonists' souls, they do emerge alive, though estranged and exiled from God's creation. In *Le Jour*, Josephine Knopp believes "this estrangement becomes complete." If, therefore, we accept David Williams's general notion of the images of exile "as amputated member and as creature without dialogue," then we must acknowledge the evolving degrees of exile in the Trilogy as steps toward the ultimate, silent extreme of exile as uncreator: Death.

This evolution poses a fundamental problem: That of the silencing of the Jewish ethos on a purely personal level. *La Nuit* banishes Eliezer's faith; *L'Aube* replaced the divine law of life with human will; *Le Jour* appears to shatter the ideal of Jewish respect for life. This idea is graphically illustrated in the story of Golda, a woman hidden in a bunker, whose child—a symbol of life and continuance—will not stop crying.

> Alors les autres, auxquels Golda elle-même s'était jointe, se tournèrent vers Shmuel et lui dirent: «Fais-le taire. Occupe-toi

> de lui, toi dont le métier est d'égorger les poulets. Tu sauras le faire sans qu'il souffre trop.» Et Shmuel s'était rendu à la raison: la vie d'un nourrisson contre la vie de tous. . . . Il avait pris l'enfant. Dans le noir, ses doigts tâtonnants avaient cherché le cou. Et le silence s'était fait dans le ciel et sur la terre.
>
> That's when the others, including Golda herself, turned to Shmuel and told him: "Make him shut up. Take care of him, you whose job it is to slaughter chickens. You will be able to do it without making him suffer too much." And Shmuel gave in to reason: the baby's life in exchange for the lives of all. He had taken the child. In the dark his groping fingers felt for the neck. And there had been silence on earth and in heaven.

This episode exemplifies the crisis upon which Wiesel strikes in *Le Jour*. The sanctity of life is one of Judaism's most fundamental beliefs, one which supersedes faith in God and all aspects of the law. It is this reverence for life that the narrator places in question. The protagonist's attempted suicide and his protracted desire to die while in the hospital amount to the most supreme challenge yet found in Wiesel's fiction. The protagonist has tired of hollow protestations against God's silent injustice; he has, more effectively, rejected the past. Knopp believes *Le Jour* represents "the ultimate defiance of God, the final rejection of God's role in history." It seemingly depicts the absolute victory of silence's negative role. And yet, by the novel's conclusion, we are impressed by the radical alteration in the protagonist's character. For the first time in the trilogy, a Wieselian protagonist is brought to tears. This reaction marks the beginning of renewal. The nameless protagonist has moved from the sterility of death toward the warmth of human feeling and emotion.

The theme of silence in this novel appears on several levels with varying complexity. In a manner of speaking, this novel is the silence after the horrific scream vocalize by the texts of *La Nuit* and *L'Aube*. *Le Jour* delineates those sharp, tense seconds after the articulated sound has ended, a moment charged with the silent echoes of the scream, which prolongs and intensifies the physical act. The elements of *La Nuit* and *L'Aube* are here synthesized and crystallized, transformed into new and more threatening forms of silence. Not only is the protagonist reluctant to speak about his past, but when he does vocalize his memories, the listener is threatened by those words and stories. What he recounts does not inspire understanding or hope, but merely engenders hatred that evolves from the listener's having been drawn into the hell expounded by the narrator. Silence would seemingly be safer for both parties. The protagonist comes to view himself as "un messager des morts parmi des vivants"; "just a messenger of the dead among the living," and he is on the side of the dead.

If, as earlier stated, the human voice represents life, then *Le Jour* immediately underscores the protagonist's tenuous hold on life. "On parlait avec difficulté"; "It was difficult to speak." Gestures prove difficult to accomplish. "Faire le moindre geste, c'était tenter de soulever la planète. J'avais du plomb dans les bras, dans les jambes"; "The slightest gesture was like trying to lift a planet. There was lead in my arms, in my legs."

The accident, which we later learn was a deliberate act of self-destruction, reduces the protagonist to a mute, his voice having temporarily been silenced. Moreover, he now finds himself excluded from all human contact and any bodily movement by the plaster cast and bandages that literally shroud him. In this specially designed cocoon proceeds the struggle between life and death. And yet, the protagonist's situation of extreme physical/metaphysical alienation that manifests itself in vocal and physical paralysis still permits a near-animal instinct to seize him. "Je fis des efforts surhumains pour crier"; "I made a super-human effort." This raging against death, represented by his desire to break the silence, is indicative of a shift in attitude. It is the initial phase of a radical metamorphosis. And, when finally he does speak:

> Ma voix n'était qu'un murmure. Mais je pouvais parler. J'en ressentis une joie qui me fit monter les larmes aux yeux. . . . La preuve que le pouvoir de la parole ne m'était pas ôté m'inonda d'une émotion que je n'arrivais pas à dissimuler.

> My voice was only a whisper. But I was able to speak. This filled me with such joy that tears came to my eyes. . . . But the knowledge that I could still speak filled me with an emotion that I couldn't hide.

There is a fundamental paradox in this novel. For the first time in Wiesel's fiction we encounter two diametrically opposed forms of silence. The first represents the negation of life as exercised in *La Nuit* and *L'Aube.* In effect, this silence signifies separation of an individual from the group and a denial of a social or moral contract. The very existence of this negative silence, however, proves to be the germinating factor for a new and regenerative silence absent in the preceding novels. It is this more positive silence that produces the revolt against death, providing support for the protagonist's burning desire to speak. Thus in this novel, the text alternates between the negative silences of the Holocaust and those that produce joy at being able to speak.

The novel does witness, however, the birth of another degree of negative silence: The lie. Lying becomes a part of the protagonist's nature, as it allows him to exist in the realm of the living. Sartre defines lying as "a renunciation of expressing an impossible truth and using words not to get to know others but to be accepted, to be loved." A liar knows something but chooses to conceal it in a willful silence. By lying, the protagonist believes he will be marginally accepted by society, while his authentic self will pass undisturbed beneath the falsehoods. The question here is what truth does this protagonist choose to hide? An initial response would be that the horrors of the Holocaust lurk submerged beneath the placid surface of his language and actions. There is also the reality that his mind focuses on one abiding truth—death. But, more to the point, his frightening secret is his attempt to take his own life. For these reasons, the truth must be concealed.

Thus, when asked to recount his past, he flatly refuses. This imposed silence must be seen as a lie, as it obliterates and betrays the echoing voices of the countless dead. And, when some partial truth is spoken, either hatred or silence are the residual effects. Truth only appears to injure and to deform. Truth forces the protagonist to become a torturer who inflicts misery on those individuals as yet unscathed directly by the horrors of the *anus mundi.* As a result, the protagonist resorts to prevarication. The lie denotes an abandonment of one's responsibility to express the truth. In order to conceal the unspeakable, lying becomes an active adoption of euphemisms, or words possessing multiple meanings, or silence itself. Veracity emerges as another victim of the *shoah.*

Even if the protagonist were to discover those words that might best express his plight, they possess a degree of impotence and ambiguity that would require further elaboration. Thus, lying or silence would be best. As he tenuously exists in the realm of the living, he opts for speech, carefully, shrewdly choosing his words and phrases. His articulated lies easily silence truth. But, as with most liars, the protagonist lives in fear of discovery. In the novel, he himself is unsure whether under sedation this facade of lies had been shattered by a subconscious desire to purge himself of the many sublimated secrets he conceals. One example should suffice to illustrate this point. When he is no longer critically ill, his doctor, Paul Russel, initiates his own investigation into the protagonist's desire to die. "—De quoi donc avez-vous peur? A nouveau, j'eus l'impression qu'il me cachait quelque chose. Se pourrait-il qu'il sût? Avais-je parlé dans mon sommeil, pendant l'opération?"; "What are you afraid of, then? Again I had the impression that he was keeping something from me. Could he actually know? Had I talked in my sleep, during the operation?" The text plunges into a dense silence that conceals the protagonist's thoughts. His anxiety mounts with every query and each statement. This painful tension—transpiring as it does in silent Proustian undercurrents—produces its own piercing, threatening silence that tortures the protagonist. The hospital room becomes, by extension, another of the many symbolic prisons in which the early Wieselian protagonists find themselves. Moreover, the room signifies the continued existence of the *univers concentrationnaire* and of its menacingly negative silences that impose an impotent muteness on the protagonist. Unable to express his emotions, his tongue has become paralyzed. His silence signifies nothing more than a lie and, as such, represents a victory for the powers of death and evil. The world beyond his hospital room ironically echoes within, enticing him to join the living—an invitation he rejects. Russel strives to dislocate his patient's morose facade, only to encounter further silence. Even when queried if he loves his mistress, Kathleen, the protagonist mutely considers before asserting the fidelity of his love. An obvious crisis arises between the conflict between the animal desire to live and the survivor's need to reject life. His affirmation of love for Kathleen, therefore, persists as nothing more than a lie; and, once he has stated this, a potent authorial silence imposes itself upon the text. "Rien ne bougeait plus. Le silence était complet"; "Nothing stirred. There was complete silence."

The various elements of silence do indeed stifle the aspects of life represented by Dr. Russel, the unseen world beyond the hospital room, and Kathleen. Kathleen especially represents life. Her verbal imperatives have continually pressed the protagonist through the motions of existence. When she visits him in the hospital, her incessant talking is juxtaposed to the protagonist's deathly silences. Thus, it is Kathleen who suffers most from the lies that mask the profound hidden secrets. One particular episode best exemplifies this situation. She happens to ask about the enigmatic Sarah. After some initial disquietude, the protagonist replies that Sarah was his mother's name, an answer embracing an element of truth while still subsisting as a lie. Sarah also happened to be a young girl whom the protagonist had encountered in Paris long before knowing Kathleen. More to the point, Sarah is the antithesis of Kathleen. She symbolizes death and the terror of the *univers concentrationnaire.* Forced at the age of twelve to become a prostitute in the camps, the innocence of her childhood torn from her, she is an extension of the protagonist's own tormented psyche. Her story haunts him and drives him to hatred. Sarah's regulated monotone voice and her prolonged, intense silences torment him from the depths of the monstrous silence of oblivion to which he believed the memory exiled. But Kathleen remains ignorant. Sarah, the silence of Auschwitz, will be Kathleen's eternal rival.

The lies and their accompanying silences imply other elements of the same night in which all early Wieselian characters exist. Arguments for life are negated by silence. Dr. Russel argues that life wants to live, to continue, to struggle against death. His logic merely draws an awkward silence. The protagonist unquestionably realizes the danger he represents for Russel. And yet, even this drama of interrogation ensues in nothingness, its conclusion a cold, disastrous silence. Thus, Michael Berenbaum would apparently seem correct in postulating that

> Death ultimately triumphs. Though the correspondent does rage against death and though he does outwit death a second time, the external forces of death and his own desire for death remain. The ashes of the past will inevitably return to haunt him as they have haunted him before. All being is being unto death. In *Le Jour* Wiesel exposes a world in which God is at best absent in the struggle between life and death. At worst, God may even be an ally of the forces of death.

Yet despite such firm support for death's supremacy, evidence exists within the narrative that underlies the evolution of silence's role from a purely negative pole to one in which it becomes a positive presence.

The protagonist's silences change to more transparent forms as Kathleen attempts to understand him through the medium of silence. While he has been ill, she has attempted to interpret his silences, daring to invade the reserved region. With his defenses down, she has been able to penetrate the shadowy void; or, has she been allowed to enter owing to an alteration in the type of silence that predominates? For whatever the reasons, the protagonist's ten-week physical isolation and recuperation have imposed changes, and have prepared the way for spiritual regeneration. The catalyst appears to be personified in the character of Gyula, who alone appears capable of comprehending the meanings and directions of the protagonist's silence.

Gyula represents life, but unlike Kathleen, whose timidity often borders on the passive, he is a celebration of life. His name in Hebrew means redemption or redeemer. Gyula transforms the protagonist's words and silences into a portrait, a metaphorical mirror, in which the latter is finally able to recognize himself and his absolute estrangement from life. In the concluding pages of the book, Gyula stands at the center as he emphasizes life, offering the protagonist redemption from death. Gyula's initial protestations appear merely analogous continuations of those so strongly voiced by Dr. Russel and Kathleen. What element in the friendship between

Gyula and the nameless protagonist passes in silence, unnoticed, a factor that will favor the former with a degree of success? Gyula is also a survivor, a factor based on two textual clues. First, the statement that only Gyula has been able to divine the protagonist's secrets suggests that he alone possesses some special quality allowing him to comprehend the hidden significance of the protagonist's words and silences. Second, Gyula comes to see the protagonist daily, in the afternoon. The key-word here is afternoon. It offers sufficient insights to explain Gyula's ability to fathom the text's morphological silences, and similarly establishes his connection to being a survivor.

This time of day corresponds to one of the daily services of the Jewish liturgy: *minha.* Tradition attributes the institution of this religious service to Isaac, a survivor. In *Célébration biblique,* Wiesel relates:

> Isaac a survécu. . . . Devenu poète—il est l'auteur de l'office de *minha*—il ne rompt pas avec la société, il ne s'oppose pas à la vie. . . . Il s'établit dans son pays . . . il se marie, ii a des enfants, il fonde un foyer; le destin n'a pas fait de lui un homme amer et aigri.

> What did happen to Isaac after he left Mount Moriah? He became a poet—author of the *Minha* service—and did not break with society. Nor did he rebel against life. . . . He married, had children, refusing to let fate turn him into a bitter man.

Isaac like Gyula is a survivor who has come to accept life. The names *Isaac* (he who laughs) and *Gyula* (redemption) speak of joy, redemption, and a sense of life. Gyula, himself a survivor, is imbued with a sixth sense that assists him in understanding the protagonist's dilemma. It similarly explains his relative success in the wake of Kathleen's and Dr. Russel's failures.

Through his words, his own particular silences, and eventually his portrait of the protagonist, Gyula forces a transformation. He endeavors to convince the protagonist that suffering is given to the living; only the living can derive significance from suffering. Before the dreadful pictorial representation of the protagonist, Gyula's words resound like an incantation of exorcism: "Kathleen est vivante. Moi, je suis vivant. Il faut penser à nous"; "Kathleen is alive. I am alive. You must think of us." The protagonist has come to the brink. Gazing at himself in the portrait much as Eliezer had viewed his spectral reflection in the mirror at Buchenwald—and as Elisha had seen himself in the pane of glass—the nameless protagonist must choose. "Tout était dit. Le pour et le contre. Je choisirais les morts ou les vivants";

"Everything had been said. The pros and the cons. I would choose the living or the dead." As a coup de grace, Gyula burns the portrait, leaving only its ashes. But the novel's conclusion is far from inconclusive. The tears the protagonist now sheds reflect a limited return to life, a regeneration of the emotions of a living man.

Berenbaum's aforementioned statement that "death ultimately triumphs" in this novel now has limited validity. Man must die; life's expected culmination is death: "For dust thou art, and unto dust shalt thou return" (Genesis 3:19); "Man born of woman is short-lived and sated with trouble." (Job 14:1) Yet, despite the bitterness and negativity of the text, *Le Jour* reflects a subtle resurgence of and toward life. The essence of silence, its metamorphosing significance, create a tension that leads to speech, and this action eventually erupts in fire and water, both archetypal symbols of purification. Though crushed, the nameless protagonist is not defeated. He can now prepare to be born into an imperfect world where he must continue the struggle.

CONCLUSION

Wiesel's trilogy guides us on an exploration of hell and its aftermath. The three protagonists exist within the void of Auschwitz, amidst the destructive silence unleashed there. The *nihil* that destroyed their lives and beliefs reaches beyond 1945 and corrupts them, annihilating bodies and souls. Though they have survived, though they live in a lifeless exile, they too become victims. Their voices cry out as a single one. Moreover, the various levels of silence do evolve in the course of the trilogy and effect alterations in the protagonists.

As exiles, the three might appear shattered and lost. Yet Emile Cioran emphasizes that "it is a mistake to think of the exile as someone who abdicates, who withdraws and humbles himself, resigned to his miseries, his outcast state." Eliezer remains alone, isolated, exiled from God and humanity. His world has been shattered by the greater silence of Auschwitz. Elisha, the survivor, opts for action in order to free himself from the painful solitude of his Parisian room. Ironically, the negative silence that predominates transforms his choice into an act of deicide. Both protagonists are victims of the Holocaust and its aftermath.

Initially, the same appears true for the nameless protagonist of *Le Jour*. Yet the silences at play in this novel crystalize into actions that reflect both negation and regeneration. The attempted suicide is symbolic of the most destructive silence: Death. But the protagonist demonstrates a faint though inexplicable desire to live. Despite his lies and silences, he does speak and, as Parain recognizes "speaking implies that one is not alone." His is no longer a vegetative life where negative silences stifle words, thoughts, and deeds. The protagonist has recognized that life can be lived, though of necessity its essence will be monumentally altered by the events of the past. The words and silences of this third novel return to their origin in the Holocaust, and then emerge with a new sense of vigor and direction. *Le Jour*, bleak though it appears, promises a renewal of life and its unique dialogic relationships. The ambiguous conclusion does indeed present a possibility of "return"; the protagonist has shed the chains imposed by the negative silences of Auschwitz in order to accept the yoke of different silences. No longer tied down, he can progress. He emerges, in a peculiar way, a victor. Max Picard suggests: "In silence . . . man stands confronted by the original beginning of all things: everything can begin again, everything can be re-created." If we accept the *nihil* of Auschwitz as the beginning of Wiesel's literary universe, which is a creation wrenched from that absolute nothingness by the Logos, then Picard's statement does indeed offer hope. The victor's hope will be realized in unique acts of *teshuva*, return, in Wiesel's fourth novel, *La Ville de la chance* (*The Town Beyond the Wall*).

Chronology

1928 Born on September 30, on the Jewish holiday of Simchat Torah, in Sighet, Rumania. Sighet is located in the region of Transylvania, which is annexed by Hungary in 1940 and reverts back to Rumania in 1945.

1934–1944 While living in Sighet, Wiesel attends *heder* (primary school) and later the yeshiva, where he becomes immersed in the study of the Torah and the Talmud.

1944–1945 Elie Wiesel is imprisoned in various concentration camps (Birkenau, Auschwitz, Buna, Buchenwald) from April 1944 to April 1945.

1945 On April 11, Elie Wiesel is liberated from the Buchenwald concentration camp. He is then sent to France with other children who have survived the concentration camps.

1946 Travels first to Taverny and then Paris, where he rents a room in Porte Saint-Cloud. Earns money as a choir director and Bible teacher.

1948–1951 Elie Wiesel studies philosophy, literature and psychology at the Sorbonne. Camus, Kierkegaard and Kafka are among the writers who influenced him the most.

1948 While working as a journalist, Wiesel visits Israel to report on the Israeli struggle. During the following years, he continues to live in Paris while working as a newspaper correspondent.

1956 Elie Wiesel settles in New York, where he still lives today. *Un di velt hot gesvign* (*And the World Has Remained Silent*), an account of Wiesel's experience in Auschwitz, is published. Wiesel states that this account is the foundation for all of his subsequent books.

While working as a correspondent to the United Nations for the Israeli newspaper, *Yediot Aharonot*, Wiesel is struck by a taxi in Times Square. Later, unable to get his French travel documents extended, Weisel applies for American citizenship.

1957 Works for the *Jewish Daily Forward*, a New York Yiddish newspaper, as a writer of feature articles.

1958 *La Nuit* published in Paris. Translated and published as *Night* in 1960 in the United States.

1960 *Dawn* (*L'Aube*) is published.

1961 *The Accident* (*Le Jour*) is published.

1962 *The Town Beyond the Wall* (*La Ville de la chance*) is published. Wiesel wins the Prix Rivarol and the National Jewish Book Council Award.

1963 Elie Wiesel becomes a United States citizen.

1964 *The Gates of the Forest* (*Les Portes de la forêt*) is published. Wiesel now devotes himself full time to writing and lecturing.

1965 Wiesel visits the Soviet Union during the Jewish High Holy Days and writes a series of articles on his impressions of Soviet Jewry for *Yediot Aharonot.*

1966 The articles on Soviet Jews from the previous year are collected and published as *The Jews of Silence: A Personal Report on Soviet Jewry.*

1968 Wiesel's first drama, *Zalmen, or the Madness of God,* is published in France. It is first staged, as *The Madness of God,* in Washington, D.C., in 1974. *A Beggar in Jerusalem* is published and awarded the *Prix Medicis,* one of France's most distinguished literary prizes.

1969 Wiesel marries Marion Erster Rose, a Viennese, who is also a survivor of the concentration camps. Marion becomes a translator of most of Wiesel's books.

1970 *One Generation After* is published on the twenty-fifth anniversary of Wiesel's liberation from Buchenwald.

1971 *Souls on Fire* (*Célébration hassidique: portraits et légendes*) is published, consisting of lectures originally given at the Sorbonne and at the Young Men's Hebrew Association in New York.

1972 Appointed Distinguished Professor of Jewish Studies at the City College of the City University of New York. Wiesel's son, Shlomo Elisha, is born.

1973 *The Oath* (*Le Serment de Kolvillàg*) and *Ani Maamin* are published.

1976 *Messengers of God: Biblical Portraits and Legends* (*Célébration Biblique*) is published.

1978 Elie Wiesel is appointed Andrew Mellon Professor of Humanities and University Professor at Boston University. *Four Hasidic Masters and Their Struggle Against Melancholy* and *A Jew Today* are published.

1979 *The Trial of God,* Wiesel's second drama, is published. Weisel also appointed Chairman of the President's Commission on the Holocaust. Awarded an honorary degree by Wesleyan University.

1980 *Le Testament d'un poète juif assassiné* published; translated as *The Testament* in 1981. Awarded an honorary degree by Brandeis University.

1981 Awarded an honorary degree by Yale University.

1983 *Le Cinquièeme fils* published in Paris. Translated as *The Fifth Son* by Marion Wiesel and published in New York by Summit in 1985.

1985 *Against Silence: The Voice and Vision of Elie Wiesel,* three volumes, edited by Irving Abrahamson published in New York by Holocaust Library. *Signes d'Exode* published in Paris by Grasset et Fasquelle. Receives the Congressional Gold Medal of Achievement from President Reagan.

1986 October 14 wins Nobel Peace Prize for *Night.*

1987 *The Night Trilogy: Night, Dawn, The Accident* published in New York by Farrar, Straus & Grioux. L*e Crépuscule, au loin* published in Paris by Grasset et Fasquelle.

Contributors

HAROLD BLOOM is Sterling Professor of the Humanities at Yale University and Henry W. and Albert A. Berg Professor of English at the New York University Graduate School. He is the author of over 20 books, including *Shelley's Mythmaking* (1959), *The Visionary Company* (1961), *Blake's Apocalypse* (1963), *Yeats* (1970), *A Map of Misreading* (1975), *Kabbalah and Criticism* (1975), *Agon: Toward a Theory of Revisionism* (1982), *The American Religion* (1992), *The Western Canon* (1994), and *Omens of Millennium: The Gnosis of Angels, Dreams, and Resurrection* (1996). *The Anxiety of Influence* (1973) sets forth Professor Bloom's provocative theory of the literary relationships between the great writers and their predecessors. His most recent books include *Shakespeare: The Invention of the Human*, a 1998 National Book Award finalist, and *How to Read and Why*, which was published in 2000. In 1999, Professor Bloom received the prestigious American Academy of Arts and Letters Gold Medal for Criticism.

LAWRENCE L. LANGER is a professor of English and holder of the Alumnae-endowed Chair at Simmons College in Boston. He is the author of *Preempting the Holocaust* (1998) and *The Game Continues: Chess in the Art of Samuel Bak* (1999).

MICHAEL BERENBAUM is a contributing editor of *Witness to the Holocaust* (1997) and *The Holocaust and History: The Known, the Unknown, the Disputed and the Reexamined* (1998).

JOHN K. ROTH is a professor in the Department of Religion and Philosophy at Claremont McKenna College, Claremont, California. He is an editor of

Holocaust: Religious and Philosophical Implications (1989) and *From the Unthinkable to the Unavoidable: American Christian and Jewish Scholars Encounter the Holocaust* (1997).

ELLEN S. FINE is a professor of French at Kingsborough Community College, City University of New York. She is the author of "The Absent Memory: the Act of Writing in Post-Holocaust French Literature" (1988) and "Women Writers and the Holocaust: Strategies for Survival" (1990).

ROBERT MCAFEE BROWN is the author of *Spirituality and Liberation: Overcoming the Great Fallacy* (1988) and *Gustavo Gutiérrez: An Introduction to Liberation Theology* (1990).

COLIN DAVIS is a professor of History at the University of Alabama, Birmingham. He is the author of *Michel Tournier: Philosophy and Fiction* (1988) and *Levinas: An Introduction* (1996).

ORA AVNI is a professor of French at Yale University. She has published extensively on nineteenth and twentieth century French theory and literature. She is the author of *The Resistance of Reference: Linguistics, Philosophy, and the Literary Text* (1990) and *D'un Passé l'autre: aux portes de l'histoire avec Patrick Modiano* (1997).

DR. SIMON P. SIBELMAN is an Associate Professor of French Language and Literature at the University of Wisconsin-Oshkosh. He has received numerous faculty development grants as well as a research grant from the Memorial Council for Jewish Culture. He has been published in a variety of journals, including *The British Journal of Holocaust Studies* and *European Judaism*. His book, *Silence in the Novels of Elie Wiesel*, was published in 1995. Currently, Dr. Sibelman is completing the manuscript of *Circumscribing Swann's Nose*, a study of Jewish self-identity, as well as co-editing a book called *Fractured Images* which looks at how France has chosen to remember the Second World War.

Bibliography

Abramowitz, Molly. *Elie Wiesel: A Bibliography.* Metuchen, N.J.: The Scarecrow Press, 1974.

Alexander, Edward. *The Resonance of Dust: Essays on Holocaust Literature and Jewish Fate.* Middleton, Conn.: Wesleyan University Press, 1979.

Alter, Robert. *After the Tradition.* New York: E. P. Dutton, 1969.

Arendt, Hannah. *Eichmann in Jerusalem.* New York: The Viking Press, 1963.

Bar-On, Dan. *Legacy of Silence: Encounters with Children of the Third Reich.* Cambridge: Massachusetts: Harvard University Press, 1989.

Berenbaum, Michael G. *The Vision of the Void: Theological Reflections on the Works of Elie Wiesel.* Middleton, Conn.: Wesleyan University Press, 1979.

Berger, Alan L. *Crisis and Covenant: The Holocaust in American Jewish Fiction.* Albany: State University of New York Press, 1985.

Berkovits, Eliezer. *Faith After the Holocaust.* New York: Ktav, 1973.

Bettelheim, Bruno. *The Informed Heart.* New York: Avon Books, 1971.

Brown, Robert McAfee. "The Holocaust as a Problem in Moral Choice" in *Dimensions of the Holocaust.* Evanston: Northwestern University, 1977: pp. 47–83.

———. *Elie Wiesel: Messenger to All Humanity.* Notre Dame: University of Notre Dame Press, 1983.

Cargas, Harry James, ed. *Harry James Cargas in Conversation with Elie Wiesel.* New York: Paulist Press, 1976.

———, ed. *Responses to Elie Wiesel: Critical Essays by Major Jewish and Christian Scholars.* New York: Persea Books, 1978.

Davis, Colin. *Elie Wiesel's Secretive Texts.* Gainesville: University Press of Florida, 1994.

Dawidowicz, Lucy S. *The War Against the Jews 1933–1945.* New York: Bantam Books, 1976.

Estess, Ted. *Elie Wiesel.* New York: Frederick Ungar Publishing Company, 1980.

Erzahi, Sidra DeKoven. *By Words Alone: The Holocaust in Literature.* Chicago: University of Chicago Press 1980.

Fackenheim, Emil. *God's Presence in History.* New York: Harper Torchbooks, 1972.

Fine, Ellen S. *Legacy of Night: The Literary Universe of Elie Wiesel.* Albany: State University of New York Press, 1982.

Friedman, Maurice. *To Deny Our Nothingness: Contemporary Images of Man.* New York: Delacorte Press, 1967.

Frost, Christopher J. *Religious Melancholy or Psychological Depression?: Some Issues Involved in Relating Psychology and Religion as Illustrated in a Study of Elie Wiesel.* Lanham, Maryland: University Press of America, 1985.

Glatstein, Jacob, Israel Knox and Samuel Margoshes, eds. *Anthology of Holocaust Literature.* New York: Atheneum, 1975.

Green, Mary Jean. "Witness to the Absurd: Elie Wiesel and the French Existentialists." *Renascence* 29 (1977): 170–184.

Greenberg, Irving and Alvin Rosenfeld, eds. *Confronting the Holocaust: The Impact of Elie Wiesel.* Bloomington: Indiana University Press, 1978.

Halperin, Irving. *Messengers from the Dead.* Philadelphia: The Westminster Press, 1970.

Hilberg, Raul. *The Destruction of the European Jews.* New York: Franklin Watts, Inc., 1973.

Kahn, Lothar. "Elie Wiesel: Neo-Hasidism." In his *Mirrors of the Jewish Mind: A Gallery of Portraits of European Jewish Writers of Our Time*, pp. 296–300. New York: Thomas Yoseloff, 1968.

Knopp, Josephine. "Wiesel and the Absurd." *Contemporary Literature* 15, April, 1974: pp. 212–220.

———. *The Trial of Judiaism in Contemporary Jewish Writing.* Urban: University of Illinois Press, 1975.

Lang, Berel, ed. *Writing and the Holocaust.* New York: Holmes & Meier, 1988.

Langer, Lawrence. *The Holocaust and the Literary Imagination.* New Haven: Yale University Press, 1975.

———. *Preempting the Holocaust.* New Haven: Yale University Press, 1998.

Paterson, David. *The Shriek of Silence: A Phenomenology of the Holocaust Novel.* Lexington: University of Kentucky Press, 1992.

Rabinowitz, Dorothy. *New Lives: Survivors of the Holocaust Living in America.* New York: Alfred A. Knopf, 1976.

Rittner, Carol. *Elie Wiesel: Between Memory and Hope.* New York: New York University Press, 1990.

Rosenfeld, Alvin H. *A Double Dying: Reflections on Holocaust Literature.* Bloomington: Indiana University Press, 1978.

Rosenfeld, Alvin H. and Irving Greenberg, eds. *Confronting the Holocaust: The Impact of Elie Wiesel.* Bloomington: Indiana University Press, 1980.

Roth, John K. *A Consuming Fire: Encounters with Elie Wiesel and the Holocaust.* Atlanta: John Knox Press (1979).

Sherwin, Byron L. "Elie Wiesel and Jewish Theology." *Judaism* 18, Winter, 1969: pp. 39–62.

———. "Jewish Messianism and Elie Wiesel" in Byron L. Sherwin, ed., *Perspectives in Jewish Learning–Volume Five.* Chicago: Spertus College Press, 1973: pp. 48–60.

Sibelman, Simon P. *Silence in the Novels of Elie Wiesel.* New York: St. Martin's Press (1995).

Steiner, George. *In Bluebeard's Castle: Some Notes Towards the Redefinition of Culture.* New Haven, Conn.: Yale University Press, 1971.

Stern, Ellen Norman. *Elie Wiesel: Witness for Life.* New York: Ktav Publishing House (1982).

Walker, Graham B., Jr. *Elie Wiesel: A Challenge to Theology.* Jefferson, N.C.: McFarland (1988).

Wardi, Dina. *Memorial Candles: Children of the Holocaust*, translated by Naomi Goldblum. London and New York: Tavistock/Routledge, 1992.

Wiesel, Elie. *All Rivers Run to the Sea: Memoir*. New York: Knopf, 1995.

———. *And the Sea Is Never Full*. New York: Knopf (1999).

Acknowledgments

"The Dominion of Death" by Lawrence L. Langer. From *Responses to Elie Wiesel*, ed. Harry James Cargas. © 1978 by Yale University Press, Inc. Reprinted with permission.

"The Experience of the Void" by Michael Berenbaum. From *The Vision of the Void: Theological Reflections on the Works of Elie Wiesel.* © 1979 by Wesleyan University Press. Reprinted with permission.

"In the Beginning" by John K. Roth. From *A Consuming Fire: Encounters with Elie Wiesel and the Holocaust.* © 1979 by John K. Roth. Reprinted with permission.

"Witness of the Night" by Ellen S. Fine. From *Legacy of Night: The Literary Universe of Elie Wiesel.* © 1982 by State University of New York. Reprinted with permission of the State University of New York Press.

"Darkness That Eclipses Light (*a moral journey—1*)" by Robert McAfee Brown. From *Elie Wiesel: Messenger to All Humanity.* © 1983 by University of Notre Dame Press. Reprinted with permission.

"The Conversion to Ambiguity (Early Works)" by Colin Davis. From *Elie Wiesel's Secretive Texts.* © 1994 by the Board of Regents of the State of Florida. Reprinted with the permisson of the University Press of Florida.

"Beyond Psychoanalysis: Elie Wiesel's *Night* in Historical Perspective" by Ora Avni. From *Auschwitz and After: Race, Culture, and "the Jewish Question" in France*, ed. Lawrence D. Kritzman. © 1995 by Routledge Inc. Reprinted with permission.

"Victims to Victors: The Trilogy" by Simon P. Sibelman. From *Silence in the Novels of Elie Wiesel.* © 1995 by Simon P. Sibelman. Reprinted with permission.

Index

Adorno, Theodor, 1
Akeda, 35–56, 58, 156–57, 158
Alienation, and *Night*, 22–23
Alvarez, A., 146
Ambiguity
and *Dawn*, 105–9
and *Le Jour* (*The Accident*), 105–9
and *Night*, 95–105
and *The Town Beyond the Wall*, 107, 109–27
And the World Has Remained Silent, 89
Anne Frank: The Diary of a Young Girl, 5–6
Antipsalm, 153–54
Art, definition of, 3–4, 5
Auerbach, Erich, 3
Auerhann, Nanette, 134–35, 136
Avni, Ora, 129–43

Barthes, Roland, 152
Beggar in Jerusalem, A, 70, 76, 101
Beginning
of *Dawn*, 76
of *Le Jour* (*The Accident*), 42–46, 76
of *Night*, 130, 132, 137–39, 140–42
of novels, 75–76
of *The Town Beyond the Wall*, 76
Beginnings
and *Dawn*, 36–42
and *Night*, 31–36
Behaviorist approach, to *Night*, 134, 135–37
Berenbaum, Michael, 17–30, 169, 171
Berger, Peter, 17
Bettelheim, Bruno, 6
"Beyond Psychoanalysis: Elie Wiesel's *Night* in Historical Perspective" (Avni), 129–43
Bildungsroman, reversal of, 12–13, 15, 129
Blanchot, Maurice, 49, 159
Bloom, Harold, 1–2
Boak, Denis, 96
Boy, hanging of, 12–13, 34–35, 64–65, 74, 99, 155
Brown, Robert McAfee, 69–93, 95–96
Buber, Martin, 88, 96

Camus, Albert, 7, 12, 15, 81, 84
Cattle wagons, night of, 51
Cayrol, Jean, 151
Celan, Paul, 2
Céline, Ferdinand, 146
Central tension, and narrative technique, 98–105
Christianity, and *Night*
and hanging boy, 74

and relations between God and world, 33, 34, 36
Cioran, Emile, 171
Cognitive approach, to *Night*, 134–35, 136
Cohn-Bendit, Daniel, 132
Concentration camp philosophy, 58–62
"Conversion to Ambiguity (Early Works), The" (Davis), 95–127
Crucifixion, and hanging boy, 64–65, 74, 155

"Darkness That Eclipses Light (a moral journey–1)" (Brown), 69–93
Davis, Colin, 95–127
Dawn, 17, 69, 70, 115, 123, 126
and ambiguity, 105–9
beginning of, 76
and beginnings, 36–42
and executioner, 77–80
and silence, 159–63
and theodicy, 17, 24–26
Death, and *Night*
life displaced by, 3–16, 32
ritual, 12–13
Deliverance, theme of in *Night*, 97
Deputy, The (Hochhuth), 8
Des Pres, Terence, 59, 133
"Dominion of Death, The" (Langer), 3–16
Drumer, Akiba, 24, 155

Eichmann, Adolph, 50
Eliahou, Rabbi, 59–60, 61, 99, 157
Eliezer (narrator)
and credibility of own narrative, 101
and death of father, 15, 48, 54, 57, 58, 59, 61–62, 63–64, 75, 156–58
details introduced by, 99–100
direct comment by, 98, 99
effect of violence on, 48
and erosion of faith, 53, 72–74, 152–54, 155–56
father abandoned by, 58–62
father rescued by, 57–58
and father-son theme, 51, 54–62, 99, 102–4, 156–58
and father's rescue of, 56–57
and father's unfinished story, 62–67
fictionalization of voice of, 105–6, 108, 109–10
function of, 97
and hanging boy, 64–65, 74
and "items" of reality, 9
and Juliek, 63
and liberation, 16
name of, 105–6
and night, 11–12, 49–54, 72
piety of, 97
and religious values, 8, 14
and respectful human dignity, 154
retrospective viewpoint of, 99
and Rosh Hashanah, 22–23, 53, 73, 155–56
and self-recognition, 97
and shattered future, 77
and shattering of self, 74–75
silence crushing essence of, 152–53, 171
and staring corpse, 62, 77, 97, 104, 139–40, 158–59
and survivor guilt, 61–62, 99, 103
and *The Town Beyond the Wall*, 113
voice of, 65–66
and Yom Kippur, 14, 23, 156
Ending, of *Night*, 97, 139–40
Entre deux soleils, 108
Estess, Ted, 95–96
Evil, *Night* as response to, 70–77
See also Theodicy
Executioner, and *Dawn*, 77–80
Exile, theme of in *Night*, 97

"Experience of the Void, The" (Berenbaum), 17–30

Faith. *See* God
Father
  death of, 15, 48, 54, 57, 58, 59, 61–62, 63–64, 75, 156–58
  Eliezer rescued by, 56–57
  Eliezer's abandonment of, 58–62
  Eliezer's rescue of, 57–58
  and father-son theme, 51, 54–62, 99, 102–4, 156–58
  silencing voice of, 152
  speech of, 102–4
  unfinished story of, 50–51, 62–67, 100–101, 103–4, 156–57
Father-son theme, 51, 54–62, 99, 102–4, 156–58
"Final Return, The," 114
Fine, Ellen S., 47–67
Fire, theme of in *Night*, 51–52, 72
Flight, and *Le Jour* (*The Accident*), 81–86
Frank, Anne, 5–6
Future, shattering of, 75–77

Gates of the Forest, The, 69–70, 76, 107
Ghetto period, 51
God, and *Night*
  death of, 64–65, 72–74, 99
  erosion of faith in, 18–24, 31–36, 53, 72–74, 152–56
  and hanging boy, 34–35
  relations with, 31–36
  silence of, 154–56, 158
  See also Theodicy

Hartman, Geoffrey, 1–2
Hasidism, and time, 151
Hecht, Anthony, 8
Hegel, Georg, 18
Heimler, Eugene, 146
Heschel, Abraham Joshua, 147, 149
History, and *Night*, 100
  reader's knowledge of, 98
  self-positioning of subject in, 129–43
  seriousness of, 20–21
  and spiritual drama, 96–97, 104
Hochhuth, Rolf, 8
Humanity, erosion of notion of, 154
Hungarian Jews, expulsion of, 50

I and Thou (Buber), 88
Imagery, in *Night*, 9–12
Imagination, and *Night*
  and death, 15
  reality *versus*, 7
"In the Beginning" (Roth), 31–46

Jarry, Alfred, 146
Jew Today, A, 100
Johnson, Paul, 96
Jour, Le (*The Accident*), 17, 69, 70, 76, 115, 118, 126
  and ambiguity, 105–9
  beginning of, 42–46, 76
  and flight, 81–86
  and silence, 164–72
  and theodicy, 17, 26–29
Juliek, 63

Kaddish, 22, 52, 73
Kafka, Franz, 47, 146
Kahler, Erich, 3–4, 5
Kasack, Hermann, 5, 12
Katz, Bela, 58, 99
Katz, Meir, 57
Kazantzakis, Nikos, 82

Kazin, Alfred, 65
King Lear (Shakespeare), 5, 6, 8, 9
Knopp, Josephine, 164, 165

Langer, Lawrence L., 3–16, 64
Language, in *Night*, 12
  mistrust of, 101–4
  silence evoked by, 152
  truth *versus*, 7
Laub, Dori, 134–35, 136
Life, and *Night*
  as choice, 36
  and voice, 65
Lifton, Robert Jay, 62
Literature, Holocaust transmuted into, 1–2
Longest Shadow: In the Aftermath of the Holocaust (Hartman), 1–2
Loss, theme of in *Night*, 101
Loss of the Self in Modern Literature and Art (Sypher), 55

Madness, in *The Town Beyond the Wall*, 89–93
Mauriac, François, 48, 65, 154, 160
Messengers of God: Biblical Portraits and Legends, 56, 170
Messiah, and theodicy, 19–21
Moché the Beadle
  critique of answers to post-Shoah difficulties offered by, 142
  deportation of, 8, 49, 71
  disbelief of story of, 8, 49–50, 98–99, 100, 129–30, 137–39, 140–42, 148, 151
  faith of before ordeal, 8, 130
  language of, 101–2
  and saved from death by miracle, 104–5
  and silence, 100
  and silencing of time, 148
  songs of, 97
  as witness, 49–50
"More Light! More Light!" (Hecht), 8
Myth of Sisyphus, The (Camus), 7

Narrative technique, of Night, 98–105
Neher, André, 55, 155, 163
Nietzsche, Friedrich, 64
Night
  and ambiguity, 95–105
  as autobiography, 105–6, 107
  and beginnings, 31–36
  and cycle, 106. *See also Dawn; Jour, Le*
  and displacement of life by death, 3–16, 32
  Eliezer (narrator) as witness in, 47–67
  in historical perspective, 129–43
  publication of, 68
  as response to evil, 70–77
  victims in, 70–77
  void in, 17–24, 29–30
Night, theme of in *Night*, 48–54
  and beginnings, 31–36
  and cattle wagons, 51
  and end and beginning, 66
  and first night, 11–12, 31–32, 49, 51, 52–53, 72
  and inner night, 52
  and last night, 49, 51, 54
  and theodicy, 18–24
  and voice, 63
Nightmare, reality *versus*, 10–11, 13–14

Oath, The, 76, 119–20
"Old Acquaintance, An," 61
One Generation After, 131
Ozsvath, Zsuzsanna, 96
Parain, Brice, 161, 172

Parry, M., 160
Past historic tense, in *Night*, 98
Picard, Max, 172
Plague, The (Camus), 84
Prayer book, and theodicy, 19
Premonition, and narrative technique, 98–99
Primary trauma, 1–2
Providence, theme of in *Night*, 97
Psychoanalytic approach, to *Night*, 133–37, 142, 143
Punctuation, silence evoked by, 152

Raba, 19
Reality, and *Night*
  acceptance of, 8
  imagination *versus*, 7
  items of, 8–9
  nightmare *versus*, 10–11, 13–14
Religion, and *Night*
  futility of, 14
  silencing traditions of, 148–49
  See also God, and *Night*
Rescue, theme of in *Night*, 56–58
Rosh Hashanah (New Year), in *Night*, 14, 22–23, 53, 73, 155–56
Roth, John K., 31–46
Rousseau, Jean-Jacques, 161
Rousset, David, 146, 155
Rubenstein, Richard, 72

Sabbath, silencing of, 148–49
Sachs, Nelly, 9
Sartre, Jean Paul, 162–63
Satz, Martha, 96
Saussure, Ferdinand de, 141
Schächter, Madame, 51, 71, 99, 151–52
Schizophrenic art, 13, 16
Scholem, Gershom, 20
Secondary trauma, 1–2
"Selection," 14
Self, and *Night*
  destruction of, 147
  shattering of, 74–75
Self-positioning, in history, 129–43
Shoah narratives
  and Moché's return, 129–33
  therapeutic explanations of, 133–37, 142
Sibelman, Simon P., 145–72
Silence
  and *Dawn*, 159–63
  and *Le Jour* (*The Accident*), 164–72
  and *Night*, 145–59
Spectator, in *The Town Beyond the Wall*, 86–89
Speech, and *Night*
  direct, 102
  silence evoked by, 152
  See also Language, in *Night*
Spiritual drama, and history, 96–97, 104
Steiner, George, 152
Style, of *Night*, 98
Sun, as counterpart to Night, 51
Survivor, The (Des Pres), 59
Sypher, Wylie, 55
Szklarczyk, Lillian, 164

Telegraphic style, of *Night*, 98
Testament, The, 76
Theodicy
  in *Dawn*, 17, 24–26
  in *Le Jour*, 17, 26–29
  in *Night*, 18–24
Thibaud, Paul, 145
Time, in *Night*, 52–53
  silencing of, 147–51
  See also *Night*
Totentraum (Kasack), 12
Town Beyond the Wall, The, 69, 70, 154, 172

and ambiguity, 107, 109–27
beginning of, 76
madness in, 89–93
spectator in, 86–89
Trauma, primary and secondary, 1–2
Trial of God, The, 76
Truth, and *Night*
language versus, 7
silencing of, 151–52

Uncertainty, and *Night*, 33
Unfinished story, of father, 50–51, 62–67, 100–101, 103–4, 156–57

Verb tense, in *Night*, 98
Victims, in *Night*, 70–77
"Victims to Victors: The Trilogy" (Sibelman), 145–72
Voice, in *Night*
silencing of, 152, 154
theme of, 63–66
Void, in *Night*, 17–24, 29–30

Wangh, Martin, 134, 135–37
Warning, and narrative technique, 98–99
Williams, David, 164
Witness, in *Night*
Eliezer (narrator) as, 47–67
Moché as, 49–50
"Witness of the Night" (Fine), 47–67
World, shattering of, 71–72

Yom Kippur (Day of Atonement), 14, 23, 156

Zohar, 21
Zola, Emile, 153
Zorba the Greek (Kazantzakis), 82